KNOWLEDGE AND WISDOM IN BITS AND PIECES

Doug Huffman

ISBN 979-8-9897112-9-1 (paperback)
ISBN 979-8-9897112-8-4 (eBook)

Printed in the United States of America

Contents

Chapter 1

A Little Salt at the Tomb

No doubt you've heard the well known *axiom*; "*Take it with a grain of salt*"? Well, when it comes to the New Testament, we must remember to **not** *forget* to bring our *salt* shakers. To make this point **crystal** clear; according to one of the **leading** *experts* on the *writing* and *compilation* of the *New Testament,* Professor Bart Ehrman, most of the NT was written after *decades* of **oral** *tradition;* that is, *passed* **orally** from *person* to *person* until finally being **written** *down.* With that in mind, just *how* **much** does the *story* or *message* get **tweaked** after being *passed* from **person** to *person?*

Well, no one knows exactly how many people the *content* of (most) the NT books *passed* **through** until finally *written* down. Doubtless they are *laced* with invaluable *truth,* but we can be sure, it's **not** a **word** for **word** *record* like a modern *recording*! Personally, I do **not** *accept* anything in the New Testament without it *being* **supported** and **substantiated** by the *Old.* On the other hand, only a fool *throws* the entire NT *away* as the Jews have done. Unfortunately, it's their loss.

With that said, let's take a New Testament *stroll* to the *tomb* of the Hebrew *Messiah* at His *resurrection*. What an *interesting* little *walk* when we closely **compare** the *four* accounts! First in **Matthew** 28 we find "*Mary Magdalene*" and "*the other Mary*(?)" arrive at the tomb. "*Then there was a great **earthquake** and an **angel** of God **descended** from **heaven** and **rolled back** the **stone** and **sat** on it*".

Continuing in verse **4**, *guards* are mentioned, which "*shook with fear*" and "*fell down like dead men*" (*feinted*). Then the *angel* tells the Mary's; "*He is not here; for He is risen*". He then **showed** them where He had *lain* in the *tomb* and *tells* them (v.7) "*He is on His way to **Galilee** and to go quickly and **tell** the **disciples** they would will **see Him there***". Verse 9 then tells us Yahshua *met* the Mary's **before** *Galilee* and told them to *go* **tell** the *disciples* they would *see Him* in **Galilee**". Already, we see a glaring problem in the angel *telling* the Marys' they would **see Yahshua** in *Galilee*, *not* **on** *the* **way** there!

Now, in **Mark,** chapter 16, we find "*Mary **Magdalene**, Mary, the **mother** of **James** and **Salome** coming very early on the first day of the week bringing spices to anoint Him*". Verse 3, has them "**asking** *each other* **who** *would* **roll away** *the* **stone** but *then they* **looked up** *and saw it was* **already rolled away***".

They then "**entered** *the* **tomb** *and found a* **young man** *in a* **long** *white* **robe**" *telling* them Yahshua "*was* **raised**" and "*showed them where* **He had lain**". They then "**fled** *the* **tomb** *in fear and* **told no one**" (v.8).

The angel then told them to "*go* **tell** *the* **disciples** (and Peter) that *He was going* **before them** *to* **Galilee; there** *you* **will see Him**". Now verse 9 gets very strange; "*Now when **He** rose **early** on the **first day** of the week, He appeared **first to Mary Magdalene**" (no others) who went and *told* the disciples, who "*didn't believe her*". He later *appeared* to them. Even here, it seems we have *a* **different** *account* that **doesn't** *mesh* with the account in **Matthew**; that is of the *angel* sitting on the *stone* and with only the "*two Marys*" there. Plus, there is **no** *mention* of the *soldiers* in *this* account either.

Next is **Luke's** account, *where we find "Mary Magdalene, the mother of James, Joanna and <u>other</u> women went to the tomb"* with the tomb **already** open (unlike Matt).

Again, here in **Luke**, there was **no** *body,* but *not **one*** *angel* (sitting on the stone) but <u>**two**</u> and now *"in shining garments"*! Again, the **angels** *said; "He had risen and was not there"* and to **inform** the *disciples, b*ut, this time the *women <u>did **not** meet Yahshua</u> on the* way! And, upon meeting the disciples who did **not** *believe* them, *Peter "ran to the tomb" to see for himself,* where *"he saw the empty tomb and linen cloths"* and **left.**

Again this account is **drastically** *different* from the *others.* There were **more** *women* this time and **two** angels. Plus, here **no** one **saw** *Yahshua* until He *appeared* to the (**two**) *disciples* on the *"road to Emmaus".* (Not Galilee) Unlike the *first* two *accounts,* they did **not** *recognize* Him until *after **much*** conversation, including the Mary's telling them they had a *"<u>vision</u> of angels"* who *informed* them. Again, *parts* of these accounts mesh, but other parts *don't* even *come* **close**!

And finally, we have another *radically* **different** account *rendered* in **John**! There, in chapter 20 we find **only** *Mary Magdalene* **arriving** *at* the *tomb* (while still dark) and when she didn't find Yahshua's *body,* she **ran** to *Simon* **Peter** (and the *other* **disciple** Yahshua loved) and lamented that Yahshua was *gone* and asked *where* they *took* Him. There is **no** *mention* of **angels,** and *Peter* with the *"other disciple" ran to the tomb* (v.4) finding the linen *cloths* (folded) but *no* body. They then *left* and went **back** *home.*

In verse 11 then, we find **Mary** *weeping* and *looking* in the *tomb.* Again she sees **two** *angels* **sitting,** only this time *one* was *sitting* at the *head* and the other at the *feet* of where Yahshua had been laying. They asked her *why* she was *weeping,* to which she exclaimed, while turning to *confront* **Yahshua,** whom she **didn't** *recognize.* She thought He was the *gardener* and asked if He had *taken* the *body* and *where* He put it. He then said *"Mary"* which she *recognized* and *exclaimed "Rabboni"*!

He then tells her to *not **cling*** to Him as He had *not* yet *ascended* to His Father and to *go **tell*** the *disciples* (except Thomas). Then in verse 19, He came (through the wall) and stood in the *middle* of His *disciples* and *showed* them His *wounds*. He then "*breathed on them*" and said; "<u>*recieve the*</u> (YHWH's) ***Spirit***". In verse 26 then, we find Him *appearing* to *Thomas **eight*** *days* later. (The "*doubting Thomas*" story)

Now, this is *where* it gets ***really*** *strange* in chapter 21. There we *find* a *whole **different*** *account* of His *meeting* with His *disciples*. Simon (Peter) Thomas, Nathanael, the sons of Zebedee and two others *fishing* with no luck. Yahshua (whom they didn't recognize) shows up and asks *if they had any food.* He then tells them to *cast* their net on the "*right side of the boat*" *where* they got a *full* catch. Getting back to shore, they found a ***fire*** *burning* and Yahshua instructing them to put some of their *fish* on it. It then states in

v.12; "*none of them **dared** asked **who He was**".*

Apparently they *suspected* it was Him, which is very *strange* considering

v.14 tells us that this was the ***third time*** He *appeared* <u>to them.</u> Did they *forget* what He ***looked*** like after *seeing* Him ***twice*** *before* and *having* ***received*** "*His Spirit*" which "*He breathed on them*"? Unfortunately there is something very ***wrong*** with this *picture*! John's account is about as *different* from the others as you can get! (They are all different) But, we must remember the gospels were *written* from ***oral*** *tradition* and to keep our ***salt*** *shakers* handy and ***not*** *throw* the baby *out* with the *bathwater* as did the Jews. After all, the NT is *proof* the Spring OT Feasts (harvest) were ***rehearsals*** for the ***real*** *thing*!

Chapter 2

Ancient Hatreds and Agendas

Many *great* (and wise) men such as Winston Churchill, *echoed* the oft quoted *axiom*; "*Those who do **not** learn from history are doomed to **repeat** it*". There's great *wisdom behind* that statement considering even the *wisest* man in history, Solomon, gave it *credence*; "*There is **nothing** new under the sun*". (Everything repeats)

Unfortunately, *never* in history has that ***wise** sentiment* been more ***ignored**!* It seems the *prevailing **attitude*** in our modern society (at least in the Western, *modern **Israelite*** nations) is we are *paving* "***new** ground*" but are we; *really?*

Ironically, one of the *most **valuable** sources* of *history* known to man is one that's mostly *rejected* as ***fable,*** Biblical! You see; if an *enemy* wants to *infiltrate* with the *intent* to ***destroy*** a *nation,* what better way than to get the people to *forget* their *enemies* in the *past?* After all, do *ancient **hatreds*** ever really go *away?* An *honest* look into *history **confirms*** they don't!

To that end, there's a scripture that *far **exceeds*** its *weight* in ***precious** jewels*; it's **II Peter** 3:8. This scripture gives us such amazing *insight* into the "*whys*" of ***current*** conditions; "*with the Lord* (YHWH) ***one day is as a thousand years** and a **thousand years** is as **one day***"! Wow, what a shocking *mouthful* of *insight* when fully *comprehended*!

Unfortunately, after 40 years of *listening* to preachers *pontificate*, rarely heard was a commentary on **what** II **Peter** actually *says*, much less *implies*! On the surface, it indicates an obvious *difference* between the *time* **continuum** we *know* and *exist* within, and the Creator's. What Peter was clearly **instructing** His *disciples* (and us indirectly) is that **time** in our *dimension* passes *blindingly* fast compared to *time* **passing** on **the** *other* **side** of the *curtain*.

The *truth* is, from the perspective of our *spiritual* **adversaries**, the *Garden* of **Eden** was *just* **earlier** *this* **week**!! Unfortunately, we in this **time** zone simply *fail* to *grasp* the *depth* of that **reality**! We (as a whole) have *relegated* the **activities** and **attitudes** of our *adversarial*, **demonic**, *enemies* to the *dusty* shelves of **fables** and *myth,* whereas from *their* perspective, their **anger** and **hatred** for the Creator YHWH and **His** *people* is as *fresh* as a **few** *days* ago! We can be sure there's *nothing* **dusty** about *that AT ALL*!

The obvious *point* here is; for Israel's *ancient* **spiritual** *enemies* to *cause* us to **forget** *them* and **their** *agendas*, they need only *wait* a *few* **days** (from their time perspective). Doubtless, their *jealousy,* **anger**, and **hatred** towards *YHWH* and *mankind* hasn't *diminished* in the least; of that we can be sure!

To *relegate* ancient Bible history *to* **irrelevant** *fable* and *myth,* as modern Israel (and mankind) has *done*, is a *monstrous* **travesty** and will be the *undoing* of **Western** *nations* and the *world* as a whole!

Considering YHWH's *Plan* for His *Family* and people has **not** been *completed*, there can be no doubt His *demonic* adversaries' *evil* **agenda** to *destroy* His *Plan* and **us**, is as blazing a *wildfire* in their *hearts* as ever! In fact, the Great *Flood* that **drowned** the *watchers* **children** was just **earlier** *this* **week**! Are they not *lusting* for **revenge**? We must also *not* forget that all the *pagan* nations (puppets of the demon spirits) that *conquered* and *enslaved* Israel are **still** *around* and are still *enemies* of (modern) Israel.

An extremely interesting (and short) *study* is to look into *"who"* all those people (nations) are in this **present** *age*. The shocking *result* of that *query* is that they are virtually across-the-board, modern *Muslim* nations! In fact, a very telling *example* of that ancient hatred *still* being **alive** and well, is found in the *attitudes* the Arabs *express* towards the *modern **Jews*** and the ***US***! It's plainly *seen* in the fact they have never given even the *slightest* <u>**valid**</u> reason for their **blind** *hatred*! In spite of their *hatred*, the Jews have only *treated **them** well* extending to them every *benefit* of *doubt*.

In fact, the Jews gave the *Arabs* **control** of the temple *mount* and *Gaza* when they *didn't* **have** *too*! But, interestingly, this time the Arab peoples are *determined* not to just *enslave*, but to **exterminate** *modern **Israel***! (voiced by the Ayatollah of Iran) Obviously, the Arabs' **irrational** *hatred* can only be *coming* from a *high* (other dimensional) *place* and it's *not* just for the *modern **Jews***! They call modern *Israel* (Jews) *"little **satan***" while *labeling* the *United* **States** (modern Ephraim) *"the great **satan**"*! They have been *telling* the *world* after they *run* the *Jews* *"**into** the sea"* they are going *after* the US!

What a shocking coincidence (not really) considering the ancient *patterns*; it's *Ephraim* (Joshua) with his *faithful* partner *Caleb* (Jew) that led **ancient** *Israel* into the **Promised** *Land*! That ancient *example*, as I **Corinthians** 10:11 explains, was a *type* and **rehearsal** of the **real** *thing* *"for **them** upon whom the **ends** of the **ages*** (age) *have come"*! The demon *adversaries* (literally-*"satans"*) fully knowing the *reality* of *that* **truth,** are *gathering* their *pawns*, modern Muslims and a few *others*, in an all out last ditch *effort* to *stop* YHWH's *plan* for **Ephraim** (US) and **Judah** (Jews) to *lead* His *modern* **People** into the *"New Promised Land"*!

We conclude from ancient *history* that YHWH was *forced **over*** and *over* to *allow* Israel's *enemies* to *enslave* them in order to *turn* them *back* after continually *turning **away** from* Him.

Reading those *accounts* in **Judges** is like listening to a *broken* record; happening *over* and **over** and *over* again! They just did not learn! Has anything *changed* today? Has modern Israel's *inclination* to *turn* **away** from and **reject** *YHWH* and His **torah** *instructions,* **changed**? The answer to that one is blatantly *obvious* to anyone with *open* eyes!

At the same time, has *YHWH changed,* even though **Malachi** 3:6 says He *doesn't*? That said, will He not once **again** *turn* His *back* and *allow* the **same ancient enemies** to **again** have *their* **way** with *modern* Israel? Again, those who *ignore* **ancient** Biblical *history* are certainly *doomed* to **repeat** *it*! In fact, our *ancient* **enemies** are currently *swarming* into our *modern* **Israelite** *nations* behind the *scenes* like a *tsunami;* to *do* what they've *always* **done** in the *past*; **subdue** and *enslave* (thankfully for the *last* time)!

To conclude this mind blowing mini-study; is it any wonder why the *controllers* (puppet masters) of this world are also **poisoning** us with their **inoculations, medicines, genetically modified foods, fluoridated** and **chlorinated water**; not to mention *teaching* our young *women* (and men) to be **promiscuous** and **murder** their *unborn babies*? That's not to mention the blatant *promotion* of **Sodomy** (Homosexuality). They are literally turning us into a *modern* **Sodom** and *Gomorrah,* and most know **how** that*ended*! They are doubtless expecting the **same** end for us!

Chapter 3

What the Heck is Anti-Christ?

One of my favorite *profound* sayings states; "***The truth is stranger than fiction***"! This mini-study is a perfect *example* of that *very* concept. That said; religions, like Christianity *teach* and *believe* so many *absurdities*. For example; they *celebrate* the *birth* of *their* Messiah on a day called (named) "*Christ **killing***"!? ("*Mas*" is the root of massacre) Plus, they *believe* and teach the **Hebrew** (Jewish) *Messiah* had a **Greek** *name*; not just *any* Greek *name*, but *one **dedicated*** to the **chief** God of the *Greeks,* **Zeus**! (A name was *dedicated* to Zeus by *attaching* the *last **two*** *letters* of Zeus's name.)

Honestly, how could the *Hebrew* Messiah have a *Greek* name, one *dedicated* to Zeus at that, considering the scriptures show *Him* and His *family **in*** and *teaching* in the temple? You see, someone with a *Greek* (Hellenistic) *name* would never be *allowed **anywhere*** near the temple! In fact, as far as the Pharisees were concerned, all of the **Hebrew Diaspora** (scattered ten tribes) were now *Gentiles,* let alone *those* of the diaspora with **Gentile** (like Greek) *names*!

Considering such absurdities, this mini study is going to take a *peek* into an even greater *absurdity*; this one called *"Anti-Christ"*! That said, just *who* or *what* is an **"anti-Christ"** anyway? Well, ask 50 Christian ministers and you will probably get *50* **different** *explanations*. The *problem* is those 50 *different* ideas are all based to one degree or another on private interpretation.

What *confusion*; but the scriptures tell us *"confusion"* is **not** of the Creator. That means *confusion* has to be of the *devil*, right? Is that where **this** anti-Christ confusion is *originating*? Well, most *believe* the *anti-Christ* is the *devil* or *someone* **possessed** by the *devil*; an *assumption* that would be well *founded*, except there's a *problem*!

The *confusion* of this *supposed* Biblical concept (teaching) takes absurdity to a *whole* **new** *height* when we take an **honest** *look* (like the name *"Christ-mas"*)! First of all, considering the *first* part *"anti"* would indicate someone *antagonistic* or *opposite*. If that's true *"anti-Christ"* would mean being **opposed** to or *against* *"Christ"* right? Well, when we look into *what* this **title** or *name* **is** and *where* it *originates*, it gets very *strange* very quickly!

You see *"Christ"* is an English translation of the *Greek* word *"Christos"*. Christos is the Greek word meaning *"anointed"* or *"anointed one(s)"*. Well, that all sounds *well* and *good* until we do a little *investigating* into the *Greek* **gods**. You see, *they* were **all** *"Christos"* i.e. **anointed** ones, with Zeus being the *chief* **anointed** one, or **Christ**! Wow, what a bombshell that bit of *understanding* (truth) is!

Well, the common *explanation* is *"Christos"* means the *same* thing as the **Hebrew** word for *"Anointed One"* **"Mashiyach"** but, the **Hebrew** *Messiah* could *never* be *Christos* (Christ) because it's a **Gentile** *designation* which made (makes) it **unclean** to the Jews (Hebrews).

A Jew, or *Hebrew*, could **never** be *Christos* (Christ) as it's an oxymoron; *Hebrews* are *not **gentile** Greeks* and were given a completely **different** (separate-set-apart) *anointing* (*commission*) than the Gentiles!

YHWH made it abundantly clear **His** *people* (Israel) were "**set apart**"- exclusively ("*qodesh*"-badly translated "*Holy*") for a **special** *purpose*, which was to be a **priesthood** to the *Gentiles*! Obviously, the *Greeks* (Gentiles) are *anointed* (Christos) for a completely **different** *purpose* than the *Hebrews* (or Jews) so **only** a **Greek** could be *given* the "*Greek*" **designation** of "**anointed one**" or "**Christ**"!

On the *other* side; only a *Hebrew* (Israelite) could be given the *Anointing* of *Mashiyach,* which is a *commission* YHWH clearly *gave* **His** *people* (Israel) in **Exodus**19:6; to be a *priestly* (priesthood) people to the *Gentiles*!

It's *they* who were, and still are, **anointed** (commissioned) to *lead* the *Gentiles* (like the Greeks) to YHWH! That's *what "Mashiyach"* means! No *Greek* Messiah (Christ) can ever *take* upon *himself* (or his people) the *commission* **YHWH** *gave* His *set-apart* people, **Israel**!!

Well, that brings us back to the *concept* of *anti-Christ*. It would literally be someone *opposed* to a **Greek** *messiah* or **Greek** *anointed one* (not Hebrew). That said; who's more *anti-Christ* (anti-Greek gods) than *YHWH* or His *set apart-**exclusive**** people? Like I said in the beginning, how more unbelievably *absurd* can it get? "*The truth really is **stranger** than fiction*".

But, that shocking truth should *not* seem *strange* considering the translators also *exchanged* the **Hebrew** Messiah for a *Greek* one; "**Iesus**" (Jesus)? After all, by *replacing* the **Hebrew** Name of the *first-born* **Son** of YHWH, **everything** is **changed**; the entire "**big**" picture **Plan** of YHWH is *destroyed* and **lost**!

You see, Yahshua, the ***actual*** *name* of the ***Hebrew*** *Messiah,* means; "*YHWH* (the Father) *is Salvation*"! Again, the translators (puppets of the demon muses) getting us to *accept* a *false* **Greek** *Messiah* is no *different* from getting us to *accept* "*Christ*" as the ***true*** *designation* of the *Jewish* (Hebrew) Messiah!

Not to *stray* too far from topic, we can add even more *emphasis* to the absurdity of the *concept* of *anti-Christ* by witnessing how the translators *exchanged* the Creator's special *Set Apart* Name, *YHWH* for "***Baal***"! Wow, *how* was that even *possible*? Of course, ***Baal*** translated to *English* is "***Lord***"!! The "*Lord*" is the very *god* the Israelites were constantly getting in *trouble* for *worshipping* back in ancient times! Talk about shock upon shock!

Again, if we're to *accept* the *designations* (titles) at *face* value, the *anti-Christ* would be someone *opposed* to the ***Greek*** *gods*, like the ***Hebrew*** *Messiah* and His (Creator) Father *YHWH*; not to mention all YHWH's people!

But, obviously, the *original* word for *anti-Christ,* before the ***demon*** *inspired* translators got hold of it, would have been "*anti-Mashiyach*"; that is, anyone *opposed* to the ***Hebrew*** *Messiah,* Yahshua, and *what* He was *Anointed* (Mashiyach) for; that is to be *High Priest* of ***Israel***, who in turn were *Anointed* to be the *Priesthood* to the Gentiles; to lead them to YHWH! Besides, the Apostle John *proclaimed* that "***many*** *antichrists had* ***come***" already in the *first* century! We find that in I **John** 2:18! He goes on to say in verse 26, he was telling them "*because of* ***those*** *trying to* ***deceive*** *them*"!!

Chapter 4

Angelic Animals?

I'm sure most everyone has heard the term (even if not understood) *"the white **elephant** in the room"*. Personally, I don't know where the saying *originated*, or how, but most of us *understand* what it means. For those few who may not; the white *elephant* in the room is a reference to a huge *problem obvious* to everyone, but without anyone *willing* to *address*. I'm sure everyone can site at least one such white *elephant* in their families and/or associations over the years.

With that in mind, there is a Biblical ***white*** *elephant* (among the many I address) that is quite puny (pun) considering the *title* of this mini study; that of *angelic **animals***! Even though it's *plain* as the noses on our faces, I've ***not*** *heard* a *single* person or Bible teacher *address* or *question* it! In fact, most upon hearing it, would have a *cow*! (Pun intended again) But, for anyone to be unwilling to *acknowledge* what is so ***plainly*** *revealed* in scripture. is an incredible *mystery*!

Think for a moment; just how many people you know (including yourself) are willing to acknowledge the *concept* of "***angelic***" animals? After all (especially those of Christian backgrounds) all we have ever heard about *angels* is they are *humanoid* in appearance (baby or adult) usually with *wings*. That, of course, should prompt the *question*; just where did such an *angelic **concept*** originate?

Well, we have many *examples* of angels *appearing* to people in ancient times, but always as *humans* dressed in white. But *what* of the *wings*; *where* did they *originate*? Actually, it is somewhat obvious considering the *descriptions* of the *Seraphim* in **Ezekiel**, chapters 1-3. But, before going there, let's consider the *first* and most *familiar "**angel**"* of all mentioned in scripture; the so-called *"serpent"* in the Garden of Eden.

Why does virtually everyone *ignore* the **obvious** *description* of this *creature*; that of a very **intelligent** and *"talking"* (reasoning) *creature*, which is obviously **not** *human* or *humanoid*! It is also *plainly* states this *creature* (Nachash) was the most *cunning* of all the "*beasts*" (of the field)! **Beasts**? Obviously, this *beast* (not human) was **not** *alone*, there were (are) *many* like it! Also obvious, is the fact this *Nachash* was not like the **dumb** *animals* we have all around us today.

So, *what* exactly was this *Nachash*? Well, to begin with *"serpent"* (snake) is not the *correct* translation considering *"Nachash"* means *"divine enchanter" "shining one"* and/or *"burning one"*. In fact, the **fiery *serpent*** (seraph) Moses was *instructed* to *erect* in **Numbers** 21:9, was a *Nachash*. Snakes are not exactly **burning** *ones*, but we do have further *descriptions* of this *Nachash* creature in **Ezekiel** 28. There we read of a *perfectly* created being, *clothed* in *jewels,* also called "*the Cherub that covers*" (YHWH's throne).

On each side of the Ark of covenant (a *replica* of YHWH's throne) was a gold rendering of a **winged** *creature*! According to the lament, this **perfectly** *created* **creature** (Ez.28) *defected* (rebelled) from its *created* *purpose* and *position* as one of YHWH's *winged* Cherubim *covering* His *throne,* to *become* what we have come to *know* as *"the devil"*. (Chief adversary)

Satan, by-the-way, is simply the *Hebrew* word for *"adversary"* and *"adversity"* and is **not** a *name* at all. Strangely, we have *no* other *descriptions* other than the *one* in **Revelation** 12 of the appearance of a Cherub, but we do have many *descriptions* of its first *cousins,* the *Seraphim* in chapters 1-3 of **Ezekiel**.

A close *look* at the *Seraphim* in **Ezekiel** shows they were more *animal* (beast) than human. In fact, one description shows them to have *four* faces (three animal) many *wings* and eyes, and **hooves** for *feet*. One thing's for sure, there's almost *nothing* human (or humanoid) about them except for the *one* human *looking* face!

Well, we have the best *evidence* of the *appearance* of *angels* in **Genesis** 1 with the *creation* of the **animals**. It says they were *"created* **after** (in the image) *their kind*! Well, the only *"kind"* in *existence* at the creation of the *physical* animals were the **angels** (and the Elohim, which is another study). Plus, if we *incorporate* that bit of understanding with the *Nachash* in the Garden, it all begins to come together quite amazingly!

We must *not* forget the strange event of the *"Sons of the Elohim"* in **Genesis** 6 (*"Watchers"* as they are called by Enoch) who *vacated* their *posts, descended* and *procreated* with *human* women. How interesting, their offspring were *bizarre* creatures called *"nephilim"* (badly translated *"giants"*) which were *superhuman* **hybrid** *creatures,* (but did include *giants*)

But, another white *elephant* in the room is the fact that **all** the **ancient** *cultures* **worshiped** *animals* as **gods**! Hmm, whatever *possessed* them to do that if the *animals* were the *lowly* **physical** *creatures* of which we are now *familiar?*

Well, here's where it get very interesting; according to the most *ancient* writing we have, the Book of Enoch (taken out of the OT canon after 500 years by the Catholics) documents how 200 of these *beings* (watchers) *vacated* their *realm* and *posts* (see Jude 6 also) to **establish** *themselves* and their *offspring* as **gods** and *kings*!

In fact, the Hebrew word most often translated "*angel*" is "*Malak*" which curiously also the word for "*king*"! What a coincidence considering the gentiles (pagans) not only *worshiped* **animals** but *loved* the *concept* of ***kings***!

Is it also just a *coincidence* that YHWH (Father Creator's personal Name) *condemned* the *concept* of a **king** to His people while also *forbidding* them to *worship* the *demons* (angelic animals). Interestingly "*angels*" are also **described** as "*shinnon*" in **Psalms** 68:17. *Shinnon* means "*changeable*" or in modern vernacular; "*shape-shifter*"!

No doubt, the *animal* watchers that *descended* and *procreated* with humans most likely *presented* themselves as *human* but after *combining* angelic *animal* DNA with *human*, the *truth* was out of the bag. After all, from just where did all the *half-***human**; *half-***animal** *creatures* appear? Don't forget, these creatures; like *Anubis* (human with Jackal head) and Ra (human with bird head) were worshipped by the Egyptians as *gods*!

Well, getting back to the *Nachash* in the Garden, we have one last *description*, which is perfectly *supported* in **Job** 41 (Leviathan) "*a DRAGON*"! Yes, that *immortal*, *winged*, *scaled*, *fire*-*breathing* and *talking* *dragon* is *described* **perfectly** with Leviathan! Read it carefully and you will find every one of those draconian *descriptions*! (Also Rev. 12)

Understanding all this, can there be any doubt ***why*** we are *acting* more and more *like* **animals** after having been *taught* we **evolved** from them? Oh yeah; let's not forget where the big push for **animal** *rights* and *veganism* is *originating*!

Chapter 5

A Story as Old as Time

A very *popular* movie, which *originally* came out as a Disney *cartoon* film was one called "*Beauty and the Beast*". It was a *cute* little film (supposedly fiction) that was very popular with *children* and many adults. A couple new versions were produced using *real* actors along with the *animated* **candle** stick, **teapot**, *silverware*, **plate** *ware*, and *dresser*. But, a most interesting line used in the *promotional* song was "*A tale as old as time*"!

How shocking to discover that *statement* is *more* **true** than not! To understand, and set the *stage* (no pun intended) we need to go back in *time* and *investigate* some *things* that *happened* and were *happening*. To that end, we find a few *scriptures* in the Bible showing one of the ***first*** *things* the Creator's created was the **angelic** world. This is *reinforced* in a much greater way in a book called "***Jubilees***".

Judging by the *bits* and *pieces* of **ancient** knowledge, the pre-Earth era, with just the Creators and Their immortal **angelic** *creations*, may have spanned *millions* of years. We have no *record* of the length of this *epoch*, but we know it was *extensive*. Then, at some point, the Creators *created* the Earth and *humanity*, which They said was *perfect*! (Not desolate or in vain) Again, there seems to have been a *long* period of time to *elapse* until an inner *planetary* **cosmic** *war* erupted.

We find the first hint of this in **Ezekiel** 28:15-16 of a ***perfectly created*** being (angel) the "***King*** (ruler) ***of Tyre***" (Mars) of whom it states; "*you were perfect in your ways from the day you were created til iniquity*" (pride) *was found in you*". The chapter goes on to *chronicle* how this *being* (creature) was *corrupted* by its "*trading*" (merchandising) and was consequently *thrown* to *Earth*. (v.17) That *action* was a *solar* **system** *destroying event* which *included* the *destruction* of *Earth*. (Isa. 14–Rev.12)

Jeremiah speaks of a *time* when YHWH *surveyed* His *perfectly* **Created** *Earth* (**Jeremiah** 4:23) and *found* it now "***without form***" (*tohuw-destroyed*) "*and* **void**".(*bohuw-empty*). It goes on to state in v.25 how He "*beheld and indeed there was* **no man**" (v.26) *and the birds of the heavens had* **fled**" and that "*all its* **cities** *were* **broken down**" and in *ruins*. Those verses were continued in **Genesis** 1:2 where it states that the world "*was* (had become) **without form** *and* **void**" which is "*tohuw* and *bohuw*" the exact same words *used* in **Jeremiah** 4:16. Then in **Genesis** 1, He goes on to *restore* the Earth and *recreate* mankind.

Well, few people are *willing* to *accept* these *scriptural* **truths** but we do have *secular* **proof** of these events to back up the scriptures. In fact, after sending the *probes* and *rovers* to **Mars**, we know *Mars* once had **oceans** and **civilization** until it was **struck** by a *moon* **sized** *object* in its *southern* hemisphere. This *collision* all but *split* the *planet* in **half,** *causing* it to *careen* **out** of its *orbit* into the *inner* **solar** system to all but *collide* with Earth! NASA, *JPL*, and the *British Journal* of *Nature,* all discovered by *reverse* **computer** *mapping* of the *solar* system, this **extinction** *level* **event** of Earth's life is an *ancient* ***fact***! How interesting then this "***King*** (Queen) *of Mars*" (Tyre) addressed in **Ezekiel** 28 had a **trading** *empire* (apparently including Earth) when it was *destroyed.*

Having *its* trading **empire** and home world *destroyed* and being *thrown* to Earth (Ez. v.17) we can only imagine the **seething** *hatred* in *its* heart *towards* the *Creator*. Now being filled with a *spirit* of **revenge**, it shows up in the *Creator's* **Garden** of *Eden* (v.13). Apparently the **best** *revenge* it could *contrive* was to go *after* and **corrupt** the *newest creation* of *YHWH*, which was **Adam** *and* **Eve**! (The *apples* of His eye-pun intended)

In the **Book of Enoch** (part of the OT canon for some 500 years) we find the account of *200* **watchers** (angels) *discussing* the *idea* of going *down* to *humanity* and taking *wives* for *themselves* (which they did). **Genesis** 6 *briefly* refers to this *event* also. It seems these *creatures* (like the *nachash* in Eden) had the ability to **shape shift**.(Shinin in Hebrew) No doubt they *showed* themselves to the **human** *women* as *handsome* **young** *men*, but their high-bred *offspring* revealed the *truth*. Half *human* and **half** *animal* creatures began *appearing* everywhere!

Eve was one of those *impregnated* by one of those *angelic* **watcher** *creatures* as well as Adam. (Cain and Able were twins (Olaf Hagee) We know this because of *what* YHWH asks Cain (Quain) after he *slew* Able, in **Genesis** 4:6. There YHWH asked him why his *countenance* (face) was *fallen* (a mistranslation) which is "*nephal*" in the **original** *Hebrew*. The *nephal* were the high-bred offspring of the watcher (angels). According to Bible Historian Olaf Hagee, there are many ancient Hebrew writings saying "*Quain*" (Cain) had **glowing** *eyes* (and skin) *grew* **horns** and became a giant! He became the first "*mighty man*" (nephilim giant) on Earth, with many more to come!

What virtually everyone reading **Genesis** reads right *over*, is the *fact* the *animals* were created "*after their kind*". (Gen.1:25-KJ) What *kind* **preceded** *them*? Well, it was the **angelic** *kind*! The *animals* were all created as **spirit** *animals* (angels) **first,** and considering these creatures were *like* **gods** to *physical* humans, they naturally were *worshipped* as **gods** *and* **kings**! In fact, "*Malak*" (angel) in Hebrew means both "*angel*" and "*king*". What a coincidence!

Well, now we get back to the *title* of this paper which is *a **story** as **old** as **time***; "*Beauty and the Beast*"! We must keep in mind it was *beasts* who anciently "*took*" **human** *women* as mates! So, there's **nothing** *new* about *that* movie! In fact, it shocked archeologists to *unearth* ancient *relics* from the most *ancient **South** American* people called the "*Moche*" *depicting* on their *pottery* the same **animated** *housewares* as *portrayed* in the film! How shocking is that!?[Professor Edwin Barnhart-Lost Worlds of South America-]

According to those *ancient* writings, there was a *Jaguar* (watcher king) who **took** a *human **woman*** to be his *wife* and *queen,* who then spawned a **human** *baby* with a ***Jaguar*** head (like the Minotaur). But, unfortunately, the ancient version did not have the *happy **ending*** Disney portrays.

No, in the ancient version, the *half-breed* child with the ***Jaguar's** head,* grew large and one day, turned and **devoured** its *mother*! So much for *happily* ever after! The *Jaguar **headed** monster* then went on to become the **new** *god* of the *Moche* people! Sorry, that is not the *standard* Disney *happy* ending at all, but that's the "***real***" *world* of ancient times! (For more on this subject, see "The Grand Trans-dimensional Delusion")

Chapter 6

The Age of *"Feelings"*

There was a song back in the seventies called *"Feelings"* which was (as you might have guessed) all about *feelings!* In fact, it seems everywhere we *look* these days, people are talking about their *"feelings"* and/or being *offended.* It's amazing to see all the ***therapists,*** *teachers,* and even *parents* focusing on *feelings;* how a person or child *feels;* **how** something (that happened) *makes **them** feel.* In fact, there's been a whole *revolution* promoting the *importance* of *feelings* (like racism) and a *push* to get in *touch* with *those* feelings! The 64.000 dollar question is why? Where's this *really* coming *from?*

Is this a *good* trend or not? I will have say with utmost confidence that *understanding* and *caring* about the *feelings* of *others* is very important! In fact, treating others with *respect* to their *feelings* is no doubt a ***large** part* of the *command* to **love** others as *ourselves.* But, one thing's for sure, it's ***impossible*** to live in this world and ***not** offend* anyone. In fact, it seems many these days, ***insist*** upon *living* in a *constant **state*** of *offense.* Others are *offended* for simply ***not** getting* what they *think* they *deserve!*

At any rate, the worlds' *obsession* with ***feelings*** has ***red flags*** flying all over it! After all, is it *evil* for a child to ***feel*** bad for ***losing*** a *game* (or an adult) or not getting as *good* a *present* as someone else? Are we really to *shield* them from such *experiences* as our society is *advocating lately?*

Another *side* to this *feeling* issue is the *push* to "***follow** our hearts*" especially when it comes to *relationships*. I don't think I've seen a movie or tv show that doesn't **condemn** a person *following* their **head** *versus* their *heart*. Even more *disturbing* is to *hear* that very same *promotion* in the *pulpits* of churches! But, maybe that *place* of *teaching*, being called "***pulpit***" ("*pulling into the pit*") isn't a coincidence!?

Even in the congregation I was raised "*self-esteem*" was *taught* as being so very important. In fact, some in my own family came at me with the argument; *how* can we *love* someone unless we *first **love** ourselves*? That almost seems a *logical* argument until we incorporate *scriptural* teaching and a little **common** *sense*! The *admonition* to *love* others as we *love **ourselves***, does *not* mean people *don't* (for the most part) love *themselves* as I have had *friends* and **loved** ones argue!

What's obvious to anyone with an **open** *mind* and *eyes,* is to realize *self- love,* is *inherent* in **all** *people.* It's a little *thing* called "*selfishness*". From birth, our primary motivation is to **take** *care* of **ourselves, our** *needs* and **our** *wants.* It's having to *learn **how*** to *love* and *think* of *others* the way we *think* of *ourselves* that's the *problem.* People who *claim* to *hate* themselves are *decieved.* What they *hate* is **their** *perception* of how **others** *view* them; that they are **not** *loved* or *valued* they way *they* think *they **should** be!* In fact, I have no doubt the *chief **source*** for *suicide* is *excessive **self** love!*

People who ***truly** hate* themselves would **not** *care* what *other* people **think** of *them.* They would **not** *eat* the food they *like* or *wear* the *clothes **they** like.* But that's not the way it is with the so *called **self**-haters.*

They are *obsessed* with *self-comfort* and **self** *pity*. But, a person who truly *hates* him or herself, will have **no** *pity* for *themselves*. One *does* **not** *pity* someone or *something* it **hates**! Well, there's a very obvious *explanation* for such *self-deception* and *behavior found* in **Jeremiah** 17:9 which *dogmatically* states; "*The **heart is deceitful above all things**"*! That's a *mountain* of a scripture very few are willing to *accept*! After all, how can the "*heart*" be **deceitful** above "*ALL things*"? But then, isn't the devil a "*thing*" to be included in "**all** *things*"? Can the *heart* be more *deceitful* than the *devil*?

Well, the *truth* to this *conundrum* is found right *there* in the *Garden* of *Eden*. But, before looking at it, we must understand it's the **heart** that's the *seat* of our *feelings* and **emotions**, and, anyone who's been *around* for any time at all, understands how **fickle** *feelings* and *emotions* can be.

This is especially true for children and *bi-polar* adults. They can be *crying* **one** moment and *laughing* the next! The *reason* for that is our *emotions* (our hearts) **lie** to *us*. I'm not saying *emotions* are not *real* or should be ignored. No, they are very real, but need to be properly implemented and *controlled*.

A good *example* is the *emotion* of **loss**. It's a very real *emotion* and should *not* be *ignored*. When *improperly* dealt with, *grief* can *destroy* relationships, and turn people to **drugs** and *alcoholism*, and even *murder*. Emotions are extremely *powerful,* but again, must be *kept* in **proper** *perspective*.

The only way to understand *emotions* of the *heart* is to understand "**why**" they are so *unpredictable*. To understand, we need again go back to *see* exactly what *transpired* in the *Garden* in **Genesis**. There we find Adam and Eve *partaking* (and embracing) the *Tree* of *Knowledge* of *Good* and *Evil* (the dragon). What's rarely understood is **what** they *really* **did**; accept the "*spirit*" of that *reptilian* god. They unwittingly gave the Nachash the *permission* to **fill them** and their descendants with its' *spirit* of "**PRIDE**"!

Pride is the **opposite** of YHWH's *Spirit* of **humility**. Pride is a **lying** *spirit* that *destroys,* and brings *destruction* and *death*. It makes us *believe* every **lie** about **ourselves** *possible*, like how **generous** we are, or how *patient,* **loving,** *self-controled,* and/or **righteous**! I can go on and on, but whether we like it or not, we are all from birth, filled with that *proud,* **controlling**, and **destructive** *spirit*. Our duty in this **physical** *life* is to *identify* that *spirit* of *pride* (leaven) and **replace** it with *YHWH's* **Spirit** of **humility** and *truth*!

Getting back to the *title* of this study *"feelings"* the point should be obvious by now. The greatest *tool* the demons have to **manipulate** *us* is **pride,** with which they have **filled** our *hearts*. It's *through* **our** emotions they are able to **control** the *attitudes* and *behavior* of mankind. In fact, every *sin* and *evil* is *rooted* in **pride** and **emotion**. It was through *emotion* the Nachash (dragon) was able to *manipulate* Eve into *partaking*.

It knew Adam could *not* be *manipulated* so *easily* by his emotions (women are much more emotional) so it **targeted** *Eve*, who it *knew* would then be able to *manipulate* Adam through *his* **love** (emotion) for her, which is *exactly* what happened! It was though the *emotions* of **jealously** (turning to hatred) the *dragon* was able to *manipulate* Cain into **murdering** *Able*. So, is it any wonder why our current age is putting such *emphasis* on **feelings**.

This emphasis on *feelings* is being *facilitated* to *steal* our *national* and **personal** *freedoms* and **destroy** us! An extremely valuable scripture we would do well to remember is **Psalms** 119:165. It states; *"Great peace have those who keep* (practice) *your **Torah** and **nothing** shall **offend** them."*

Chapter 7

Amazing Chronology of Revelation

One of the greatest *keys* to understanding the **strange** *book* of **Revelation** is to *realize* it's **mostly** *chronological.* Due to the *fact* the Jews *founded* Christianity (first 15 popes were Jewish) and *hated* Yahshua and **His** *Apostles,* they **rewrote** *first* **century** *history* and *erased* the fact Yahshua **did** *return* for His *Priesthood* (including His Apostles) in the **first** *century* as He **promised** *them!*

Once we *understand* and *accept* **that** *truth,* everything begins to *fall neatly* **into** *place.* Understanding the *letters* to the **seven** *cities* (congregations) in *Asia,* in the first *three* chapters of **Revelation,** were to *warn* them *Yahshua's* **return** was **eminent** and they all *had* **problems** to *correct* to be *ready* for His **first** *century* **return.** These letters were certainly **not** for *people* (churches) **thousands** of *years* in the *future;* that's simply *absurd!*

Next, *understanding* Yahshua was in **heaven** *preparing* to **return** for His *Priesthood,* the next *two* chapters *fit* **perfectly.** In chapter 4, we're *given* a *picture* of *24* **elders;** no doubt the **saints** of *old* **resurrected** *with* Yahshua (Matt. 27:53) now *seated* **around** the *throne* in heaven, having *earned* their *crowns* and *positions* of *authority.*

Chapter 5 then, is about *opening* **judgement** *seals* of both **destruction** and **salvation** for the **completion** of the **spring** *harvest* (first century) and *beginning* of the **human** *fall* harvest. Then, there's a **leap** *forward* to the *initiation* of the *fall* **harvest** *season* in chapter 6, beginning with the *ride* of the **four** *horsemen*. The four *horsemen* kick off the **tribulation** *years* that *began* with the *Feast* of *Trumpets* **arriving** in **real** *time* **fulfillment** in 2017.

The **white** *horse* seems to denote *false* **righteousness** while **the** *rider* of has a *bow* (with arrows) and a *crown* which *depicts* **conquering**. The *white* horse no doubt *includes* **false** *religion* and no doubt includes **lying** *political* leadership. But, the "*crown*" is very interesting, considering the *globalists* used the "**crown virus**" to literally **conquer** *most* of the *world*! Plus, the crown *led* to the *shots*. Are this *horseman's* **arrows** a *picture* of the vaxes?

The *second* **red** *horse* no doubt *depicts* the *civil* (national) *wars* that **erupt** *shortly after*, which apparently *morphs* into a third **world** *war*. Naturally, **world** *war* brings a whole *host* of *evils*, which the *third* **black** horse *chronicles*. The **fruits** of *war*, are obviously **famine**, and *disease*. The **final** *horse* then, is **death**, which is *estimated* to be 3/4's of the **worlds** *population*. But, before the *ride* of the *red* horse, chap. 7 is *injected*.

With chapter 7, then, there's an *interlude*, where the **war** *horse* is **momentarily** *halted* until 12 *thousand* of each of the 12 *tribes* of Israel (144,000) are given a **seal** of *protection* to **survive** the ensuing *hell*.

Connecting the *dots*, this 144,000 have to be the **seeds** for the *new* **Promised** *land*, the *one* the OT physical **promised** *land* **pictured**, or *what* I've *dubbed*; "*the* **New** *Eden*"! This *fulfills* the **Ezekiel** 37 prophecy of the *tribes* of Israel *becoming* **one** *nation* again!

Even though the *chronology* has been *perfect* so far, for some reason, chapters 11 and 12 (and 19) are **out of place**. The events of chapter 12 *should* be right *after* chapter 5 by the fact the *supernatural* **Revelation** 12 "*sign of the woman in heaven*" was **seen** in **real** *time* during the *Feast* of *Trumpets* in 2017! That *sign* **confirmed** that Donald *Trump* (his name) *initiated* the *Feast* of **Trumpets** in **real-time fulfillment**, *September* 2017.

We don't *know* just **where** chapter 11 *fits*, but seems to flash forward *to* the **end** of the **millennial** *period* of the New *Eden*, which is actually only 800 years from now. (Pictured by the **8** days of the Feast of Tabernacles)

Then, we have *chapters* 8, 9, and 10, which **contextually** *follow* the **Revelation** 12 *sign* of the *woman*. That **sign** is the *announcement* of the *coming* of the *dragon* who is *coming* to **destroy** the *woman* (YHWH's Elect) who's *whisked* **away** by the great *Eagle* (Michael?) to a *place* of **safety** for *three* and one *half* years. That 3 and 1/2 years begins in **2024**, after the *second* **solar** eclipse, forming the *Hebrew* **letter** *Tav*. But, the *dragon* spews out a *great* **flood** after her, which the Earth *opens* its *mouth* to **swallow**. (Apparently the invasion of China)

Plus, about the *same* **time**, there is a *water* **flood** caused by the *second* **trumpet** *plague* in **Revelation** 8 which is an **asteroid** *that* falls into the *pacific* ocean. NASA is currently *tracking* **it** and named it Apophis. Chapters 8-10 *depict* in **great** *detail*, the *arrival* of the *Nemesis* **solar** *system,* which will *arrive* in 2024, which means "**Just** *instrument of* **punishment**"!

Then, in chapter 10 the **bottomless** *pit* is *opened* and the **imprisoned** *watchers* are **released** and the *world* is **forever** *changed*. Chapter 13 *details* a **new** *beast* (no longer the dragon) and **its** *kingdom* while chapter 14 is apparently the *completion* of the *fall* harvest. Chapters 15-18 *detail* the *judgement* of that *kingdom*, which **Zechariah** tells us is the **rebuilt** *Babylon* and apparently including the *new* **tower** of *Babel*.

Chapters 18 and 19 *foretell* of the *release* of the dragon, (from the pit) which is shown to have been *imprisoned* in chapter 20 (the last out *sequence* chapter). Chapters 21-22 then chronicle the **new** *heavens* and Earth along with the *new* **House** of **YHWH** descending *from* heaven.

Chapter 8

Angel of Light

In II **Corinthians** 11:14, we find a *strange* passage telling us "*the devil masquerades as an angel of light*". First of all, *what **is** an "angel* of *light*"? Considering, we don't find a *reference* to an *angel* of **light** anywhere else in the scriptures, how are we even supposed to *know **what** it *is*? Is it an *angel* made of *light*? Or maybe it's a *special **class** of *angels*?

Considering the many references to the **stars** being *angels,* such as **Job** 38:7, is that *what* the *stars* in the heavens **actually** are? After all, **Genesis** 1:14 tells us the *stars* were *placed* in the *heavens* to "*rule the night*"! Is "*rule*" simply a *metaphor,* or are those giant *balls* of *fire* literally *angels*? That may sound *absurd,* but we must remember, one of the *descriptions* of *angels* is "*Shinnon*" which means *changeable* or in modern vernacular, *shape-**shifter***.

We do have an *example* of such a *thing* in **Exodus**. There, we find a "*pillar of fire*" that gave the Israelites *light* and *warmth* at night and then became a *cloud* for *shade* during the day. In fact, it was that *cloud* that *lead* them through the *wilderness*, which means it was not *just* a *cloud*. No, it had to be a *shape-shifting **angel***.

Corinthians 10:11 also speaks of a "*rock*" that was "*anointed*" (christos- christ— the Greek word for *anointed*) to *follow* the *Israelites* through the *wilderness* and *provide* them with *water*. Unfortunately, the translators saw the word *anointed* (christ) and decided this had to be *Jesus*, which is an absurdity! The *truth* is, angels are *anointed* to do many *things for* YHWH.

Well, we do have a word that means "***light** bringer*" in **Isaiah**, which was **not** *original* but *added* by *Jerome* when he was *producing* his *Latin Vulgate* translation. His *memoirs* tell us he *received* an **euphony** while translating, to *change* the name "*Heylel*" in **Isaiah** 14, to *Lucifer*. Heylel loosely means "*god* of *death*" while Lucifer means the opposite; *bringer* of *light* (or life) Light many times is a *reference* to *life*, **not** *death*!

Without going into a long *dissertation* we find that *Heylel* was the dragon (Rev.12) that launched the *war* against *Michael* and His *angels* and *lost*. **Ezekiel** 28 also references this *event* and mentions how this *perfectly* created *being* (angel) was *cast* to Earth after being *corrupted* by it's *pride* and *greed* (trading) and of course, *losing* the war! It also states in **Ezekiel** 28 that this creature (dragon) was ***in*** the Garden of YHWH. It (she) no doubt was the metaphoric "*tree of the knowledge of good and evil*".

Remember, YHWH *told* Adam and Eve if they *partook* of that *tree* they would *die* (which they did)! In fact, we are told she (the devil) was the *original liar* (and murderer)! She told Eve and Adam the ***first** lie*, "*You will **not** surely **die**, but will be like the **gods*** (immortal)! But, of course, she was *lying* and they **died** as does *everyone* who *lives* by *her* spirit of *pride*!

One *thing* we see in scripture, is how YHWH would *change* someones name to *reflect* their **new** place or *purpose*. We find this with Abram, Sarai, and Jacob, just to name a few. Personally, I have concluded the *same* thing happened with *Heylel*. I *believe* her **name** *probably* originally **was** Lucifer (light bringer) **before** her *sin* and *rebellion*, which is *why* she **inspired** *Jerome* to *change* it *back*!

How amazing to see II **Corinthians** 11:14 *prophesying* she would become *Lucifer* hundreds of years before *Jerome* made the *change*! (That the *devil* would *masquerade* as an *"angel of light"*) Unfortunately, her *deciding* to make *war* against YHWH was a **death** sentence for *her* as well.

We see in **Revelation** 20:1-3 that on the real-time *spiritual* *fulfillment* of the *Day* of *Atonement*, she will be *bound* and *thrown* into the **bottomless** pit for the *duration* of the **real-time fulfillment** of the *Feast* of *Tabernacles* (new Eden). Then she will be *released* just before the *end* and the *burning* of the *Earth* that II **Peter** 3:10-12 informs us.

We don't know too much about her except she was *created* **perfect**, and was *one* of the *"covering Cherubim"* (apparently of YHWH's throne). She is also a *dragon* and the *angelic* **ruler** of Tyre (Mars). (Ez.28) Plus, she is called the *adversary* (satan-devil) and was the one in the Garden of *Eden* that *corrupted* Eve and Adam.

Thankfully, we are told that on the real-time *fulfillment* of the *Day* of *Atonement* (fall of 2027) she will be *thrown* into the *bottomless* **pit** with the angel *Azazel*. That way, during the 800 years of the *millennial* period (real- time fulfillment of the *Feast* of *Tabernacles*) she will be **unable** to *influence* and **kill** *humanity* until the *end* of that period when she will be *released* to raise *havoc* on the Earth one *last* time!

Revelation tells us *all* those that *follow* her will be **burned** *along* with the *old* Earth! Then YHWH *renews* the Earth and never again will a *creature* like the *dragon* be allowed to do what Heylel *did*.

But, we have to remember, YHWH *needed* her and her *minions* for a valuable reason, to give **us** an adversary to *fight*. You see, just to choose to **do** *right*, is only *half* of it. That *choice* has to be **fought** *for* to be truly *real*! So Heylel is literally a **necessary** *evil*! (Pun intended)

Chapter 9

Atlantean-Mars Trading Empire?

There's a very strange *account* in the Bible I have yet to hear *adequately* explained. It's found in **Ezekiel** 28; a *lament* to the "*prince*" and "*king*" of "*Tyre*". *Tyre*, of course, was the *Phoenician* **trading** capital of the Middle East which Nebuchadnezzar *attempted* to **conquer** but *failed*, considering he had *no* **navy**, which the *island* nation *possessed*. Tyre had the greatest *fleet* of ships in the *ancient* world and in fact *sailed* and *traded* over the **entire** *world*!

It's said King *Hiram*, who built **Solomon's** *temple* bought *materials* from Tyre, who brought materials from as far away as what is now called "*the America's*"! Much *archeological* **evidence** has been uncovered supporting that conclusion! Tyre was finally *destroyed* by *Alexander* the Great, who *claimed* a *silver* **flying** *ship* came out of *nowhere* and *destroyed* one wall of the Island *fortress* with a **beam** of *light*!

Getting to that "*lament*" *delivered* to the *Prince* and *King* of Tyre by **Ezekiel**, we find some very **bizarre** language and *events*. The *first* is how it was first *directed* to the "*prince*" of Tyre, obviously the **physical** *ruler* of *Tyre*. But then the *lament* strangely **shifts** to the "*King*" (Malik) of *Tyre* who is obviously **not** a *physical* **being**! (V.12) The text plainly states how *this* being was "*created* **perfect**" as (to be) a "*Covering Cherub*" (v.14) apparently one of the *winged* **creatures** that *covered* the **throne** of the *Creator*. It seems this creature was *perfect* until *corrupted* by its *vanity* (pride) and *greed* spawned by its' **merchandising** (trading)! (V.16)

The crazy *thing* is, verse 13 tells us this *winged* (reptilian) *creature* (nachash) was also in the *Garden of* **Eden**! Of course, the Christian churches all *teach* this *creature* was the "*snake*" and/or the *one* they call "*Satan*". But *Satan* is a *misnomer* considering it's simply the Hebrew word for "**adversary**" and/or "*adversity*". Somewhere along the line some *influential* **person** *removed* its' *actual* name "*Heylel*" (Is. 14) from the text and *replaced* it with the *generic* Hebrew word for "*Adversary*". Naturally, not *having* or *using* it's *actual* name has causing *great* **confusion** in Biblical understanding!

Verse 12 of **Ezekiel** 28 tells us this *perfectly* created creature was apparently the *most* **beautiful** *thing* ever created. But how did this **perfect** *creature* end up in the *Garden* of *Eden* as the Creator YHWH's (His personal Name pronounced "*Yah-way*") **adversary**?

Well, this *stunning* **reptilian** *creature,* **clothed** in *pure* **gems** (angelic scales) *became* **corrupted** by *its* **merchandising**! Obviously, there was a **trading** empire in *existence,* which we will see, was *operating* **before** the *Garden* of *Eden* and *Adam* and *Eve*!

In verses 16 &17 this *perfectly* created **creature**, *corrupted* by its' *beauty* and **merchandizing**, was *punished* by being *cast* to the *Earth*! We read that in verse 17, where the translators **wrongly** *translated* "*Erets*" (*Earth*) to "*ground*" versus its *primary* meaning "*Earth*". It also tells us this *cherub* was *humiliated* before its *peers* ("*laid before kings*"-angels) in that same verse. What the *average* person has *not* been taught is "*king*" and "*angel*" are the **same** word "*Malak*".

It seems the *original* **kings** were the *watchers*, which Enoch tells us *procreated* with humanity and set *themselves* up *as* **rulers**! That's why the Prophet Samuel was so *upset* when Israel wanted a "*king*" (literally-"*angel*") to **rule** them!

Getting back to this *reptilian* **angel** being *cast* to *Earth*, a shocking *truth* **denied** us is by *reverse* **computer** *mapping* the orbit of *Mars*, **Nasa**, *JPL*, and the *British Journal of Nature*, have all concluded that *Mars,* in ancient times, was struck by a *moon*-sized object (the remnants of which are it's current moons *Phobos* and *Demos*) was knocked into a *near* **miss** *orbit* with Earth.

It was a mass *extinction* event that's referenced in **Jeremiah** 4:16. There, we see how all *humanity* and its *cities* were *destroyed* and the Earth *rendered* "*Tohu and Bohu*" which is the *condition* we find in **Genesis** 1:2 (The Earth had become *tohu* and *bohu*-destroyed)!

The really amazing part of all this is "*Tyre*" is the *Phoenician* word for the *Roman* name "**Mars**"! In other words, this "*King*" or Angel of *Tyre,* was also the ancient **ruler** of *Mars* who had a **trading** *empire* that was *destroyed* (apparently involving Atlantis according to Plato). Also, it's now known that *Mars* once had *oceans* that were mostly blasted into Mars *orbit* when it was struck but that wayward *moon*! With that in mind, **Genesis** 2:5-6 tells us that the Earth was *watered* by a *mist* **before** the *flood*. Before the flood, there apparently was not enough *ocean* to cause *rain*? When we think about it, the *water* levels *rising* **above** the *mountains* by *rain* was *impossible* considering *rain* comes **from** the *oceans*.

It could *rain* for a *hundred* years and *not* raise the **ocean** *levels* **one** *inch*! So, *where* did all **that** *water* come *from*? Putting the picture together, it becomes obvious the *great* **flood** was the *final* **descent** of the *ice* that had been *collected* in **Earth's** *orbit* by the many **close** passes of *Mars,* until eventually *returning* to its **original** *orbit*. In fact, the Book of **Job** speaks of a "*swaddling band*" that caused thick *darkness* on the Earth at some *period* in the past! (Job 38:9)

It's also been *discovered* the *Mediterranean sea* was *once* **farmland***!* The remnants of **terracing** and *farming* (Ancient Aliens) have been found in the *low* parts of the valley. So, again, more proof we got water from a **non-** *Earthly source*! That said, was the *flooding* (and sinking) of *Atlantis*, really just a *myth*? Plato wrote of a *super* **race** *living* in Atlantis who apparently had *flying* (space) *ships*.

Did Plato just pull *Atlantis* out of his *rear* or was there some *truth* to *his* writings? Was *Atlantis* (the *source* of the *name* of the *Atlantic* ocean) a part of the ancient **trading** empire before *being* destroyed by *Mars*? Were these *super* beings (god-like) the *peers* of this *Nachash* described in **Ezekiel** 28?

With that *mountain* of information, can there be any doubt as to *how* that *Nachash earned* its *reputation* as YHWH's *adversary*? After all, *she* (a female according to the Book of YHWH) would have had a *monstrous* **chip** on her shoulder (pride was her downfall) for having her **trading** empire and world, **destroyed** and being *humiliated* before her *angelic peers*? That said, could she have possibly found a more *perfect* **revenge** than to go *after* the *apples* of YHWH's Eye, the *pinnacle* of His Creation; *Adam* and *Eve*?

Also quite interesting, is how this **reptilian** *creature* was also the angelic *ruler* over **Tyre,** which was the **trade** *capital* of the ancient world! In fact it's a good bet, the technology for their *fleet* of *ships* likely *originated* with this **angelic** *queen,* who had a *trading* empire with *oceans* on her home *world.* Considering she's *immortal,* is it any *surprise* that *after* Tyre was *destroyed,* Rome became the **next** *world* **trade** *empire?* In fact, if we take a *close* look, our *new* **one** *world* **government** is *nothing* but a **new** *worldwide* **trading** *empire!* (Ten trade states) Can there be any doubt our modern *global* **trading** *empire* is simply **another** *attempt* by the *queen* of **Mars** to *resurrect* her **ancient** *trading* empire?

Chapter 10

Born to Die?

In the Messianic *Christian* sect I was *raised*, we were *taught* death was **"*mandatory*"** (at least *once*)! In fact, I don't know of a Christian (or any other) denomination that teaches any *differently*. Are they *correct?* Were we really *born* to **die**? Well, the *denomination* in which I was *raised* used a Bible scripture to "*prove*" this was the case; that we all have at least one **required** appointment with **death**! The scripture **supposedly** proving *that* conclusion is found in NT book of **Hebrews**.

Well, I for one have always had a *problem* with the "*God* of *Life*" **condemning** His creation (children) to **mandatory** *death*. It seems to be a bit of an *oxymoron*, but maybe that's just me! Considering Adam and Eve were told they could eat "*freely*" of the "*Tree of Life*" in the Garden of Eden, it seems *rather* obvious this *partaking* of the *Tree* (of Life) did **not** involve **death**. That *notion* is further *reenforced* by the *admonition* that if they *partook* of the "**other**" *tree*; "*The Tree of the Knowledge of Good and Evil*" they would "*surely die*"; showing the *Tree of Life* did **not** *involve* **dying**!

In fact, after Adam and Eve's *ill-conceived* and *foolish* choice to *partake* of that *Tree* of **death** (knowledge of good and evil) the *notion* the *Tree of **Life***; quite literally being the *Tree of **Immortality*** (no death involved) was *established*. But, what *happened?* Did Adam and Eves' foolish *choice* **condemn** and *doom **all*** of their *descendants* to the **same** *fate?* Did the Creator YHWH really *deny* all humanity the *choice* of the *Tree* of Life which He *offered* Adam and Eve, just because of **Eve's** (and Adam's) *foolish* choice?

Again, maybe it's just me, but I have a bit of a *problem* with *such a* conclusion! I like to think the Creator (Yahweh) is not so *cold* and *cruel* as to *punish **all*** of *humanity* for a foolish *decision **we*** had **nothing** to *do* with! That said, it seems to me such a *cold **heartless** god* would also not have a problem in *punishing* (torturing) people (possibly for eternity) for some little *mistake* or *foolish* choice! Honestly, I want *nothing* to do with such a *vicious* and *merciless* god!

In spite of the "*supposed*" *evidence* (ie. proof) found in the book of **Hebrews**, I can make a case many times *greater* just *the **opposite*** is the **real** *truth*; that our amazing God of *mercy, love* and **life**, did **not** *create* us to **die**, <u>but *to **live***</u>! In fact, he *plainly* states in **Ezekiel** 18 He takes **no** *pleasure* in the "*death of His people*" (wicked or righteous)!

This case can easily be made by *doing* what the *Bereans* in **Acts** 17:11 did; *searching* the (OT) *scriptures* to *see* if *what* the 1st. Century (NT) teachers were *teaching* was **true**. You see, **Malachi** 3:6 tells us YHWH does **not** *change*, so if we want the **real** *truth*, it's in His **"*original*"** *teachings*. That's *what* the *Bereans* were *searching*; the **OT** *scriptures*, which is **all** they *had* at that point.

Looking in those scriptures, we not only *have* **immortality** *offered* in the Garden, but at *Mt.* **Sinai** as well. After Moses, led Israel to YHWH's *Mountain*, YHWH *offered* them that **same** basic *offer* He gave Adam and Eve! We find it in **Deuteronomy** 30:19; *"I call heaven and Earth as witnesses today against you, that I have set before you* **life** *and* **death**, **blessing** *and* **cursing***; therefore* **<u>choose</u> <u>life</u>** *that both you and your descendants may* **<u>live</u>**.*"* (Not die)

It's *rationalized* **what** was being *said* in that scripture was *"life"* is just a reference to a *"good"* and *"blessed"* existence versus a *cursed* and *miserable* one; **<u>before death</u>**. Honestly though, can we really *accept* the Israelites (and us) **had** to *die* in order to receive YHWH's *offer* of **life**? What kind of *trickery* would that be; to *offer* the people a *choice* of *life* **or** *death,* which are *opposites,* but then **require** them **die** in order to *receive* their (our) **choice** of *life*? What nonsense!

Well, He adds to this concept of *"life"* meaning *"immortality"* through the Prophet **Ezekiel** in verse 21 of chapter 18; *"But if the wicked man turns from all his sins, which he has committed,* **keeps all my statutes,** *and does what is* **lawful** *and* **right***, he shall* **surely <u>live</u>***; he shall* **<u>not die</u>**.*"* This is a very *plain* scripture, which makes it very clear *"life"* does **not** mean *"* **after** *death"*! It also tells us **why** *everyone* is **dying**!

He goes on to further *reinforce* that conclusion in verses 31-32; *"Cast away from you all the transgression which you have committed, and get yourselves a* **new** *heart and a* **new** *spirit; for* **why** *should you* **die***, O house of Israel? For* <u>*I have* **no pleasure** *in the* **death** *of one who* **dies**,</u> *says YHWH* (our God) *Therefore* <u>*turn and* **live**</u>! (Not die)

If one is *inclined* to *dismiss* the *Old* Testament as if YHWH *failed* and *started* **over** with something *"new"* there's a scripture in **John** that echoes the same concept of **Deuteronomy** and **Ezekiel**.

It's found in chapter 8, verses 51-52; *"Most assuredly I say to you; if anyone **keeps** my word* (s) *he shall **never see death**"*. That statement is *reinforced* in verse 52; *"If anyone keeps My word* (s) *he shall **never taste death**'*! (NKJ) I don't know how more **plain** a *scripture* can *be*, but unfortunately, a *misunderstanding* of a scripture in **Hebrews** has led people *completely* in the **opposite** *direction*; it's verse 27 of chapter 9.

Again, we must keep in mind YHWH (the Father Creator) *does **not** change*. Since the New Testament came *later* (mostly by oral tradition) the only way we can be sure **our** understanding of a scripture true, is to *compare* it to *YHWH's* OT **instructions**, which He *gave **earlier*** (like the *Bereans*)!

That scripture in **Hebrews** states; *"And as it is **appointed** for men to die once, but after this the judgment—"* This scripture **seems** to *imply* we *have* to **die**, but obviously **Genesis** and the scriptures just quoted, clearly *show* we **don't**; that we can *choose* **immortality** *over* **death**. In fact, we even have *examples proving* **Hebrews** does **not** mean what it is *interpreted* to mean. That *example* is **Enoch**, and **Elijah** who **didn't** *die* (apparently Moses and others)! Obviously, the current teaching of **Hebrews** 9 is proven a *lie* because of *those* that did **not** *die*.

Actually, *what* that scripture in **Hebrews** is telling us is we are *allowed* to *choose death* **once** (even by default) and *still* be **resurrected**. But, as **Revelation** 20:14 tells us, the "**second**" *choosing* of *death* will be the **final** *one*; to be "*thrown into the lake of fire*"!

The real *problem* here is the *demons* want us **dead** and have been *feeding* us the **lie** that we **must** *die*. The primary way they have *sold* this **lie** is with **another** *lie*; the **immortal** *soul* **lie** told in the Garden of *Eden*! After all, if *death* only *means* "**changing** *places*" **death** *is ok*, right?

The bottom line is, if the demons can **convince** us that we *don't* **have** the *choice* of physical *immorality*, we **accept** *death* by **default**! In other words, if we **don't** *believe* we can *choose* **life** (immorality) we simply *die* **without** *question*! I believe the demons are hoping *beyond* hope that YHWH's **lying** about His *promise* of **resurrection** as well.

Chapter 11

Badge of Compliance

There's been many badges especially *metaphorical,* worn for many reasons over the centuries; such as *badges* denoting **honor** or *courage.* Other *well **known** badges* of *merit* are the boy and girl scout *badges* given for their many *levels* of *achievements.* There are also many metals of *honor* and *achievements* awarded in the *military,* but all for *good.*

On the other hand, there've been many **negative** *badges awarded* as well, such as the *star **arm** bands* the Jews were *required* to *wear* during the *Weimar* Republic in Germany. With that *band* they were only *allowed* to *live* in certain *parts* of the cities (ghettos) and shop in *certain* stores. That badge even *restricted **what*** they could *buy.*

Another type of *badge* is the "*mark*" that was, and is to be *placed **upon** people* in the Bible. The first of those is seen in the book of **Ezekiel** 9 where these angels were sent into Jerusalem to place a *mark* upon all the *righteous **found** there.* (Those lamenting the evils) The **death** *angels* were then *sent* in to *kill* everyone **not** *bearing* the *mark*!

On the *other* hand, the Bible book of **Revelation** (c.13;16) speaks of **another** mark that shows **compliance** to a *powerful* **world** *ruling* entity called "*the* **beast**". Personally, I believe that *beast* is a **literal** (angelic) *beast*, probably *disguised* as a *man* (or human). But, it's said *there*, **all** who do **not** *receive* that *mark* of **allegiance** to that **governing** *power*, would not be *able* to *buy* or **sell** *anything*!

There have been myriad *speculations* as to *exactly* **what** that *mark* **is** and *how* it will be *administered;* some say a **chip** *under* the *skin*, while others say it will be an electronic tattoo. Still others believe it will be as simple as a *world* **ID** *card* such as a drivers *license* or *passport*. (Or a vax card) The frightening part is we're told in **Revelation** 19 (v.20) all those that *receive* "*that mark*" will **burn** in the **lake** of *fire*!

Regardless of the *speculation*, it seems we've already been given a *precursor* of **that** *mark*; the **masks** that were *required* for all *merchants* and *clerks* to **wear** in order to **sell** *anything*. In fact, much of the world also *required* anyone *entering* any kind of mass transportation (even *restaurants*) to also *wear* that *mask* **of** *compliance* as well!

At the same time, everyone was told to stay at least **6** *feet* **apart** due to this *virus* and to *contain* its spread. How strange considering, the CDC's own guidelines for "*social* **distancing**" to curb the *spread* of virus's is only **three** *feet*! So, what's really going on? Well, in 2015, then US secretary of state, stood up in a public *speech* and told us the US needs to be more **like** *China*.

Well, I for one, had *no* idea *what* she was *saying* until now. You see, China has a **monitoring** *system* in their *cities*, **tracking** *citizens* 24-7. Then, for every *slight* **infraction** *noticed*, such as *J-walking*, **littering**, *parking* in a **no** *parking* **zone**, a fine is *leveled* in the form of *deductions* from their personal **credit** *scores*.

When their *credit* **score** gets **low** *enough,* they can **no** *longer* **use** *public transportation* beginning with *airline* travel. Then it's *trains,* **busses,** and even the *ability* to have and/or *drive* **cars.** Of course, it doesn't stop *there,* but trickles *down* to *where* they can *go, shop,* and even **what** they are *allowed* to *buy* regardless of how much *money* they *have!*

Back to the **demanded** 6' *distancing,* insiders *told* us the **reason** for that *absurd,* **redundant** *distancing,* has **nothing** to *do* with a (the) virus. After all, with *everyone* **wearing** *masks* and working **behind** *shields* in retail, the *staying* 6' *apart* becomes ridiculously *pointless,* unless what the *insiders* told us **is** *true.*

Again, they're *telling* us the governments are *implementing* China's 24-7 citizen *monitoring* system with the *erection* and *implementation* of **5-G** *cell* **towers.** These towers finally have the *incredible* **band** *width* to literally *track* and monitor **all** *citizens,* at least those within *tower* **range.** The problem is, until fully *implemented* and *bugs* worked *out,* people congregating *closer* than 6' could cause *confusion* with the *tower's* function.

What's so *frightening,* with that *system,* even here in the US, they will be *monitoring* all **our** movements and literally **controlling** *everything* we *do.* With the *aid* of our **smart** *devices,* all our *conversations* are also being *monitored* and *recorded.* And, for every little *infraction,* **more** of our **freedoms** will be *removed,* just as in China!

Apparently, the *reasoning* of the new *global,* **communist,** *dictatorship,* which has now *taken* **control** of most of the world, is **all** *uprisings* will be *detected* and **stopped** *before* they *begin.*

Besides, they *plan* to only *allow* the *average* citizen to have the "**bare** *necessities*" as the *globalist* **propagandist** *film,* "*Jungle book*" announced in the middle of that children's cartoon.

The children were ***told*** *there* to *forget* about their *worries* and *cares* (including responsibilities) and just be happy with the *"bear* (bare) *necessities"* their *socialist* government *provides* for them! Unfortunately, 99% of those watching the film ***failed*** to *notice* that *macabre,* and ***dire*** *directive* and its *implications.* In this ***new*** *global,* ***communist*** *dictatorship,* there will be only ***two*** *classes*; the *rich* ***ruling*** *elite* and the *poor* ***enslaved*** *peasants.*

Plus, part of ***that*** *plan* is to *reduce* those working *serving* ***peasants*** to less than a billion. Another part of the *plan* is to *eliminate* all the *weak,* leaving only the *super* ***strong*** (biologically) to use as *breeding* stock and *slaves.* This is to be *accomplished* by *developing* special *injections* (falsely called *vaccines)* that will ***kill*** off the *weak,* ***infirm,*** and *elderly,* leaving only the *"ubber mench"* or ***super*** *people.*

In fact, that's exactly what *Hitler* was attempting to *accomplish* with his ***blond,*** *blue-****eyed*** *ayrien* nation! Unfortunately, due to the ***dumbing*** *down* of the people in the ***Weimar*** *Republic,* the *experiment* passed with ***flying*** *colors*! Because of that, the *communist* ***globalists*** are getting away with *doing* the ***same*** *thing,* only now, on a world-wide scale! In fact, the *machinery* to *accomplish* this has ***already*** *been* ***set*** in *motion* by simply using the *simple* ***element*** of ***fear***!

How interesting to have witnessed the *theft* of the *personal* ***freedoms*** of the *Western* nations by simply creating a *pandemic* of *"****fear****"*. They *stole* all our *freedoms* without *firing* a shot!

And because of it, the only ***true*** *freedom* we still have left is to say *"how* ***high"*** when told to *"****Jump****"*! How clear it now is why the *list* of those *destined* for the lake of *fire* in **Revelation** 20, begin with *the* ***fearful***! To have a ***true*** relationship with our Creator (Creator's) we have to be able to *place* ***complete*** *trust* in *Their* ***protection*** and *provision*! Fear has ***no*** *place* there!

Chapter 12

The Basket Woman

In **Zechariah** 5, we find some really *strange* passages, which make no sense at a glance. In verse 5 of chapter 5, **Zechariah** is being told to "*lift his **eyes** and **see** what goes **forth***". He then asked; "*What is it?*" "*A basket*" he was then told, which apparently was a *common* thing (basket) *throughout* the earth.

In verse 7, **Zechariah** is shown there was a *woman* called "*wickedness*" *sitting* in the basket with a ***lead*** *disc* over the *top* to keep her *sealed* in. What a bizarre few scriptures! What on Earth do *these* scriptures *mean* and do they have any *value* for us?

Well, in an *attempt* to *answer* that *question*, it's usually *helpful* to get some *background*. Zechariah was born of a *priestly* family in Babylon toward the end of the *captivity* and was then brought to *Jerusalem* by His *grandfather*. Tradition tells us he had begun *prophesying* at a young age.

Of course, the question arises; for *whom* were his prophecies *intended*? Was it for the ***post*** *Babylon* Jews or for people much *further* ***down*** the *road*? After all, many prophecies in books such as **Ezekiel**, **Isaiah**, **Daniel**, **Revelation** and others, have many *prophecies* that still have *not* come to *fruition*.

With that in mind, let's continue *reading* those bizarre *passages* in **Zechariah** 5. Verse 9 tells us *Zechariah* then *looked* **up** to see two **winged** *women* (angels?) who seized the *basket* with the **evil** woman and *lifted* it into the air. So Zechariah asked the *angel* **where** they were *taking* the *basket*. He was told, the *basket* was being *taken* to **Shinar**, *where* the city of *Babylon* was. (Babylon had not been destroyed yet)

Remember, in **Genesis** 11 we find the *tower* of *Babel* was also *built* in the *plains* of *Shinar*. Obviously, the *woman* in the *basket* called "*wickedness*" was once again going to be **restored** in *Babylon,* as we are told in verse 11 of **Zechariah**. There, in answer to Zechariah's *question* as to *where* it was being taken, the *angel* states; "*To build a **house** for it in the land of **Shinar**, when it is ready, the basket will be set on its base.*"

That's very interesting considering a *base* is a ***foundation***. By the *time* that *prophecy* was to come to *fruition*, Babylon would have long been *destroyed* and in need of *rebuilding*. **Revelation** 17 speaks of a **woman** *riding* a scarlet (red) *beast* who's called "*The mother of harlots and of abominations*". Is that the **same** *woman* in the *basket* **called** wickedness?

After all, **Revelation** 18 references the fact Babylon had been *rebuilt* and had become the *jewel* of the Earth and, the *merchants* of the Earth had become *rich* by her.

Interestingly, verse 18 tells us *she*, the "**woman**" is a reference to the rebuilt **Babylon**. But, then she's (Babylon) *destroyed* and the whole Earth *morns* her *destruction* (Rev.18:9). Interestingly, going back to chapter 17 and verse 8, we're told; "*The **beast** that you saw **was, and is not**, and will send **out** of the **bottomless pit** and will go to **perdition***". (Lake of fire)

That gives us *two* clue's as to *who* the **beast** Babylon **rides** is, or from which she gets her *power*. We see that during the *trumpet* plagues (the fifth trumpet) the pit is **opened** and all those *imprisoned* there are *released*, including the **king** of the *pit*, **Azazyel**.

But, after the *Atonement* ceremony in **Leviticus**, 13, Azazyel is ***thrown*** back into the *pit,* but *not* alone. **Revelation** 20 tells the *great dragon* (devil) whose been *ruling* this world since the Garden of Eden, will be *thrown,* ***chained,*** into that *pit* along with *Azazyel.*

Then, in **Revelation** 20:3 we're told the *dragon* will once *again* be ***released*** after the Millennium (the New Eden). So, now we have ***two beasts*** who could be the *power* of Babylon; Azazyel and/or the *dragon.* Of course, that fits perfectly with *what* we find in **Daniel** 7, where the last ***beast*** *kingdom* is the *kingdom* of the ***dragon***! Apparently, she is the *wickedness* that *rebuilds* and *restores* Babylon.

Also, we see **Revelation** 17 and 18 mentioning *"merchandising"* where she has made the *merchants* of the Earth very *wealthy.* With that in mind, if we go back to **Ezekiel** 28, we find the *one* ***thrown*** to Earth, ending up in the *Garden,* was due to *"merchandising".* Obviously, this *dragon* does not *learn* any ***new*** tricks. In fact, we can trace her *influence* all through ***Bible*** *history,* where she has *attempted* to ***reestablish*** her ***trading*** empire with *nation* after *nation,* from *Tyre* to the *NWO* (one world trading empire).

This *new "One World Order"* the globalists are *establishing* (but will fail due to Nemisis) have *divided* the world into *ten* ***trade*** regions. In fact, I was shocked to see a map hanging in a bank *showing* those **10** *trade* ***regions.*** (States) These ten *global* ***trade*** states will be *governed* by a *centralized* ***world*** government.

Of course, this global (socialist) government will come with *its* ***own*** *police* force and *court* system! If that doesn't send a *chill* down your spine, it's possible you don't *have* one?! It certainly does for me.

The conclusion to the *affair* is, at the end of the Millennium (New Promised Land or Eden) all that will be *left* on this Earth will be the *dragon*, her **rebel** *watcher* co-horts, and all the *people* who have *refused* to *embrace* the Creator *YHWH* and His *Torah* of **Love**. As II **Peter** 3:10-12 tells us, the Earth and *heavens* will **melt** with *fervent* **heat** and all will be **burned** *up*. **Revelation** 21:8 alludes to this event calling it a "*Lake which burns with fire and brimstone*".

Of course, this is *where* Christianity gets its *idea* and *belief* of an **ever** burning **hell** *fire*. Fortunately, this *fire* will be *lights* **out** for those *burned*, not an ever-*lasting* **torture** *chamber*. That shows the *mercy* of the all *merciful* Creator YHWH!

Chapter 13

Baptism, What is it?

There's a strange *ritual* in which most churches *ask* their parishioners to *participate*, called *"baptism"*. But, *what's* that all about? After all, most churches give it great *reverence* but **differ** vastly in *why* and *how* they incorporate the *practice*. For instance, the *Catholics* perform this ritual on newborn babies by *sprinkling* water on their foreheads (although some of the orthodox churches actually dunk the babies). On the other hand, most Protestant churches *baptize* only adults and usually by **complete immersion,** while yet others, **disregard** *it* altogether.

What then is this *strange* custom and *why's* it *performed?* Where did it *originate* and *why* do most **Bible** *believing* churches see it as so important? They claim it's *Biblical* and to be *performed,* but *why* and *how?* Obviously, with the many ways it's *practiced,* not everyone can be *correct* on the procedure.

One of the greatest *reasons* for the *ceremony* is the New Testaments' *example* of one who went around *baptizing* people, called **"John the Baptist"**. In fact, even the *Messiah* **requested** John **Baptize** *Him* in **Matthew** 3:13-17! Apparently, the *ceremony* was so *critical* that even the *first-born* **son** (Yahshua) of the *Creator* (YHWH) felt He *needed* it *done* for Him; *something* He apparently could **not** *do* for Himself!

The Messiah's *example* shows us there's *obviously extreme* **importance** *attached* to this strange *ritual,* and if we *exercise* **wisdom**, shouldn't we extend the *same* credence to it? That seems to be the *wisest* choice, but where to begin? Obviously the most logical place to *begin* is to make sure the translators did a **correct** *translation*. Unfortunately, *improper* *translation* has **hidden** the *truth* as we see in so *many* cases throughout the scriptures. Improper translation and/or *failure* to *translate,* does all of us a major *injustice;* leading to all kinds of *improper* and *false* conclusions.

To begin with, the translators *failed* to *translate* the original **Greek** *word* "*baptizo*" into its' proper English meaning, "*immerse*". A similar *disservice* done to us was their *failing* to *properly* translate **other** words such as "*Satan*" which is **not** a *name*, but a Hebrew *word* meaning "*adversary*". The same goes for "*God*". It is *not* a name at all, but a *title* (adjative) for *deity*. An even more **injurious** *lack* of translation was their *failure* to **properly** *translate* "**Christos**" into *one* of its **three** English *meanings*.

Christos like its *Hebrew* counterpart "*Mashiyach*" has **three** *meanings* derived by context, which are; "*Anointed* **One**" "*the* **Anointing**" (of YHWH's Spirit) or "*the Anointed* **ones**" as in those who had *received* YHWH's great *out-pouring* of Spirit. By *failing* to correctly do their jobs, the translators effectively rendered much of the NT into pure *nonsense,* as we see in such phrases as "*In Christ*" which actually means to be *filled* with **YHWH's** *Spirit*.

Again, the same sort of *problem* was caused by the translator's *failure* to render the Greek word "*baptizo*" into its English meaning "*immersion*". John (Yahshua's' cousin) was not "*John the* **Baptist**" but "*John the* **Immerser**"! Obviously, using the word *immersion,* immediately does away with all the "**sprinkling**" *rituals.*

Understanding the *"washing"* *ritual* included *immersion*, gives us a *clue* as to *what* it's *about* and *where* it *originated*. With that in mind, and referring back to the temple *rites* (Leviticus) we see the priests were **forbidden** to *enter* the temple unless they were *fully **washed*** (clean). So, outside the temple was a huge *brass **pool*** (laver) supported on the backs of *twelve* brass bulls, in which the priests would *disrobe* and *fully **immerse*** (wash) themselves before *entering* the temple (the Creator's house). The idea was they were not to come *before* YHWH (the Creator) *unclean* (dirty).

Physical *uncleanness* was a *metaphor* for **spiritual** *uncleanness* or *sin*, but there's *additional* meaning. But, if **physical** *uncleanness* is a *metaphor* for **spiritual** *uncleanness* or *sin*, why did the Messiah, of whom it's written *"had no sin"* need to be *immersed* (cleansed-baptized)? Obviously, there's additional *meaning* most are *missing*.

Another *aspect* to *baptism taught* with *scriptural* support, is we *need* to be **baptized** (immersed-cleansed) before we can *receive* YHWH's *Spirit*. Again, it makes perfect sense that we need to be *cleansed* of our *sins* (repentant) before we can receive YHWH's pure *Spirit* of *Truth*. But, once again, that leaves us with the *problem*; *why* Yahshua, of whom it says *had **no** sin*, *needed* to *be **cleansed*** (baptized)?

I was *given* the *answer* to this *conundrum* in a very surprising and *unexpected* way. Many years ago, I would stop in and do *odd* and *repair* jobs for an elderly widow. One day her daughter dropped in and we all sat to have some cake and milk. Somehow the subject of the Bible came up and they asked a very *good* and *unexpected* question.

They were wondering why Yahshua (the Hebrew Messiah) needed to be *baptized* when He obviously **had** the *"Holy Spirit"* from birth. After all, our church taught that *receiving* the *Holy Sprit* was the **actual** *purpose* of *baptism* and no one could **have it without** being **baptized**.

Well, I had no more than told them I had **no idea**, when suddenly the answer was *coming* **out** of my mouth! The amazing part is I had **never** *heard* or *imagined* the *answer* I found my own mouth *telling* us! It seems that YHWH's *Spirit* was **speaking** *through* me just as Yahshua had *promised* His disciples would *happen*!

Anyway, the *answer* (given us) was that *baptism* (immersion) was **more** than just being *cleansed* before going into the temple (YHWH's presence) or being given *YHWH's* **Spirit**. Yes, **those** *requirements* were *necessary*, but there's *additional* meaning to the ceremony. That *meaning*, which *emanated* from my mouth (like the donkey that spoke to Baalim) was that *baptism* (immersion) is also a personal **contract** with our Creator *YHWH*!

That *contract* (covenant) we make with YHWH at *baptism* is a **complete** *dedication* to *Him* and *His* **Torah** *instructions*. It's in *essence*, a *commitment* to a **righteous** (sinless) *life* that we have **committed** *ourselves* too. It's then YHWH gives us *a* "**helper**"; **His** *Spirit*, which **gives** *us* the actual **ability** *to* **fulfill** that *covenant* (contract). That said, the reason Yahshua asked John to *baptize* Him was simply a *formality;* the *signing* of the *contract.* After all, Yahshua had been living *up* to that *contract* since His birth! But, if we are *immersed* (baptized) into *pagan* and/or *false* names, obviously the whole issue become *nonsensical* and *mute.*

Chapter 14

Christian Questions

Concerning beliefs, is it not only *logical* that we all *need* to **defend** our *beliefs* and be able to *honestly* and *logically* **answer** *questions* posed of them. Otherwise, of what **real** *value* are our beliefs? Shouldn't anyone calling themselves a *Christian* be willing to *answer* the following *list* of very *logical* and **legitimate** *questions,* especially considering the very *scriptures* they *claim* to **adhere**, *advising* us to *always* be *ready* to *give* an (*honest* and **logical)** answer when someone *asks.*

It seems like a *fair* **test** considering the Creator tells us He does not **give** true *understanding* to those who *worship* **pagan** gods and *ignores* His Torah. ("*A good understanding have all those who "**do**" His commandmfents"*-**Psalms** 111;10) The following then, is a list of *legitimate* **questions** any true *Bible* adherent should be able to *honestly* answer.

To begin; how is it *the God* Christianity **claims** to *worship, shares* the *same* **generic** *title* **name** as all the **other** *gods* (angels and demons) even though He says that *His* Name is *Qodesh*; that is, "*Dedicated*"-"*Set Apart*" and "*Exclusive*"? How can His Name be Qodesh if He is just a "*one size fits all*" god that *shares* His **exclusive** (set apart) *Name* and *title* with all the **pagan** *gods,* only spelled with a capital G?

A *closely* **related** *question* is, *how* can the **Hebrew** *Messiah* have a *generic* **Greek** name (and title) when His *advent* and *sacrifice* was *established* *"From the foundation of the world"* as **Revelation** 13:8 states? Did His Father really *decide* that a **Hebrew** *Name* was **not** as *good* as a *generic* **Greek** *one*? After all *"Iesus"* (the Greek before it was changed to Jesus-17th century) is just a *generic* Greek *word* (title) that means *"savior"*. That means **"that** *savior"* could be **any** *god* the **people** *decide* to *worship* in hopes of **saving** *them* (like Zeus)!

In this same *vein*, how is it the **Hebrew** *Messiah* was also *given* a **Greek** *designation* (Christos) versus a *Hebrew* one? Yes, one of the *meanings* of *Christos* is *"anointed one"* but then, **all** the **Greek** *gods* were **"anointed ones"** (Christs) Zeus being the *chief "anointed one"* of the *Greek* **olympian** *pantheon*! In fact, when someone wanted to **honor** *someone* or *something*, they would *dedicate* that *name* to *their* **favorite** (chief) *god* (christ) by *attaching* the last **two** *letters* of *Zeus* as in *Ies-us* (Jesus). We see that fact demonstrated in most *important* **Greek** names! *"Did the God* **of** *the* **Hebrews** *really dedicate the* **Name** *of His first-born* **Son** *to* **Zeus**"?

With *Greek* Names in mind, another *teaching* of Christianity is that *"God"* **lost** *ten* of His **chosen** *tribes*. Problem; what *kind* of *inept god* **loses** His own **chosen** *people*? Hmm!? Is He like the *Greek* gods who had a **lousy** *reputation* for their *hit* and *miss* ways of taking *care* of their people?

Then, there is the *other* argument; that *God's* **people** *Israel,* **failed** *Him,* so He decided to give the *Gentiles* a **try** *instead*. Of course, that means the Creator was so *naive* that He *didn't* understand the *choices* His people would *make* and *failed* to *have* a **contingency** *plan*! (Unless you argue the gentiles were) Was He really as *incompetent* as we humans tend to *be*, or is *His* **plan** for **His** people **Israel** still on *track*?

If the Creator (YHWH) *failed* with His people, did He also *fail* with His *Law* (Torah) as well? Did He *make* all these *laws* that were just **too** *hard* for His people; *forcing* Him to **switch** to a *plan* of "*grace*" instead? Again, what does that *say* to **ineptness**? Did the all-wise "*Ancient of Days*" really not understand that His **Torah** outline for *human* **behavior** was going to be just *too* **hard** for His People, *forcing* Him to **change** His *covenant* (plans) with them?

Of course, the Creators' Torah (Law) also *included* His *Sabbaths,* which scripture tells us were *to* **be** *observed* **forever** (throughout their generations). Was He also *forced* to *abandon* **those** *Sabbaths,* which are the *outline* of *His* **plans** for His *people* and the world? What *kind* of a **weak** god is *forced* by *His* **own** *creation* to **abandon** His *plans* for them?

In light of **abandoned** *plans*; did the Creator *inspire* the *inclusion* of 14 (or ten currently) *scrolls* in the *Septuagint* Bible (270 BCE) only to then *inspire* the *translators* of the *King James* to *later* **remove** them? In fact, the chief *instigator* of this *move* was Martin Luther, who not only took out some *ten* books, but wanted to get *rid* of the Book of **James** as well. He called **James** an "*epistle of straw*". That begs the *question;* did the Creator make a *mistake* by *inspiring* those so-called *Apocrypha books* to be **included** in the *canon,* or, did He *make* a **mistake** by having them *taken* **out**?

The *same* **questions** can be *applied* to the *translations*. Did the Creator really *inspire* the translators, considering there *hundreds* of very **different** *translations*? In fact, many argue the **1611** *King James* translation was the only *correct* one, but if true, why is the name *Jesus* **not** *there*?

Plus, the 1611 had 10 *Apocrypha* books, which the later King James translations *deleted*. Did the Creator also *inspire* the King James translators to *remove* His **"Set Apart"** (exclusive) Name YHWH and *replace* it with **Baal** ("*the Lord*") when so there are so many *commands* in those scriptures to "*proclaim*" and "*glorify*" the Name **YHWH**?

In the New Testament, the Messiah gave a *private* discourse to *His* disciples (the twelve) in **Matthew** 24, **Luke** 21, and **Mark** 13, but in doing so, was He actually speaking **over** their **heads** to a *generation* **thousands** of years in the *future*? Considering

He *predicted* the *destruction* of the temple to *come* to **pass** in *their* generation, would not "*His* **return**" which He **also** *predicted* in the *middle* of that discourse, not *also* have **happened** in "*their* generation"? After all, His chief Apostles; *John,* **James**, *Peter,* and the writer of **Thessalonians** *all* **taught** that He **was** *returning* in "*their* generation". Were they **deceived** even *after* **receiving** YHWH's **spirit** of *Truth*?

Considering YHWH's Disciples were *teaching His* **return** in *their* generation; which Christianity *teaches* **didn't** happen, how does that **not** make them "*deceived*" and **false** *Apostles*? How does His **not** *returning* in **that** generation not make the *Messiah* a **false** *teacher* (prophet) as well? But then, a good *understanding* of the Creators' *Feasts* (Sabbaths) clearly *show* He did indeed *return* in **their** generation (and had to)!

The next related *question* is it that *John* the *Immerser* (baptist) *proclaimed* the *Messiah* (Yahshua) to be the *Lamb*. How can that *be* if He didn't **do** *what* the *lamb* in the *Passover* **rehearsal** did (save the firstborn)? How does it work to **rehearse** a *play* for *generations*, only to **change** *it* on **opening** day? Remember, the **lamb's blood** only *saved* the "**firstborn**" not *all* of *Israel* and certainly **not** the **whole** *world*!

With that thought in mind, *why* does **John** 3:16 state; "*For God so loved the* **world** *that He gave His only begotten Son—*" but 1 **John** 2:15 tells us; "*If anyone* **loves the world***, the* **love** *of the* **Father** *is* **not** *in him.*" In other words, if "*God*" **loves the world**" it's a *good* thing, but if **"we"** *love* the **world**, it's not??

Considering that word "*world*" (*Kosmos* in the Greek) *why* did the translators *choose* the *last* meaning (which doesn't fit) in the list of **possible** *meanings* of *world* when the very **first** *meaning* is "**orderly arrangement**" (order)? After all, we get our *word* **Cosmos** from the same word because the *stars* are very *ordered*. But, there's nothing *orderly* about this *worlds* **inhabitants**. That said, is not the "*order*" referred to in **John** 3:16, YHWH's (and Yahshas') *priesthood*? The *priests* were the *firstborn* after all!? Does it *not* make sense that the *High* Priest would **save** (shed His blood) for His *priesthood* (firstborn)?

Since the **one** the *Passover* **lamb** *pictured* was *slain* at exactly the **same** *time* the Passover lambs were *instructed* to be killed (3 PM) and the *wave sheaf* **happened** in *real* time *exactly* **three** *days* later (the resurrection of Yahshua and the saints of old) which signaled the *beginning* of the **spring** *harvest* (human harvest) and the *countdown* to the **completion** of the *spring* **harvest**, how is it the *spring* harvest was not **completed** "*count fifty*" *later*? (Fifty years) Or was it?

After all, the *timing* of the *Feast* **rehearsals** like the *slaying* of the *lamb* and the *wave sheaf* (graves in Jerusalem opening up-first resurrection) came to *real-time* **fruition** with shockingly **precise** *timing*, but yet the *completion* of the **spring** *harvest* supposedly *stopped* and was not *completed* after **fifty** *countdown* had *begun*? How absurd!

Then there's the issue of the **13th** *apostle* (and more). Why does **Revelation** tell us there are *only* **12**? Secondly, why was *this* apostle's *selection* (calling) so *different* from the other twelve considering **Hebrews** 13:8 tells us Yahshua does **not** *change* (*what* He *taught* and how He *does* things)? Plus, *why* does Paul make **false** *statements* such as; "*There are none righteous, no not one*" when **Hebrews** lists a whole *slew* of them beginning with "*righteous Able*"?

Also, how is it that Paul *admitted* to **"*lying*"** (Rom.3:7) to *convert* his followers when the writer of the book of **Revelation** tells us *all **liars*** will have *their **place*** in the "*lake of fire*"? Was the Messiah also *lying* to His disciples when He told them that "*false prophets*" (this includes apostles) *would come"* who were so **slick** (crafty) they could possibly "***deceive** even the **elect***"?

Where (and who) were they, if ***not** Saul* (Paul) and his *ilk*? Besides, the Ephesians in **Revelation** 2 were commended for *exposing **false** apostles*, which **Timothy** 4 tells us they did to Paul!

Unfortunately it's only when we ***fully** understand* these *basic* Bible *questions* that we will be *able* to **ask** and **answer** them *correctly*. Of course, only a *fool **answers** questions* to which he doesn't actually *know* the *answer*! These questions are the ***foundation** restored*!

Chapter 15

The Communist (Nazi)
Takeover of the World

Communist style *governments* have steadily been *taking* **control** of the Earth in these *modern* times. Up until a few hundred years ago, the norm was the *iron* **rule** of **kings** until the *Greeks* and *Romans* incorporated a *slightly* **different** *system* with *Cesars* and *senators* (Czars). A *Czar* was like a *king* minus the **absolute** *power* of a *king*. Communism is best *defined* as an *oligarchy; **complete** power* in the hands of a *small* **group** versus a *king*.

The *idea* for **communism** came in the form of a *vision* (from **Lucifer**) to an accountant named Adam Wieshaupt. Weishaupt worked for the chief **banking** *family* in Europe (Germany) the *Bauer* family, now called the *Rothschilds*, who loved the *idea* of **setting** *up* a *"One* **World** *Government"* a **plan** so *ambitious* it would span *several* **generations**. To *accomplish* this **goal** they set up many **secret** *societies*, first *calling* themselves the *"Illuminati"* meaning *"illumined ones"* (by Lucifer).

A retired Colonel named William Guy Carr became *obsessed* by this *group* and spent the last ***thirty*** years of his *life* documenting everything about them in his book "*Pawns* in the *Game*". In that stocking *tome*, he ***documented*** how these *people* took ***control*** of *country* after *country* using the *outline* from Wieshaupts' *vision*. They began with *France*, with the ***French*** *Revolution* and then *Russia* with the ***Bolshevik*** *revolution*.

They then took *control* of *Germany* during the ***Weimar*** *Republic* of the 1930's. At the same time, they began working ***heavily*** upon the US beginning with the ***illegal*** *passing* of the *Federal* ***Reserve*** *Act* in 1913. There, they began taking *control* of our *banks* and *money*, just as they did in *France*, *Russia*, and Germany. In fact, they *fomented* the *two* ***world*** *wars* to *force* the US to *heavily* ***borrow*** from them, *subjecting* us to their ***compounding*** *interest*. Again, the goal was to *bankrupt* the US, just as they did those ***other*** *nations*. After taking *control* of the *money* they were able to *control* the *Government* and ***corrupt*** it while *stealing* all they could!

The next step was to get *control* of the *medias* to *hide* and *protect* their ***illicit*** *actions* (versus *exposing* them). After all, the *original* ***purpose*** of the *media* was to be *watchdogs* over our ***political*** *leaders*. Next, was to take *control* of the *schools*, especially *colleges*, to *shape* and *mold* what the young people ***believed*** and did. Next was to *corrupt* society through *gambling*, ***drugs***, *prostitution* etc. to *destroy* the *family*.

The family is the *concrete* ***foundation*** of every *society*. Destroy the *foundation* and the *whole* ***house*** *collapses*! (Like the Roman Empire)

The *final* steps are to ***disarm*** the *population* while *exposing* the ***puppet*** *government* ***corruption*** (which they caused) to *foment* a ***revolution*** to get the people to *rise* ***up*** and *destroy* their *puppet* ***government***. At that point they come *out* of the *closet* and *proclaim* "*we got this* and will *insure* that under their (NWO) *leadership*, this kind of *thing* will ***never*** *happen* ***again***!"

To *facilitate* this end, they used their *engineered* **crown** *virus*, which was no more *deadly* than the *flu*, but very **fast** *spreading* and **unstoppable**. Using the *media*, of which they had **taken** *control*, they **hyped** the **fear** to **absurd** *levels* to get people to *wear* the **health** *destroying masks* (especially with children) and ultimately get people to take their *so* **called** *vaccinations*, which contained **deadly** *DNA* altering *Mrna* **ingredients**.

Bottom line, the chief *goal* of the NWO people is to *drop* the *population* to **500** *million* which was the first *commandment* on the *George* **Guide** *Stones,* which they *erected* in a field to *educate* the world as to **their** *plan* and idea of a *happy,* **healthy** and *prosperous World.* Then, once they got most *everyone* to take the *shot,* they *destroyed* the stones, because that was the **purpose** of the *shots.* Their idea of a *happy* and **prosperous** *world* is to have **two** *classes*; the *rich* **ruling** *elite* and 500 million **worker** *peasants*!

To **finish** *taking* **control** of the *world,* they are *pitting* the *last* **three** great *powers* **against** each *other* to get them to *take* **each** *other* **out**. First it's *China* and *Russia* taking *down* the *US* and then for *them* to *turn* on **each** *other.* It seems like a *good* **plan** but there is a **higher** *power* (supernatural) **more** *powerful* than them in *play.* Their *plan* is *guaranteed* to **fail** except for the *destruction* of the *US* and the *West.* The big *unknown* in their *plan* is the soon *arrival* of our *binary* **twin** *solar* **system**!

The US leaders have spent *trillions* of dollars building **underground** *cities* to **dive** into at the *last* moment. They *expect* the *destruction* of the *US* and *China,* but will **not** be able to **stop** *Russia.* Despite their **best** *efforts,* the *prophecies* in **Danial** 7 show us that the **Bear** (Russia) will be the *next* **world** *dominant* **power**.

Vladimir Putin, *converted* to *Catholicism,* and *outlawed* **homosexual** *unions* and **abortion** (except to *save* the Mother)! Remember, Egypt, after throwing the *babies* in the *river,* was all by *erased* from the planet and also *Judah* in the *first* century when Herod had all the baby *boys* **murdered**! Those *babies* belong to the Creator who has **not** *changed* and we can be sure the world is going to **pay** *dearly* for the *murder* of 1.4 *billon* of *the* **Creator's** *babies*!

Chapter 16

Can Demons Perform Miracles?

In the Scriptures we find many *examples* of the *Messiah* and His *Apostles* doing *miracles*. In fact, that was one of the *reasons* people *flocked* to *see* and *hear* them, hoping to be a *part* of those *miracles*! After all, performing *miracles* is a *great* **way** to **attract** attention and *establish* the **power** of a God, is it not? But, how do we *know* the *power* to **accomplish** *miracles* is coming *from* the Creator and not *from* the *demonic* realm? They are, after all, very **powerful** *spirits*! (See Eph.6)

Obviously, considering *Yahshua* and His *Apostles* **performed** *many* **miracles** and *healings*, it can't be a *bad* thing, right? But how do we know? Again, we must bear in mind the *demons* are **powerful** *spirits*, which makes them very *capable* of **performing** *miracles*! Well, we don't have to *look* very *far* in the Bible (magicians) or all around in the *religions* today to see the demons are *alive* and *busy* **recruiting** proselytes with "**their**" *miracles*! Remember what *Yahshua* told His *disciples*; "*The **evil require** a sign*" (miracle)!

That said, *what **are** miracles* anyway? If we were to *resurrect* someone from a few hundred years ago and *show* them our *society*, **what** would they *think*? Would they not look at the *things* we take for *granted,* such as electric *lights,* or *automatic **doors,*** and see them as *miraculous*? Would *automobiles* not also be extremely *miraculous*? How about something as simple (to us) as a *radio*, that is, *voices **emanating*** from a little *box,* be a *miracle* to them?

And obviously, to *see **living** people* in a *thin* flat *television* screen would be **beyond** *miraculous*!! They would probably view them as *windows* to *heaven*! You see, a *miracle* is simply something *performed* that's *beyond* our understanding. In fact, I have had many *instantaneous **healings*** *performed* on me, which most (if not all) would *agree* were *miracles*, right? But, if we ourselves *possessed* the *understanding* to **manipulate** our *own **physiology***, would it *still* be a *miracle*?

Just to *illustrate* my point, a long time friend of mine *married* a woman they call a "*multiple*". My friend discovered she had at least **4** **different** *distinct* **personalities** that all had **different** *likes* and *attitudes*. The *strangest* one was *witnessed* when he came home from work one day and was told by the woman they were *renting* a room from that he needed to get back to their room because something very *strange* was *happening*.

He went back to find her *sitting* on the edge of the bed with only the lamp on. As he sat next to her, he was shocked to see she had *scars* (like razor scars) all over her *face*. Not only that, she was very *wrinkled* and looked to be in her 70's even though she was only in her 30's. The real shock came when the woman from whom they were renting, came in and *flipped* on the *overhead* light. In *shock* and *disbelief,* they watched the *scars* and *wrinkles* just **fade** *away,* and her *return* her to her **normal** *age*.

Regardless of what conclusion one might arrive, the fact is, *someone*, either her own *subconscious* or a **foreign** entity (demon spirit) had the *ability* to **manipulate** her **physiology**! (Shape-shift) And, if we think about it, isn't that what all *miraculous* and **instantaneous** *healing* are? And, of course, just a matter of *who's* doing it!?

Just for emphasis, that story is not a *freak* or *isolated* event. My friend (and others) also said they saw her **grow** and *shrink* (in height) right in *front* of them! Again, this is *not* an *isolated* story considering I have heard *other* stories of the *same* **type** of *thing*.

One was a man with **terminal** *cancer*, who after **switching** *personalities* would see his the **cancer** *instantly* **disappear** with **no** *trace*! Another man with **severe** *diabetes* would see his diabetes *come* and *go* depending upon **which** *personality* was *dominate*!

My personal conclusion is *multiples* are **possessed** (incarnated) by **nephilim** (or rephim) *spirits*; the *offspring* of the watchers, like the *dragon* in the *garden*. Enoch wrote of how the *watchers* (like Azazel) were *imprisoned* in the **pit** and their **highbred** (giants and half human and animal) *offspring* were *drowned* in the flood. But, because the watchers (angels) were created *immortal,* their offspring had **immortal** *souls* (where humanity got the idea).

Apparently, because of the sort of *prison* (pit) in which the watchers are *imprisoned* (according to Enoch) the *spirits* of their **highbred** *offspring* are doomed to *wander* the Earth like "*clouds with no water*". (Jude 12) But, it seems they do have the *ability* to *reincarnate* themselves (possess) into *living* creatures, including humans. It seems they are only allowed to *reincarnate* if the *one* they *possess* **allows** it in *some* way. With that in mind, it seems severe *emotional* **trauma** as children, or adults *dabbling* in *occult* circles are **two** *ways* they can **take** control.

Interestingly, the greatest minds of history, minds like *Nicola Tesla* and *Verner Von Braun* (among those who *invented* the *rocket* engine and the Atomic bomb) openly admitted *their* **knowledge** did *not* come **from** *them* but "*from the* **other** *side*"!

So, to sum up this study, any honest look *around* will *confirm* the demons are real and are very much *able* to **do** *miracles*. That's why we need to pay close attention to *those* through whom the demons are *accomplishing* their miracles. Just because someone *performs* **miracles**, does not necessarily have *anything* to do with *righteousness*!

As far as **miraculous** *things* **happening** with us; many times it's simply the *result* of *faith*! An *unrighteous* person with **enough** *faith* can do *amazing* things! Remember; II **Thessalonians** 2:9 speaks of a **lawless** *one* performing "*signs and* **lying** *wonders*" which makes us foolish to *place* our **trust** in *miracles* and *those* that *perform* them. Miracles can be a wonderful **fringe** benefit of *walking* with YHWH, but must *never* be the *reason* for *embracing* Him!!

I have noticed in my own life, the *closer* I've gotten to *YHWH*, the **fewer** *supernatural* events happen. Apparently, the reason for so many **supernatural** *miracles* when I was younger because I was so hard *headed*, that's *what* it took to *lead* me to YHWH, but now as I have *matured*, such "*signs*" are no longer *necessary* for my *faith*.

With that thought in mind, let's not forget what *Yahshua* told His disciples in **Luke** 11:29, that "*an* **evil** *generation* **requires** *a* **sign**" (for their faith)! In other words, the *wicked* are *unwilling* to **commit** their *faith* without **miraculous** *signs*. Interestingly, one miracle it seems the demons are *unable* to *accomplish* is **giving** and/or *creating* **life** (resurrection)! They certainly have the *power* to **manipulate** *physiology* but cannot *produce* **life** from nothing! All life *emanates* from YHWH, the Creator!

Chapter 17

Choice Versus Commitment

Most people automatically *connect* **choice** and *commitment*. But, with a little **honest** *analysis*, we realize they are *two **different** parts* of a whole. For instance, when a couple *chooses* to get married, how many are *committed* to **make** it **last** a *lifetime?* Well, *statistics* bear out it's less than *half.* Choosing is an *easy* and **shallow** *act,* while real **commitment** is extremely *difficult,* at least in the **long** run.

How many of us really *understand* **true** *commitment?* Personally, I would say it's only *those* who have been through and *outlasted* **tough** *times.* As the saying goes, when the *going* gets *tough,* the *tough* (truly committed) **keep** *going.* That kind of *commitment* can only be understood through *experience.* It seems *failure,* to one degree or another (trials) is *necessary* **part** of *life!*

It's said "*talk is cheap*" and how very *true!* But, **what** is *commitment,* really? Isn't *commitment* a **choice** we *continually* make? When things get tough, isn't **not** *quitting* a *choice* we **again** *choose?* Like in a *marriage,* aren't there *hundreds* of **times** people *feel* like **quitting** and *walking* **away?** Of course! But, it's *then* we must *remember* **our** *commitment* and once again **choose** to go *on* versus *quitting.* To **not** *quit* when things in life become very *difficult,* sadly, is a **choice** many people simply *cannot* make!

The secret *weapon* to being *able* to *make* the **right** *choice* to *carry on*, in spite of how *hard* things have gotten, is **outside** *help*. A loving *family* is a very *good* and usually *strong* **help** in those situations. In fact, that's one of the primary *purposes* of *family*. But in many cases, there's *no* **loving** *family* to *help* and/or *encourage*, so what then? Sadly *many* family members can be *unsupportive* for one *reason* or *another,* which prompts us to ask; *what* do we do then? But, there are *always* people *willing* to **help** if *asked!*

Well, the **best** *source* of **support** *possible* is a **spiritual** *family*. Unfortunately, many, if not most, refuse to *believe* in the *spirit* realm. And unfortunately, many of those that do, have seemingly been let *down* so often, they no longer are able to *maintain* **faith** either. Of course, that's the result of *two* things. One, we put our *faith* in the **wrong** *god* or *gods*. The other is the fact that *maturity*, physical and/or *spiritual* takes **time**. Unfortunately, *tough* times (to one degree or another) are a *necessary* **evil** for *maturity*.

No-one, **not** having *experienced* **hard** *times*, is ever **emotionally** *complete*. (Mature) We must experience **both** *sides* to have a **true** *picture* of *reality*. In fact, there's a scripture telling us "*God*" **tests** or *tries* (chastens) those *He* **loves**.

The operative *word,* there, is "*loves*". Just like any **loving** *parent*, if we *shield* our children from all *harm*, we *destroy* them in the *long* run! If we *love* our children (like our heavenly Father **loves** *us*) we will let them *skin* their *knees* from time to time. But just like our true Heavenly *Father* (YHWH-Yahway) we will *always* be **there** to *lift* them back *up* after *falling!* Understanding **this** *truth* is the true **power** *behind* **commitment**!

Chapter 18

Cross of Life or Death?

As most everyone knows, one of the most *important* **icons** in Christianity is the "*cross*". In spite of the blatant *disregard* for the *second* **commandment** (forbidding the *creating* and *use* of **religious** icons) they *rationalize* the *cross* is *different* because it's not an *image* of a **person** or *creature*. But, the *real* issue is **what** it truly *represents* and its **pagan** origins. Most Christians either *reject* **that** *truth* or **choose** ignorance.

The *cross* in its *various* forms was a *prominent* **religious** symbol in *ancient* societies such as *Egypt, Chaldea, Phoenicia, India* and many others. In fact, its *closed* **loop** *top* form ("*ankh*") was a *symbol* connected not only *passage* of the *dead* into the *underworld* (crossing the River Styx) but is *connected* to the *fertility* **goddess** *Isis* or Astarte ("*Ishtar*"-Easter). Another little *known* **fact** most people **don't** *realize* for *instance*, is the Nazi *Swastika,*, is just one of the **many** *forms* of the *cross*.

What's most shocking about Christianity's *infatuation* with the *symbol* is its **literal** *use*; that of *one* of the most **horrific** *methods* of **torture** and **death** ever *imagined*! Even though the *cross* the Messiah was *hung* upon was a cross *beam* nailed to a *tree* (the late Bible historian Dr. Earnest Martin) it was still one of the most **evil** *methods* of *torturing* someone to *death*! That said, why on Earth would Christianity *adopt* such a **nightmarish** *symbol* of *pain* and **savagery**?

Well, their *explanation* is the **cross** *symbolizes* the **resurrection** of the Christ. Unfortunately, what's **not** *taught* is how the cross was *celebrated* as part of the ancient *fertility* rite of the **sex** *goddess* Ishtar (Isis). In ancient times, *Osiris* was *resurrected* in the form of *Horus*. (Tammuz) Osiris's *wife* **Isis,** told her *subjects* Osiris had been *sent* **back** from heaven (reborn) in an *egg*, which of course, is why the *eggs* are **revered** to this day in the *Easter* (Ishtar) celebration.

Bottom line, if Christ's *resurrection* is supposed to be the *focal* point for Christians, why don't they <u>wear *symbols* of the "**tomb**" *from* which their *Messiah* **emerged**</u> as their *symbol* of **life**. Unfortunately, they have been *coerced* into *worshiping* the *god* of **death** in leu of the *God* of **Life** (YHWH). It's the *reason* they are *all* **dying** instead of *receiving* **immorality**, which the Creator *YHWH* **offers**. In fact, "*Mass*" what is celebrated every Sunday morning, means *death*! It's the Latan *root* of our word **mass**acre!

In **Deuteronomy** 30:19, YHWH *offered* His people a "*choice*". That *choice* was "*Life or **death**, blessings or cursing*". What an absurd *conclusion* to *believe* that *choosing* **life** requires **dying**!? But then, if a person doesn't *realize* they can **choose** immortality (life) **without** *dying*, they are naturally *going* to **die** by *default*. Besides, **Romans** 6:28 tells us the "*wages of sin is death*". Since everyone's **dying**, *hello*!? Obviously the *penalty* for *sin* has **not** been **removed**, instead "*mass*" (death) is **celebrated** *every* **Sunday!**

To conclude this study, *Christianity's* **worship** of *false* and **pagan** *gods* has **condemned** *them* to the "**death** *gods*" **lies** (II Thes. 2:10-11) which is the *reason* the *death* gods' symbol *displayed* everywhere and *celebrated*. Christians are aways talking about how much "*god*" **loves** *them* and all you have to do is "*believe*" and you will "**die**" and *go* to *heaven*.

Chapter 19

To Curse or not to Curse

No doubt most everyone has heard of the *"mummy's **curse**"* where a *pharaoh* would *place* a *curse **upon*** anyone *disturbing* their *resting* place (tomb). Many Native Americans also fully believe *curses* will *befall* anyone ***desecrating*** their *burial* sites as well. In fact, dozens of films have been shot around this *phenomena*. And, there are many who *claim* to have *found* these *curses* to be *profoundly **real**.*

It also seems that to this day; *pronouncing **curses*** on people by whom we've been ***wronged*** is still a very *common* act *perpetuated* in places like New Orleans. Obviously, many if not most people *refuse* to *believe* in the *reality* and *power* of curses, but, there's a *fairly **sizable*** segment of humanity that ***does believe**.* (Think voodoo)

In fact, it's amazing how *powerful* and ***real*** those *curses* apparently can be, when the *subject* of ***curses*** is throughly *researched*. But, the *real question* is; is *pronouncing* a ***curse*** on someone *justifiable*? If the *idea* and *practice* is actually *illicit,* wouldn't books such as the Bible *expose* that truth? That asked, *what* do those scriptures tell us? Is there any legitement *precedent* for ***placing*** curses?

Well, obviously, if we *accept* the Bible as our *authority*, we find the **other** side primarily *promoted*, which is to *bless* people. But, we do find *cursing* as well. In fact, in **Malachi**, (2,v.2) we find the Creator *Himself* placing *curses*! With that in mind, we need to consider *what* it *means* to have a *blessing* pronounced upon us, versus a *curse*. After all, the Messiah apparently told His disciples to *bless* those who *despitefully* **used** them.

But, isn't blessing *someone* who does *evil* to us, **condoning** their *behavior*? Shouldn't we be *condemning* **that** *type* of **behavior** *instead*? And *if* we *condemn* **such** *behavior*, isn't that *equivalent* to **cursing** *someone*? Besides, if **bad** *behavior* is *rewarded* (blessed) aren't we obviously going to get more of it? Let's not forget that the wise man (Solomon) spoke of "*An* **eye** *for an* **eye** *and a* **tooth** *for* **tooth**". Can we really *escape* the consequences for **our** actions *good* or *bad*?

Obviously, the *wisest* man that ever *lived* (Solomon-according to the Bible) doesn't sound as if **all** *behavior* should just be *forgiven* cart-blanc. It sounds more like *retribution* for **bad** *behavior* is *mandatory*, that we cannot *escape* **paying** *our dues.* In fact, what is commonly called "*Karma*" seems to *prove* we do not *escape* the *consequences* of our **evil** *deeds* at all!

Of course, it's also *true* on the *other* side; we *receive* **what** we *give*, and with *interest* according to the scriptures. If that's *true*, isn't *pronouncing* a **curse** on *someone* who has **done** *evil* simply asking for him (or her) to *receive* **what** they *deserve*? Is it *wrong* to want someone to *receive* what *they* **dish** *out*?

Another *example* of *curses* (and *blessings*) being *pronounced* in the scriptures is in the account of Baalim. The King of Midian was **paying** *Baalam* a great deal of money to *pronounce* a **curse** on the nation of *Israel.* Does that not **validate** the *reality* of *curses*, at least anciently?

Whether or not they *deserved* to be *cursed* versus *blessed*, is not for us to determine, but in the story, an Angel told Baalam to *bless* them versus *cursing* them, which he did. I think it's obvious the *curse* would have been **real** considering the *Angel* **stopped** Baalam from *pronouncing* it!

Again, we find many *examples* of the Creator Himself *cursing* people. In fact, in **Deuteronomy** 30, He says he *set **before*** them *blessings* and *cursings*. And as noted before, the *Creator* (YHWH) in **Malachi** 2, *said;* "*because people do **not** give Him* (**YHWH**) *the honor **due** His **exclusive** Name, will be **cursed**.*" He goes on to say *because* people have ***not** given* him the ***honor** due* His *set-apart* (exclusive) Name, He has *cursed* their blessings!

Obviously, He has the *right* to *curse*, and ***has*** *cursed* many people, but again, the prevailing *question* is, *can **we**?* Doesn't the ***real** issue **boil** down* to simply having the ***power*** to *bless* or *curse?* Personally, I do *not* ***believe*** anyone has *that **kind*** of *power*, but those *connected* to the ***spirit** realm*, do!

Personally, with a few of the times I was *wronged*, I did *ask* that the *one* (ones) who *wronged* me *receive* their ***just** desserts*. (Whatever they may be) Even though the word *curse* was ***not** used*, *asking* they *receive back* the *evil* they put *out* is a ***type*** of *curse!* In fact, the few times I did that, the results were quite *shocking*. It really made me *realize* how *careful* we need to be with *what* we *ask* in such situations!

Personally, I have no doubt a person *connected* to the *evil* (dark) *side* of the ***spirit*** *realm*, can be given *power* to *exact **punishment*** *up*on others ***without*** *touching* them! On the other hand I also believe the *good* side *empowers* us to *pronounce **blessings*** that *otherwise* would *not* have been *bestowed*.

Chapter 20

Did the Creator Make a New Covenant With His People?

One of the *chief* cornerstones *upon* which Christianity is *founded* (besides "*Jesus*" and "*Paul*") is the "***New Covenant***". Without a ***new*** covenant (different from the *old*; i.e. *law*) their *theology* crumbles. Suddenly the ***Sabbaths*** of **Leviticus** 23 (including the *weekly* Sabbath) ***cannot*** be *ignored*. Plus, all *their* beloved ***unclean*** foods (*pork* and *shellfish, etc.*) would *no* longer be *eatable*. Worse than that, they would have to ***forsake*** *their* ***traditional*** (pagan) ***holy*** *days* so *near* and ***dear*** to their *hearts*. But, most *difficult* of all would be *taking* ***responsibility*** for *selfish* and *proud* ***behavior***! (Works)

I don't know about you, but something *smells* ***fishy*** in *Denmark*, concerning this so-called "***new*** *covenant*"! After all, their are blatantly *obvious* ***problems*** with this ***new*** *covenant*! That said, is this ***new*** *covenant* Christianity *adopted,* ***really*** *what* the Bible *teaches*, or is it merely ***private*** *interpretation incorporated* by the ***pagan*** *translators* and the Christian *churches*? Personally,

I don't see *any difference* between *Christianity's* **new** *covenant* and a **free-for-all** *philosophy*; that is, a "**lawless one**". In fact, most of those churches **openly** *teach* they are "**not** *under the law*" (i.e. the law of Moses)! But, how is that *not* **lawlessness**? That's the *white* **elephant** in the room! Besides, the so-called "*law*" (Torah) was the *Creators'* **not** *Moses'*.

Well, if the Bible seems to *contradict* itself, maybe it's a *hint* to take a **closer** *look*; that is, with an *actual* **open** *mind*. That said, did the Creator *really* **make** a *mistake* with the so-called "**old** *covenant*" which He *made* with His people *anciently*? If so, *what* kind of a god would that **make** *Him*? After all, **Revelation** 13 tells us the *sacrificing* of His son was *ordained* (planned) "*from the **foundation** of the world*".

That sure doesn't sound like the Messiah *shedding* His *blood* was **plan** B. Besides, **Malachi** 3:6 tells us that the *Creator* (YHWH) "*does not change*". If that's true, was He really **correcting** a **major** *mistake* by introducing a "**new**" *covenant* of *grace* to **replace** the *original* (old) one?

After all, isn't the *birth* and the *death* of the Messiah supposed to be a large *part* of the "**new** *covenant*" of *grace*, **supposedly** *replacing* "*law*"?

Considering His *shedding* of **blood** was *ordained* from **before** the *world*, how could His *death* not have been *part* of that **old** *covenant*, given to *ancient* Israel? Actually, there's **nothing** *new* here at all if we simply pay close *attention* to the *context*.

One of the very *misunderstood* scriptures was one Yahshua (the Messiah' Hebrew Name) gave His disciples in **Matthew** 26:28 (repeated in **Mark, Luke** and **John**) "*For this* (cup) *is the blood of the **new** covenant*" (v.29) "*when I drink it **new** (again) with you in My Father's Kingdom*". The word "*new*" in verse 29 is "*kainos*" actually meaning "*again*" not *something* that had *never* been *done* or *existed* **before**. With that in mind, the word used in verse 28 for "*new*" *covenant* is also "*kainos*" the *same* word used in verse 29 for "*again*".

Strong's Bible Concordance comments the *original* meaning of "*kainos*" is **uncertain** but has to do with "*freshness*". (To make *fresh* or **renew**) That's exactly the *way* the context of verse 29 *utilizes* the word when He *told* them He would *drink* the cup "*anew*" with them in His *Father's* Kingdom. New (kainos) was a *refreshing* or **renewing**, not something that had **not** *been* **done** *before*; just like His mention of a **new** (renewed) *covenant*. Many other NT scriptures support **that** conclusion as well.

One of those *other* scriptures supporting the conclusion that no *literal* "*new*" covenant was *given*, is **John** 13:34. Here Yahshua tells His disciples; "*A **new** commandment I give to you, that you **love** one **another** as I have loved you, that you also **love one another**.*" Again, the word "*new*" here, is the *same* Greek word *kainos*, He used it to tell them He would drink from the cup with them **again** (new) in the Kingdom. But, His telling them to *love* **one** *another* was certainly **nothing** *new*!

In **Matthew** 22, a lawyer asked Yahshua "*what was the great commandment in the law*"? He responded by *quoting* **Deuteronomy** 6. He said in verse 37; "*You shall **love** YHWH your God with all your heart, with all your soul, and with all your mind. This the **first** and great commandment and the second is like it: **you shall love your neighbor as yourself.** On these **two commandments** hang **all the Law** and the Prophets*!"

Obviously, when He told them He was giving them a "*new commandment*" to **love** *one* another, it was **not** new at all, but the **Torah** *instructions* given to ancient Israel in **Deuteronomy** 6!

Again, the proper translation should have been "*refresh*" or "*renew*" versus "*new*". Remember, the *wise* man told us "*there's **nothing new** under the sun*"!

Not to be miss-understood, there, without a doubt, were many seeming *"new" things* happening in the *first* century. Among those were the *spring* **Feasts** coming to **real-time** *fruition*. All those centuries of **rehearsing** them were *now* the "new" **reality**. They're coming to *real-time* **fruition** was certainly a **new** *thing*, but were still very much a <u>part of the</u> **<u>original</u>** (old) *Covenant* (Testament).

A good example of *what* was rehearsed anciently and *coming* to *real-time fruition*, was the *resurrection* of the **saints of old** in **Matthew** 26:57. Such a **large** *resurrection* had **never** been *seen* **before**, but that event had been *rehearsed* for *centuries* in the *ritual* of the **wave-sheaf** *offering*.

There, a *bundle* (sheaf) of green *barley* was cut and *waved* in the temple. It was first waved **down** and then **up,** *picturing* **death** and **resurrection**! But it also *began* the *countdown* to the **completion** of the *spring* **harvest** (picturing a *harvest* of *people*) which was to be *completed* and *celebrated* **50** days later. (Pentecost) Of course, for the *actual* **human** *harvest*, those 50 days represented 50 *years* in real-time fulfillment ("*day for a year*" principle often *seen* in scripture).

The Feast of *First-Fruits* (Pentecost) was also the day of the *great* **out-pouring** of YHWH's *Spirit* which had **never** *occurred* **before** (en-mass) but again, had been *rehearsed* for centuries. With all that in mind, it's rather easy to understand how Christianity (and translators) came to *believe* **what** was *happening* in the *first* century with the *advent* of the Messiah (Passover Lamb) was a "**new** *covenant*".

But, it was only their **ignorance** of YHWH's **Feast** celebrations (Sabbaths) that led them to their *spurious* conclusions. Had they *obeyed* the Creator and **continued** celebrating they would have *understood*. **Hosea** 4:6 tells us that YHWH's "*people are* **destroyed** *for* **lack** *of knowledge*". (Especially of the overall *plan* **shown** by the *Feasts*)

It's YHWH's Sabbaths that *impart* that **saving** (from death) *knowledge,* which is *why* YHWH was so *adamant* His people **not** *forget* to **celebrate** *them* **with** *Him*! But, they *disobeyed* and **forgot** YHWH and His *Torah* (Plan) just as He *said* they *would.*

Consequently **modern** *Israel* is just as *clueless* as the *Gentiles,* as to **who** *YHWH* **is** and **_what He_** is _doing_ with humanity! But, it's time for that *lost* knowledge to be

Chapter 21

Differences; Good or Bad?

One of the most major *issues* we hear *bandied* about these days, especially in **political** *circles*, is "*racism*". It's strange to understand the *original* meaning of *racism* is "*To love our race*" but it's been **turned** *around* to mean *loving* **your** race is *good* for everyone *except* the *Caucasians*. For some reason it's being *taught*, if **Caucasians** *love their* **race**, it means they **hate** all the *others*. That is patently *absurd* considering our current *reality,* as well as *history*, shows there has always been an *element* of **hatred** in **every** race, even for *their* **own**!

The primary *explanation* for the **hated** of **other** *races,* is of course, the *differences*. In fact, we see *hatred* around the world *between* the **same** *races* because of **religious** or *political* **differences**. A good *example* is the *hatred* between the *Catholics* and *Protestants* in Ireland. Both sides are *Caucasians*, but there is so much *hatred*.

Another good *example* is the *Sunnies* and *Shiites*. Both are Muslims and basically descended from the same people, but have deep seated *hated* for *each* **other**. They only get along when facing a **common** enemy, as in their popular phrase; "*The* **enemy** *of my* **enemy***, is my friend*".

One of the *primary* **solutions** *promoted,* is to simply **erase** the *differences.* That's the *real* reason *blacks* and *whites* were *integrated* into the *same* schools and why **interracial** marriage became so *encouraged* by Hollywood and our **political** leaders. In fact, a *movement* back in the 1960's was **unisex** clothes. Both *men* and *women* wearing the **same** *clothes,* by the way, was *forbidden* by the Torah.

But, these days, it's come all the way *down* to **unisex** bathrooms! Even more absurd is how *boys* and *girls* are not being told *they* can *decide* **what** sex they are, in *spite* of **their** plumbing!

Putting all the *insane* **nonsense** aside, just *where* is this *push* to do *away* **with** the *differences* in the world, *originating?* Is this *what* the Creator's *intended?* If so, why didn't They simply *create* **everyone** the **same** *color,* not to mention the same sex? But, **Genesis** and **Proverbs** tell us *humans* were **created** m*ale* and *female!* The fact They *created* the *differences,* means it's *someone* **else** that **hates** those *differences.*

So, *what's* the **real** *problem* here? Do not the *hatreds* of the **differences** boil *down* to either *jealously* and/or **self-righteous** *pride?* After all, we're told "*pride comes before destruction*" and boy, is that ever *coming* to **fruition** these days. But, wouldn't it be a *wonderful* **new** *world* if everyone can simply *learn* to **love** our *differences?*

Of course, to do that, the *ugly* **spirits** of *pride* and jealousy have to be brought **under** *control.* But, is such a *thing* even *possible?* Can humanity ever *learn* to *love* the **non** evil **differences** and not *judge* and **condemn** those *differences?* (Or be *jealous)*

One thing's for *sure,* the *world* being as it is for *thousands* of years, has made it quite obvious, **loving** the *differences* is never going to *happen* without **outside** help. Differences can and *should* **be** *appreciated,* although **too** much **difference** can be a *problem.*

It's like marrying *someone* who is so radically *different*, they're too *irritating* to be *around* for very long. Interestingly, we are *naturally* **attracted** to people *different* from us, at least *mildly*, but *too* **much** *difference*, is a problem. That's *one* reason the *different* **races** begin to *judge* each other.

In a once Old Testament *book* called **Jubliees**, we find Noah *dividing* up the world **between** *his* **three** *sons*. (Three different races) Obviously, he didn't *expect* them to *integrate* and all *live* **together**. Why is that? Well, again, people with *too* **many** *differences* **coexisting** is *not* a **good** thing. Differences can be *nice* and *fun* for a **short** time together, but **too** *much* time begins to *get* on the *nerves*.

Getting back to Noah's sons, his son *Ham* unfortunately *decided* **he** *wanted* Shem's land and *took* it. That's one reason the *sons* of *Ham* (Canaanites) were to be *driven* **out** of the *Promised* land. That land was always *intended* for the *descendants* of **Shem**. Then, after driving *out* most of the **illegal** *inhabitants* of Canaan, YHWH told His people (Israel) they were to be "*quodesh*" which means "*set apart*" (not "*holy*").

So, again, does YHWH *hate* the *differences* because He told His people to be **separate** versus *integrated*? That's *what* we are *told* these days. But, it's like having the *in-laws* come to stay for an *extended* period of *time*. At first it's great, and everyone has lots of *fun*, but at some point, they have **over**-*stayed* their *welcome*. It's not because they're *bad*, it's because they cause *too* **much** *change* to our *routine*.

Sometimes, we have *issues* we simply cannot **tolerate** for a *lengthy* period of time. It's the *same* with the *races*. The *non*-abuse *differences* are *wonderful* for a *time*, but not *meant* to be *permanent*. Again, this is no doubt *why* Noah *instructed* his sons to *settle* **separate** *lands*, and YHWH told His people to be "*set apart*" (separate). I have no doubt, in the future all the **different** *races* with have their **own** *lands*.

It's *interesting* to note that **Revelation** 21 tells us of the "*new City of Jerusalem*" (or YHWH's House) which comes down to the ***new*** Earth, has *only* ***twelve*** gates or *entrances*; ***one*** for *each* of the ***twelve*** tribes of Israel. That makes one ask; *where* are the *gates* for the ***Gentile*** *races*? Did they all get *amalgamated* into Israel? If so, we are back to square *one* with all the *problems* earlier noted. And again, it would *indicate* the Creator's made a *mistake* creating the ***different*** *races*.

Combining a few *other* scriptures with **Revelation** 21, we find ***more*** *evidence* the Earth is given ***only*** to the *descendants* of Israel. Again, ***what*** *happened* to the ***other*** *races*? Well, one *thing* we find in both **Revelation** and **II Peter 3**; the ***old*** Earth is *completely* ***burned*** and is consequently *rebuilt,* but, we are also told the "*heavens will be renewed*" as well. No doubt, our *solar system* was *created* ***perfect*** as the Earth *originally* was, as we're *informed* in the Bible *book* of **Job**.

That said, if a *second* ***sun***, such as *Jupiter* were ***ignited***, many of the *moons* of *Jupiter* and *Saturn* with *water*, such as *Europa, Ganymede* and *Titan* could become *inhabitable*! All they need is ***heat*** to develop *atmospheres*. Is *this* not ***what*** the Creator's, originally *intended*? With that in mind, will the ***other*** *races* be *given* those *moons* as their new ***home*** *worlds*?

With a little *new* ***technology***, the Earth and these *moons* will be *close* enough for *regular* ***interaction*** and *trade*! Imagine going on *vacation* spending time *sampling* the amazing ***differences*** these set-apart *cultures* would ***naturally*** *develop*! Just think how *different* the *food*, ***architecture***, *dress*, ***dance***, and *music* would be! And when all the *hatreds* are put *away*, how *wonderful* and *exciting* this *new* ***solar*** order will be!

Chapter 22

Did The Messiah Really Deceive His Disciples?

Growing up in a Messianic Christian church was a **wonderful** *experience* for me. In fact, Church was one of my *favorite* places to which I always looked *forward*. Even in my teens (including late teens) attending *Church* and learning more *about* the *Bible* was just as *exciting* as girls (or more).

After being *married* a few years and in my mid twenties, it seemed our church had *hit* the *wall* as far as teaching *anything* **new**. That left me very *frustrated* considering my **insatiable** *appetite* for all things *Biblical* and *Spiritual* (not occult).

At the same time, I was beginning to see *problems* with my Church's *teaching* of the *Bible* and its' *scriptures*. Their *scriptural* **interpretations** *prompted* many *questions*, but I never said anything or *questioned* them for some 15 years, even though the *multiplying* **questions** *increasingly* **nagged** at me.

One of the first (problems) to pop up was the Messiah's "*private*" *teachings* to His disciples. My church taught *His teachings* were for **our** (modern) *generation*; that is *thousands* of **years** after the Messiah told **His** disciples "<u>this</u> generation". This *generation* was referring to *His* "*private*" *discussion* (teaching) in **Matthew** 24 (echoed in **Mark** 13 and **Luke** 21). **Matthew** 24 *opens* with the Messiah and His disciples over-looking the Temple and Him telling them of *its* **destruction**, where "*not one stone would be left upon another*" and them **asking** Him "*when*" *the* "*temples destruction*" would **occur.** They also asked *Him* **when** "**His return**" would *occur*. Of course, His answers included a *passel* of other **shocking** *prophecies* along with *His* **return**.

Again, **what** *my* church and *virtually* **all** Christian denominations *teach*, is the *prophecies* He gave **His** *disciples*, were **not** for *them*, but for *people* **thousands** of *years* in the *future*. One *glaring* **problem** though, the **destruction** of *Jerusalem*, **did** occur "*in* <u>**their**</u> *generation*" just as He *predicted*, but *not* His **return**?

Taking a closer look at **Matthew** 24, we're told the *disciples* took the Messiah *aside* **privately** and *asked* Him "***when** would **these** things **be**"* that is, "*the **destruction** of the **Temple** <u>and His return</u>*" (for them). In fact, all through that **discourse**,

He *extolled* **them** *privately; eyeball* to *eyeball,* if you will, with **personal** *pronouns,* such as "<u>***you***</u> *shall hear*" and "*see that* <u>***you***</u> *are not troubled*" and "*they will deliver* <u>***you***</u> *up to tribulation*" etc.

And, considering His **Matthew** 24 *prophecy* of the *destruction* of the *temple* obviously *occurred* in the **first** *century*, were the others really for people *thousands* of years in the *future?* That's extremely *confusing* for me! Of course, that's *remembering* another scripture, where we're told "**confusion** *is not of God*" (YHWH-the Creator's personal Name).

Again noting the **personal** language with which He *addressed* His *disciples* in that *PRIVATE address* (read them for yourselves) how on Earth can anyone conclude He was talking **"over"** their *heads* to a *generation* **thousands** *of years future?* Seriously??

Again, let's not forget He *ended* that *"**private** discourse"* by *telling* them "**THIS generation** *will by no means* **pass away** *until* **all these things**" (He had just told them) *"are fulfilled"*. Of course, one of *"those* **things***"* He just told them *eyeball* to *eyeball*, was *"HIS **RETURN**"*!

Shockingly, He also *told* them at the outset (verse 4) *"Take heed that* **no one deceives you**"! Is that what He did? Did He really **lead** them to **believe** (deceive) He was *speaking* to *them* while *speaking* **over** their *heads* to some *far* **future** generation? Unfortunately, that's exactly *what* the Christian churches, **without** *exception,* **teach**!

Honestly, if He wasn't really *speaking* **to** *them* (about them) how was **He** *not* **deceiving** them? After all, **Peter**, **John**, **James**, and the writer of **Thessalonians**, all *preached* He *was speaking* **to** *them* and **was returning** *in* "**THEIR GENERATION**"! (II Pet.1:16—I John 2:18—Jam.5:7&8 —I Cor.15:51—I Thes.4:15-17)

His *apostles'* teachings *prove* **they** *believed* He was *returning* in *"**their** generation"* and if He didn't, and was actually *speaking* **over** their *heads,* it would have made Him a **deceiver**, no *ifs* **ands**, or *buts*! But, I for one, **know** *the* **Hebrew** *Messiah* (Yahshua) *was* **not** *a deceiver* and that His *disciples were* **not** *deceived* and He really *did* **return** in *"**their** generation"* just as *He* **promised***!*

The really *big* **mistake** made here, is to *forget* the **Feasts** of **Leviticus** 23, which the people had been *rehearsing* all those years, were finally coming to *real* **time** *fulfillment* in the **first** century.

The Feasts of **Leviticus** 23 were simply *physical* **rehearsals** of the *true* **spiritual** *fulfillments* to *come.* They were literal *rehearsals* of the *Creator's* **plan** for *humanity.*

Getting to them, the *first*, was **Passover** with the *shedding* of the Messiah's (Lamb's) *blood* to **save** the **firstborn** (His priesthood) and the *second*; the **Wave-sheaf** (resurrection of the saints of old-Matt.27:53-54) which *began* the **countdown** to the *completion* of the *spring* **harvest**, count "50" *days* (years) later.

Did the Messiah really *commence* (announce) the **spring** *Harvest* (of people) in **real** *time*, with the *real* time *fulfillment* of **Passover** and **wave** *sheaf*, but *not* **complete** that **spring** *harvest* in **that** *season*? Remember, the *spring* (priestly) *harvest* and the *fall* (great) *harvest*, are **NOT** the **same** *thing*!

For now, I'll end this mini-*study* with a *question*; "*What did the Rabbis* (religious rulers) *do after they were* **proven** *"wrong" about* **their** *teaching Messiah was a false* **one** *and wouldn't* **return** *for His followers* (in their generation)? Here's a hint; they *did* **everything** in their *power* to *bury* **that** *truth* and *regain* their **control** over the people! In fact, they were the *literal* **founders** of *Christianity*!

According to a *Messianic* **Jewish** *teacher* and *Historian*, Randy Weiss, the first 15 *popes* were *Jewish*! Let's not forget, it was the *Rabbis* that were telling everyone *Yahshua* and His *Apostles* were *liars* and **false** *teachers*, but were then left *holding* an **empty** *bag* when the *teachings* of the **Hebrew** *Messiah* and *His* **Apostles** actually *proved* **true.** It was **they**, that were *responsible* for *promoting* an **imposter** *messiah*, **apostle**, and *religion*!

They went to the ends of the *Earth* to set up their *counterfeit* **Greek** *messiah* and *religion* named **after** *that* Greek "*Anointed One*" (Christ). By the way; it doesn't take much of a study to *discover* **all** the *Greek gods* were "**Anointed Ones**" (Christos-Christs); but the **Hebrew** *Messiah* had a **Hebrew** *Name* (and title) *appointed* for Him "**before the foundation of the world**" which was "*Yahshua*" *Ha* **Mashiyach**! (Rev.13) *Yahshua* the **Anointed** *One*!

Chapter 23

Elijah and Elisha

Two very interesting *personalities* in Bible scripture are **Elijah** and **Elisha**. Elijah was a very *powerful* **prophet** and an extreme *thorn* in the side of King *Ahab*. Ahab, the son of king Omri, was the king of the *northern* kingdom of *Israel* in 874 BCE who *built* himself the *proverbial* **ivory** *palace*. (Literally, lots of ivory) I **Kings** 16:30 tells us he was the most **evil** *king* up to that time **in** *Israel*. Partly the reason, was his *marrying* the **daughter** of the **pagan** *Sidonian* **king** Ethbaal; *Jezebel*.

Jezebel *reintroduced* the *worship* of the **pagan** *god* "*the Lord*" (Baal) once again *spiritually* **corrupting** Israel. In fact, Ahab *built* a **temple** to the *Lord* in Samaria, the *capital* of Israel, for his **pagan** *wife* and *furnished* it with an **altar** of (pagan) *sacrifice*. He also *erected* a wooden *image* of the **pagan** godess *Asherah* in the temple.

YHWH then sent *Elijah* to tell Ahab he would *hold* **back** the rain *indefinitely* due to his *wickedness*. After *three* years, YHWH told Elijah to go to Ahab and *arrange* a *showdown* between the *450* priests of **Baal** (the lord) and *400* priests of *Jezebel*, whom he throughly *humiliated* before *calling* **down** *fire* from heaven to *burn* up his *water* **soaked** *sacrifice*. (I Kings 18) He (apparently with his servants?) *attacked* and *slew* them all!

He had incredible *power* in that he *stopped* the *rain* for **three** *years* not to mention how he *called* **down** *fire* to **consume** the *sacrifice* and the *water* in the ditch. The fire not only *consumed* the water, but even the *stones* of the altar! What other *man* in scripture besides *Yahshua* had the *power* to **control** the *weather* and call *down* **stone** *consuming* **fire**?

On top of that, after *killing* all the priests of *Jezebel* and *"the lord"* (Baal) he prayed for the rain to *return*, which shortly afterwards *did!* When it started *raining*, he then *outran* Ahab's *chariot* **back** to the *palace!* What *kind* of **super** *man* can do that?

A really **strange** *twist* to the story is how after *outrunning* the horses *back* to the *palace*, he suddenly became very *afraid* of Jezebel's *threats* and ran to **hide** in the *wilderness!* After *stopping* the rain for **three** *years*, killing the 850 *pagan* priests, and *calling* **back** the *rain* after **bringing** *fire* from heaven, *what* is he suddenly so *afraid* of? What happened? Well, the context shows *extreme* **discouragement**.

He then *lamented* to *YHWH* he was the *only* **one** *left* following YHWH and they were *seeking* to *kill* him, and for YHWH to *kill* him instead. The *Angel* of *YHWH* then told Him YHWH had *7000* who had **not** *bowed* (or kissed) the Lord (Baal) and sent him to *anoint* **two** *kings* and *Elisha* to take his *place* as **chief** *prophet*.

After the *death* of Ahab, his successor Ahaziah, *suffered* a *fall* and sent his servants to *petition* the *pagan* **god** of *Ekron* (Baal-zebub) for *healing*. Consequently, the Angel of YHWH told Elijah to tell Ahaziah; due to his *entreating* a **pagan** god instead of YHWH, he would *die*.

Ahaziah then sent a *battalion* of *50* **men** to *bring* in Elijah. They *found* him (and apparently Elisha) sitting up on a *hill*. Interestingly, the *same* kind of *thing* happened to *Elisha* and his servant Gehazi, but Gehazi was *afraid* and Elisha asked YHWH to **open** *his* **eyes** to the *angels* riding *chariots* above them in another dimension.

At any rate the *battalion* found Elijah on a hill and *ordered* him to come *down* with them. Elijah then tells them *if* he was a **prophet** of YHWH, fire would come *down* from heaven and ***fry*** them, which it did. So the king sent another 50 who met the *same* fate.

Finally, a third battalion of 50 came and the commander *bowed* down before Elijah and **begged** for *mercy*, which Elijah *granted*. But, Ahaziah *died* anyway, just as Elijah *prophesied*.

The next major scene was Elijah *asking* Elisha what he could *do* for him before he was *taken* (to heaven?). Elisha then asked for a **double** portion of Elijah's *Spirit* which Elijah responded was a ***hard*** thing. But, he said, if Elisha *saw* the chariot of *fire* come *down* and take him *up*, his wish would be *granted*, which is exactly what *happened!*

The amazing thing is; 7 (major) miracles were recorded *performed* by Elijah, while Elisha performed *14*; exactly *double!* The really big *question* to *arise* here is; if Elijah was taken *up*, and Elisha was given a **double** portion of *Spirit*, how is it Elisha supposedly *died?* Obviously, there's something very *wrong* with this picture.

In fact, there's a story of how a *dead* man was *thrown* into Elishas' *tomb* and was **supposedly** resurrected upon *touching* his *bones*. But, we have two major *problems* with this story. First, **why** was Elishas' *tomb* **open**?

Obviously if they had to *open* it, they would have known *someone* was **in there**. And, judging by Elisha's *notoriety* his *tomb* would have been *well* **known** and no doubt *marked!*

The second problem is; if Elisha's bones had the *power* to *resurrect* a **dead** man, how is it the *power* to **resurrect** Elisha himself, or keep him **from** *dying* (like Elijah) was not there?

Unfortunately, we can't *have* **it** *both* ways! My guess is Elisha was also *taken* **up** like Elijah without anyone *witnessing,* so *people* began telling *stories* about what *happened* to him.

We find the same kind of commentary with *Moses*. We are told in **Deuteronomy** 34:7 "*His* **eyes** *were* **not dim,** *nor* **his natural vigor abated**" but then he *died*? If his *eyesight* had **not** dimmed and he was *still* **strong**, *how* is it **he** just *died*?

In fact, chap. 32 (48-50) supposedly tells us YHWH told Moses to go **die** (in Moab) in spite of what He tells us in **Ezekiel** 18:32; "*For why should you die, O house of Israel? For I have no pleasure in the death of one who dies, says YHWH* (our God) *Therefore turn and live*!

On top of that oxymoron, we are told in **Deuteronomy** 34:6 that YHWH **took** him and **buried** him, but **no** one **knows** where! Really? If YHWH *supernaturally* took him and *buried* **him** how would anyone have *known*? (Or that he was even *dead*?)

Another thing, in **Deuteronomy** 30 the people were offered "*life*" versus "*death*" and were encouraged to "*choose* **life**". (Immortality) Considering the Angel of YHWH *tabernacled* with Moses *regularly*, are we really to understand Moses did **not** *choose* life as was *offered* at Sinai? If anyone *knew* he had the *choice* of **life**, it was Moses!

Besides, in **Mark** 9:4, we find Yahshua **talking** with *Elijah* and *Moses*. How is this possible unless *Moses* did not *die* as Elijah did not? Remember, this was before the *saints* of *old* were **resurrected** in Jerusalem! (Matt. 27:56) Again, we must remember, it was *humans* that *recorded* and *penned* the Bible

Chapter 24

The Ezekiel 38 Effect

The *advent* of the **Feast** of **Trumpets**, marks the *beginning* of the *fall* harvest (of humanity) *season*, which is soon *followed* by the **trumpet** *plagues outlined* in **Revelation** chapters 8-11. These *trumpet* plagues are all *hell* **breaking** *loose* and *raining* **down** upon a *hapless* humanity. But, it would *not* be a *hapless* humanity if they would only *listen* **to** and *embrace* our Creator (YHWH) versus their **pagan** *gods*. He *promises* (and has always *kept* His *promises*) to do *nothing* without **first** warning **His** *people* whom *He* **promises to protect**. (Amos 3) Unfortunately we can **choose** to *reject* Him and everything *He's* **doing**; including the *blessings* (promises) that *come* with Him!

Of course, one of *greatest* of those *promises* of *blessings* is **protection**. Christianity is always *talking* about **those** *blessings* He *promises*, which unfortunately **fail** to *materialize* for most; *hit* and *miss* at best. But, *why* is that? In fact, many Christians have *left* their *faith* because *things* they *expected* to be **protected** *from* (disease and accidents) **happened** *anyway*. So how can we *blame* them? But then, it's written in **Hosea** 4; "*My people are **destroyed for lack of knowledge**"*! Just **what** *knowledge is* He **referring** to?

Unfortunately, between the *Protestant* translators and the "*private interpretation*" of the *thousands* of **different** sects (cults) that **saving** *truth* has been **lost**! In fact, the **hard** *truth* is Christianity is as *pagan* as every other *world* religion on the planet. You see, Christianity doesn't really *base* their *belief's* on the Bible, but **the** *particular* **interpretation** they *force* upon it! In fact, I haven't been able to *find* a *single* **cult** (sect) that **embraces** both *YHWH* and His *Torah* (especially His Sabbaths). What a tragedy considering *what* they are *depriving* themselves of, is *what* I call the **Ezekiel** *38* **effect**!

Of *what* I speak is not *etherial* or **wishful** *thinking* considering I accidentally *discovered* and *experience* it **first** hand. It's a *reality*; a reality *shown* **anew** *virtually* **daily**! It's *like* the *manna* that *rained* down **from** *heaven* **every** *day* for our ancient forefathers along with the **rock** that *followed* them to *provide* **water**! On top of that, there was the **shade** from the *hot* sun as well as the *night* **light** (pillar of fire)! And, according to the account, their *clothes* and *shoes* didn't even wear out! YHWH's **personal** *care* of our ancient fore-*parents* was astonishing!

That said, does He really *care* **less** *about* **us** than *them*? Besides, we're told the Creator is **not** a *respecter* of persons.

The *white* **elephant** *question* in the room is; is **that** *kind* of *provision* and *protection* not *available* **to us now** even though He tells us He "*changes* **not**"? And if so, *how* can we *find* it? Well, according to **Matthew** 6:33, we are *promised* if we "*seek first His Kingdom*" He will take *care* of the *rest* of our **needs**, just like the ancient Israelites, who clearly were *not* the most *righteous* people considering their **rebellion** and *complaining*!

What's the *difference* between *them* and *us*? Remember; while in *bondage* in Egypt, they received only **minimal** *provision* and *protection,* but *something* **changed**; *what* was it? Well, in spite of their *lack* of *faith* and *complaining*, there were *two* major *differences* **between** *them* and *us*! The *first* of these **differences** was the fact that YHWH had **restored** His *Set* **Apart** (exclusive) *Name* and they were no longer *dishonoring* and *disrespecting* Him with *pagan* and/or **generic** *names* (and titles)! (See Malachi 1&2). YHWH **will not** and **cannot** *bless* the *disrespecting* of His *exclusive* (quodesh-Set-Apart) Name!

To **bless** *such* **disrespect** sets a completely *wrong* (evil) *precedent* in His Family! After all "*respect*" is "*love*" and *love* in His **eternal** *family* is *what* it's *all* about!

The next major *difference* is YHWH's *Feasts* (Sabbaths). Again, to *disrespect* or *dismiss* **YHWH's** *Sabbaths* (anniversaries') is *directly* **disrespecting** and **dismissing** our Creator! And considering *all* **His** *Sabbaths* (weekly and annually) are *all* **about** *us* and His **Plans** for **us,** why on Earth would we **not** *want* to *celebrate* those *eternal* **Plans** for *us* in His *Family*? Can you *spell* "**d-e-m-o-n-s**" *class*? Sorry about the *sarcasm,* but **not** *wanting* to *celebrate* being a *part* of *what* YHWH is *doing* **with** and **for** *us* is like *eating* **dirt** in leu of *growing* and *eating* **vegetables,** after all, *veggies* are *made* from *dirt!*

You see, when ancient Israel left Egypt, they were *introduced* to the true Creator's Name *YHWH* and His special *Celebrations* (Sabbath-Feasts)! Those **two** elements alone were *enough* for YHWH to *pour* out His *special* **protection** and **provisions** for them! It was also the major *changing* **point** for me *personally* as well.

I noticed a *major* **change** in *provision* after *embracing* His *Exclusive* Name (and Yahshua) and an even **greater** *level* of *provision* and *protection* with the *celebrating* of His **true** *Sabbaths*, which are *dictated* (weekly, monthly, and yearly) by the *moon* with the sun's help for the *seasons* and the *light!*

This takes us back to the *title* of this study; the **Ezekiel** 38 effect. If we *follow* the chronology of **Ezekiel**, we notice that by chapter 38 (and 39) Israel is now *back* **with** *YHWH* (new Eden) and **completely** *protected* and **provided** *for* as a *whole*! That's *how* it was for Israelites in the *wilderness*. We see there (in the new future Eden) they have **no army** and **no** *walls* for *protection* and are *provided* for *so* **well** that *Gog* and *Magog* (gentiles) become **jealous**!

The real *point* is; we don't *have* to *wait* until *then* to **have** *what* YHWH *provides* Israel with in **Ezekiel** 38 and 39; we can *have* it **now**! Again, I am *living* **proof** of that **fact**! YHWH had always *blessed* and *protected* me in life, but *what* I was given before is *nothing* compared to the way I'm being *cared* for now! We **don't** need to be *perfect* (*perfect* only means "*mature*") to **claim** YHWH's *amazing* **provision** *and* **protection;** we *need* **only** give Him the *respect* and "honor **due**" His **exclusive** *Name* and **not** *refer* to Him as "*lord-baal*" or "*God-El*" (as a name) or *Jesus* as His son, plus the *honor* and *respect* **due** His *true* (lunar) **Sabbath** celebrations! How simple!

Just to *remind* us of another very interesting *example* of YHWH's **hedge** of *protection* and *provision,* is Job! Remember how the *adversary* (watcher) came to *report* to YHWH and was *asked* about *Job*? YHWH told the *adversarial* watcher His servant Job was the most **righteous** *man* in the East, to which the *watcher* **responded**; "*it is only because of the* **hedge** (of protection and provision) *you have placed* **around** *Job that he* **obeys** *You*"! The *adversary* (Satan in Hebrew) then told YHWH *if* he *removed* His *hedge* of **protection** and *provision*, Job would *curse* and *forsake* Him.

Well, YHWH *tested* Job and *proved* the adversary *wrong*. We must *not* forget; Job was not exactly *innocent* considering it was he who *advised* Pharaoh to *throw* the Israelite *boys* in the river! (Jasher) Job didn't know *who* the Israelites *were*, but, YHWH *blessed* and *protected* him anyway! Again; we don't have to be *perfect* (righteous) for YHWH to put His *hedge* of *protection* and *provision* around us; we need *only* give Him the *honor* **due** His **exclusive** *Name* and *celebrate* His *true Sabbaths* **with** *Him*!

Chapter 25

Ereb and Boqer: Evening and Morning?

In **Genesis** 1 we find the creation week *outlined* with some very *curious* **details;** details *ignored* by most, but *applied* in a very bizarre *way* to *support* the *Jewish* and **Saturday** *keeping* **day,** *beginning* at *sundown.* As we so often find when *taking* an **honest** look at *religious* doctrines, most quickly fall *apart* when just a small *modicum* of the *light* of **day** (logic) is *shined* upon them.

Again, I don't think the Creator **equipped** us with *thinking,* **reasoning,** *minds,* with the *added* **gift** of *logic,* if He didn't **expect** us to *exercise* that gift! After all, does He really want **mindless** *robots* for *children?*

So, let's step back and *apply* a little of that *rare* and mostly **unused** *gift* (especially in *religions*) **logic,** starting with the Jewish *notion* the *day* **begins** at *sundown.* That's a *belief supposedly* supported by the *creation* days in **Genesis,** which honestly makes no sense, considering the time to *work* or **accomplish** *anything,* especially in *those* times without **electric** *lights,* was during the *day*! In fact, Yahshua stated in **John** 9:4; "*I must work the works of Him while it **is day;** the **night** is **coming** when **no man** can work*".

Obviously, when the sun came *up*, they had the ***light*** they *needed* to *see* and *accomplish* things, *while* the *waning* of light (the coming of *night*) was the *time* to ***cease*** work and sleep. This was the time to enjoy the evening meal and then *sleep* until the *return* of the sun and *light.*

Considering darkness *ends* the *ability* to ***work*** (without artificial light) how could *sundown* (arrival of night) in any *way*, *shape*, or *form* be considered the "***beginning***" of the *day*? It's completely absurd!

It would like *believing* ***up*** is ***down*** and *down* is *up*! But then, if it's something we *heard all* our lives, it would *seem* to make sense even though it *doesn't* to *anyone* ***exercising*** *reason* and *logic*!

The *Saturday* keeping people, like the Jews, *came* to *believe* ***evening*** begins the *Sabbath* rest (day). The "*rest*" *part* would *seem* to make sense, but *worshipping* (honoring) the *Creator* of ***light***, who's ***called*** "*light*" with the *coming* of ***darkness*** is another *absurdity*! How could anyone *conclude* *celebrating* the ***approach*** of ***darkness*** in any *way* ***shape*** or form ***honors*** the *God* of *Light*? Is it beyond the *realm* of *possibility* the Israelites *adopted* such a ***nonsensical*** *tradition* while in *captivity* of the Babylonians, who *celebrated* (worshipped) their *gods* with the ***coming*** of ***darkness***?

There's also a scripture with this bit of *illumination*; "*Woe to those who call* ***evil good*** *and* ***good evil***; *who put* ***darkness for light*** *and* ***light for darkness***"! (Is.5:20) I would say *that* scripture just about *sizes* it ***up***, wouldn't you? But, their *argument* is ***Genesis*** one ***proves*** the day ***begins*** at *evening* because the words "*evening*" and "*morning*" are listed as the ***two*** parts of the day, but there's something very *wrong* with that.

First of all, we find the *Creator* ***dividing*** the *light* from the *darkness* in versus 3-5 and calling the *light* "***day***" and the *darkness* "***night***". Right ***there*** we *find* the ***Bibles*** definition of "*day*" it's "*light*" ***not*** darkness, or ***night***! Then we see then see *the* *day* (light) is *divided* into ***two*** parts, "*evening and morning*" ("*ereb and boqer*").

So, if the **light** (day) *begins* with "*ereb*" how can that in any stretch of the *imagination* mean *evening?* That makes the *whole* thing completely *nonsensical* and *absurd!*

Obviously, by *context* "*ereb*" **cannot** mean *evening,* just as "**boqer**" (pronounced boker) **cannot** mean *morning.* In fact, looking carefully at the narrative. we see *ereb* and *boqer* on the *first* **three** *days,* but the **sun wasn't in the sky** until the **4ᵗʰ day**! Obviously, you can't have *evening* and *morning* (or sundown) with **no sun** *in* the *sky!*

By the Bibles' own **creation** *sequence, ereb* (evening) and *boker* (morning) could **not** have **meant** *evening* and *morning* in *ancient* Hebrew. As is with all languages, *Hebrew* **evolved** over *time* and *words* like *ereb* and *boker* **took** *on* new and **different** meanings. One Bible teacher *fluent* in Hebrew (Charles Missler) *established* that exact *argument.*

Unfortunately there are no *Hebrew* writings **ancient** *enough* to show us the *original* **ancient** *meanings* of *ereb* and *boqer,* but Missler is convinced those words were referring to the *rebuilding* of the Earth after it became "*tohuw*" and "*bohuw*" (*destroyed* and *desolate*) by an ancient *cataclysm.* Missler concludes *ereb* is a reference to the **reduction** of **entropy** (chaos) while *boqer* is a *reference* to the *increase* of **order** and **clarity**. Honestly, that's the only explanation I've ever heard that even comes *close* to *making* **sense.**

One last point; if *ereb* (supposedly meaning evening) *instructs* us *when* the Sabbath day *begins,* why is *ereb* and *boqer* not mentioned on the **seventh** (Sabbath) *day* after creation? Again, the ancient meaning of ereb could have had *nothing* to do with the *beginning* of the *Sabbath* **day;** although, there are *two* of the **annual** *Sabbaths* that *are* instructed to *begin* in the *afternoon* (evening) and for very *important* reasons.

The first was *Passover*, where the *lamb* was *instructed* to *slain,* in the "*ben ha erebrim*" which meant "*between the evenings*". You see, even in more ancient times, *half* the rabbis believed *evening* (going down of the sun) began as the sun *descended* over the horizon while the other half *believed* the "*going down of the sun*" (evening) was *right* **after** *high noon* as the sun *begins* its *descent.*

So "*between the evenings*" would have meant the *slaughter* of the *lambs* was to occur around 3PM, which incidentally was the time of the "*evening sacrifice*" which makes complete sense considering it gave the people about **three** *hours* of *daylight* to *slaughter,* **dress**, and *prepare* the lambs for *roasting.* To say *evening,* the time of *slaughtering* the *lambs* commenced **after** *sundown,* is *ridiculous*!

But, considering the Jew's *upside* down *belief* of *what* **"day"** (light) is and *when* it begins (especially the *Sabbath* day) is it any wonder why they not only *celebrate* the *coming* of **darkness** (picturing death) but *celebrate* a Sabbath **dedicated** to one of the *gods* of *death;* the **father** *god* of the *Titans,* **Cronos**, or *Saturn,* where we get our modern day of *Saturday?* Proof they *worship* a god of *darkness* (death) is the fact they are *all* **dying**!

YHWH is **light** and tells us the **sign** between *Him* and **His** *people* will be *His* **Sabbath** *days* (light=life) which means *His* **Sabbath** Days are **not** *darkness* (death) and *cannot* be *days* **dedicated** to a **pagan** *god* of **darkness** and/or *death* (Saturn)! In fact, Yahshua *accused* the **Saturday** *keeping* Jews that they were the "*Sons of their father the devil*"! YHWH shows us His *Sabbath* "**days**" by *His* **calendar**; the **moon**! (Gen.1:14) That is another proof, *Saturday* is **not** *YHWH's* Sabbath.

Chapter 26

Freedom; What is it Really?

We all hear the word "*freedom*" **tossed** about on a regular *basis*, but just *what* does it literally *mean*. We hear *that* word in our "*Pledge of allegiance*" and of course, our *constitution*. We have (or had) the *guarantee* of "*free*" **speech** and "*freedom*" of **religion** along with many more, but do those **guaranteed** *freedoms* encapsulate the **true** *essence* of *freedom*? With that in mind, we hear a whole *passel* of things we're no longer *free* to **say** *these* days due to *political* **incorrectness.** It seems *saying* or *doing* anything that *offends* the so-called *liberals*, gets us *labeled* "**racist**" and/or **hateful**!

Well, there's a Bible scripture adding a whole **new** element to the *concept* of *freedom* where it is stated; "*The **truth will make you free**". (Jn. 8:32) But just what in the world does *that* mean? Are we only *free* if we have "*the **truth**"? And. just *what* is that *truth* anyway? **Who** *defines* **what it is** and/or *isn't;* our government or major *media*? What about *religion*? With *religion* in mind, what about the *Bible*? Is the Bible *true* considering the hundreds of **different** *translations*? If so, which *translation* is the **true** *one*?

That said, let's go a slightly *unorthodox* direction; that the *truth* is all ***about*** *freedom*! But before going there, a great quote from president James Garfield is *fitting*. He said; "*The truth will **set** you **free**, but it will **make** you **miserable** first*!" How very true, but again, just *what is **that** truth* that makes us *miserable* and then *free*?

Does it mean we are *free* to do *whatever* we *want* or go ***where*** we *desire* and ***when*** we *want*? Once upon a time, we had ***those*** *freedoms*, but unfortunately, that's rapidly *changing* these days! We're now told we *don't* have *freedom* to *infringe* upon *freedoms that **others*** deem ***theirs***.

There's *some* truth in that *concept*, considering our so-called *freedom* of ***speech***, really does not *free* us to *say **defamatory*** *things* to or *about* others. That said, do we have the *freedom* (or right) to ***not*** be *insulted* or *defamed* by others? Isn't that *infringing* upon ***their*** *free* speech? In fact, isn't becoming *offended*, allowing *someone **else*** to *steal* a *freedom* of ours?

How about *freedom* of ***religion***, which was also a *guarantee*, is ***that*** *freedom* real? What if your *religion* is *Islam* (meaning submission) where you are *commanded* by *your **god*** to *convert* or ***kill** the **infidels*** (those who believe differently than you)? Do we really have the *right* to *exercise* that ***supposed*** *freedom*? Obviously, ***true*** *freedom* is *not* being able to do ***whatever*** we *desire*, ***when*** we ***desire*** *all* the time.

The whole concept becomes *lost* and *moot* when we ***steal*** the *freedom* and ***choices*** of *others* by ***exercising*** ours. So, it seems we are right *back* to *square **one*** of this whole *discussion*. Everyone having the *freedom* to do *what* they *want*, ***when*** they *want* would be complete *chaos*. That *kind* of freedom is *not **free*** and is *impossible*.

So, again, *what* is the "*true*" in "***true** freedom*"? That said; if we *incorporate* a little *old **fashioned** logic*, would *true **freedom*** be the ***freedom** from **outside** control?* How can ***real** freedom* exist when we are in ***some** way under **someone's** elses' **control**.* To be under someone's *control* in any *way*, **shape**, or form, simply reduces us to **slave** status, does it not? So, if we don't want to be *under* the **control** of **others**, *how* on Earth do we think we should have the *right* to *inflict* **our** control and *manipulation* upon *them?*

That's an interesting *prospect* in consideration of the *concept* of *marriage.* If we are *honest*, isn't the *source* of virtually ***all** relationship* **problems** spawned in *one* or **both** sides trying to ***manipulate*** or *force* the other to *change* to ***fit*** their idea of *how* or *who* they should be? If we are **truly** honest, we know that's *true.*

Out of *pride*, we all *want* to *believe **our** likes* and ***dislikes**, ideas*, and *ways* of ***doing*** things are the *best!* But, when we try to *mold* and *shape* our *friends* and **mates** into **our** image, **nothing** *good* results!

But then, it's written; "***Pride goes before destruction***"! Attempting to **manipulate** *others* in any *way*, **shape** or *form* is *pure **pride*** and *selfishness!* (Parents with children not included) It's a *formula* for **destruction**!

The reason for that is we were **not** *created* to be **controlled**! (By outside forces) Our very *nature* shows we were *created* to *be **free***, which again brings us *back* to *what **true** freedom **is.*** In fact, by simply *allowing* what someone *says* to **offend** us, how have we *not* become **their** *slave!*

Well, if you don't already *know*, or have *guessed*, *true **freedom*** is "**self control**"! The bottom line is; if we *control* our *own* **actions** and *behavior*, **what** *need* have we for **outside** *control!* In fact, that's the **whole** *theme* of the *Bible!* We were created to choose to *govern* (control) ourselves using the *guidelines* of the Creator's Torah (living instructions).

The whole point of *this **physical** existence* is to *make* the *choice* to ***first** treat* our Creator with *love* and *honor* and *respect* and *each **other** second*. You see, YHWH is *not* going *to sentence* His **eternal** *children* (family) to an **eternity** of *bickering, fighting* and *general **misery**!* He simply will ***not** do **it**!*

Not only are we to *choose* to *govern **ourselves*** in *love, **respect**,* and *honor* for YHWH and ***each** other,* but then *to **fight*** (the adversary) for ***that** choice.* That was the whole *reason* for YHWH first *giving* His *angels **free** moral **agency**.* With that *freedom,* He knew a *percentage* would *choose **selfishness*** and *pride* and become the *adversary* (adversaries) to *fight* in order to make our *loving **choices** real!*

So, again, ***true** freedom* is ***self**-control* using the Creator's Torah (living instructions). If we *control **ourselves*** under those guide-lines, there's **no** *need* for **external** *control.* It's only to the *extent* we ***refuse** to take **responsibility*** for and ***control*** our ***own*** *actions,* that we *have **need*** of (and are given) ***masters** to **control** us!*

In fact, all the *freedoms* the US was *founded **upon*** are based upon ***self-** governance* or ***self**-control.* The more we ***abdicate** responsibility* for *our **own** actions,* the more we are *giving* governing **authorities** to step up and *enslave* us. Bottom line; ***true** freedom* is *self* control!!

Chapter 27

The Four Resurrections

One of the most *exciting*, but mostly *untaught* Bible *teachings* is the ***two major resurrections.*** Not only are there ***two resurrections*** clearly shown in **Revelation** 20, but with incorporating other scriptures, we find *both* those two are *split* into ***two parts.*** Unfortunately, when *resurrection* is mentioned, it's virtually across the board *applied* to the ***Messiah's resurrection.***

But, truthfully, most Biblical references to *resurrections* cannot be *applied* to the **Hebrew** Messiah (Yahshua) at all. But, accepting the Bible's actual *resurrection* teachings *changes **everything**,* literally! If Christianity, not to mention ***all*** *religions,* taught this ***basic truth,*** the world be an *entirely **different** place!*

We have a few *minor* **resurrections** mentioned, such as Elisha *raising* up the little dead *boy,* and Yahshua *resurrecting* a young girl, as well as Lazareth, the brother of Mary, but no ***mass resurrections*** until **Matthew** 27. There we find the *graves* in Jerusalem *opening* (at the same time Yahshua came out of the tomb) and the *saints* of **old** (Abraham, Isaac, Jacob, etc.) coming ***out*** *of* their *graves* and into the city.

But, back to the *two **major** resurrections* **Revelation** 20; *what **are** they* and *when* do they *happen*? In fact, we're told there, death has **no** *power* over those which are part of the ***first** resurrection;* but, did ***it** happen*, or is it *still **future***?

That asked, **Ezekiel** 37 speaks of a *resurrection* consisting of the "*whole house of Israel*" *which* we can safely *assume* is a ***future** event*. But, are we actually told *when*, or is it just a *big **guessing** game*? Would the Creator really *promise* (predict) these *resurrections* but not give us any *indication* as to *when*?

Considering ***dead** people* obviously ***don't** care*, but if a person's *soul* is in *heaven*, as most ***believe***, and *resurrection* means *receiving* a ***new** body*, wouldn't it be important to *know **when*** that ***new** body* is *coming*? But that raises the obvious *question*; if people live in heaven ***without*** a *body*, why do they even *need* one? Is that not a very ***relevant** question*?

Let's take a look at another *resurrection* outlined in II **Thessalonians** 4, commonly called the "*rapture*" that causes much controversy. Again, *did* it ***happen*** or is it *still* a *future* event? Well, the *place* to begin would be to have a *full **understanding*** of the **big** picture and how the *resurrections **fit*** into ***that** picture*.

We're told in **Isaiah**, *truth* comes in *bits* and *pieces* ("*here a little and there a little*"). But, *how* to ***assemble*** those *bits* and *pieces* (like a puzzle) is the ***real** issue*. It begins with understanding the Bible does ***not** teach* going to ***heaven*** or the *proverbial **hell*** when we *die* at all. Those beliefs are *traditional,* ***not*** *scriptural*.

Besides, if we are *able* to go to *heaven* or *hell **without*** our *bodies*, why do we *need* our bodies ***resurrected**?* On the other hand, if we ***actually*** do *die* and go into the *ground*, the *need* for *resurrections* becomes so much more obvious and *understandable*!

Well, taking an *honest* look into the scriptures, we find the *first **mass** resurrection* (saints of old) literally *occurring* in the ***first** century*. After all, how could the graves *opening* and ***many** people **coming** out, not* constitute a ***mass** resurrection*, and the ***first*** one at that? That said, and going *back* to the *spring* and *fall **harvest** festivals* in the old Testament, we find a temple *ritual* that *explains* volumes, called the "*wave-sheaf*".

A *bundle* of *green barley* (before the spring harvest) was *brought* into the temple (three days after Passover) *waved **down*** and *up*, symbolizing the ***death*** and ***resurrection*** of the *group* of *people* that *sheaf* of *barley **represented***. They were **not** in *heaven **before*** their resurrection! Considering the *saints* of ***old*** (Abraham, Isaac, Jacob, itc.) as well as the **Hebrew** *Messiah* came *out* of their *graves* on *the **exact** day* of the wave-sheaf, tells us without a doubt just *who* that *sheaf* of barley *represented*.

In fact, we have *secular **proof*** of that *shocking **event*** in the **Pilot** *letters*, which he *fired* off to Cesar *Tiberius* currently *residing* in the British museum of Bible history! A little more *investigating* shows us the *wave-sheaf* was the "*first-fruits*" of the ***first-fruit*** (spring) *harvest*. (of people) The smaller *spring* harvest was called the ***first-fruit*** harvest with the *fall* **harvest** called the ***great*** harvest.

Of course, the ***physical*** grain harvests are *typical* of **human** *harvests*. But, *before* each **main** harvest could commence, *first-fruits* had to be *brought in*. So, the *wave-sheaf* **resurrection** was the *first-fruits* of the spring **harvest**. Again, the *first-fruits* were a **minor** *resurrection* before the **major** (second) *resurrection* which **Revelation** 20 refers.

We know the *full **first** resurrection* occurred in the *first* century considering the *wave-sheaf* **resurrection** *announced* the *countdown* to the **completion** of *that* **spring** or first-fruit *harvest*, **fifty** years later (represented by the ***fifty*** *days* celebrated in the *physical rehearsal*).

No doubt, what *happened* in II **Thessalonians** 4 was "*that*" *resurrection,* which beings us to the *fall,* or *second* (great) *resurrection.* Not to go into it too much here, but Donald Trumps' **miraculous** *election* along with the **Revelation** 12 **impossible** "*sign of the woman*" being *seen* in **real** time during the literal *Feast* of **Trumpets** in 2017, *announced* the **commencement** of the *Fall **Harvest** season.*

According to the *physical* **rehearsal**, there were **ten** *days* between *Trumpets* and *Atonement,* which *translates* to *ten* **years** in *real* time. The *bringing **in** of the first-fruits* of the **fall** harvest is also *a* **minor** *resurrection* with the **balance** to **come** *later.* Shockingly, we're even told *approximately* **when** that great *resurrection* of **Ezekiel** 37 will be.

In **Hosea** 4, is a *prophecy* given to the ***northern*** nation of ***Israel*** just *before* the *Assyrian* **captivity** (approximately 715 BCE) that they would be "*stricken and torn*" but would be "***revived** after **two** days*". Obviously, *two* days did not mean *two **literal** days,* but 2000 years as II **Peter** 3:8 *tells* us; **one** *day* in the *spirit* realm is like *1000* years here in this *physical* realm. How amazing then to see the *reviving* of those *Israelite* (tribes) nations commencing **two** *thousand* **years** *later,* with the beginning of the *renaissance* in the 13th century!

That *prophecy* was **right** *on,* but there was *more.* Israel was *told* in the last part of that prophecy, after being *revived* after *two* days, they would be "*raised up*" on the "***third** day*". Obviously, the *third* day would be another ***1000*** years after the *reviving* in the 13th century. Doing the math puts the "*raising up*" of the **whole** *house* of *Israel* in the neighborhood of 2260!

Of course, the **exact** *year* **cannot** be *established*, but at least the *general* **era** can. The *reason* for such a **time** *span* is *obvious*, considering *preparation* for the *resurrection* of **millions** if not *billions* of people is going to be a **great** *undertaking*. They will all need *places* to *live*, not to mention **clothing**, *food* and the general *necessities* for *living*. Personally, I don't think those *things* are going to be *part* of **their** *resurrection* but must be *prepared* **for** *them* **in** *advance*.

Chapter 28

Faith

We hear people throughout every *walk* of life and *religion* citing *something* called "*faith*". But the **real** question is; *what* **is** *faith; really?* That asked, is *faith* the *trust* we place in *everyday* **things,** such as *faith* that the *chair* we *sit* on will **hold** *us,* or that our *houses* will not *fall* on us, or that our *cars* will *start* and get us *where* we *want* to *go?* Are those *examples* of **faith** any *different* from the *kind* of *faith* **religious** *people* are usually *referring* to? After all, all *religions* are called "*Faiths*"!

One of the most oft *quoted* and *heard* statements, refers to having *faith* in "*God*". But, "**who**" or "*what*" **is** *God* and "*why*" should we *put* our *faith* in this **being?** In fact, in a *reference* to *God,* we are told; "*Without faith it's impossible to please Him*" (Heb.11:6) Is **that** faith our God is *actually* **real,** or *faith* in some *other* **aspect** of that God. Or, maybe it's about *what* He will **do** *for* **us?** In fact, ask a *hundred* different people from *different* **faiths,** and doubtless, you'll get *100* **different** answers.

Well, no doubt *some* will be *close,* but the *truth* is, virtually **no one truly** *knows* just **who** the *gods* actually **are,** or of the **spirit** *world* in which the "*Gods*" **reside.** Of course, that's not to mention their *interaction* with us. We all have *ideas* and *bits* and *pieces* of **that** *realm, passed* to us from a *hundred* **different** directions, but *what's correct?*

Again, in just which of peoples *concepts* of God (or gods) should we *place* our *faith*? Does *faith* in *just **anything*** or ***any*** *god **work***? Besides, ***why*** should we put our *faith* in a *god* in the ***first*** place? Assuming our *faith* in this *god* of ***ours*** (that He exists) is *correct*, isn't the *real **point*** of *faith* (in a *god*) about *what* that God can and/or will ***do*** for *us* and give us *what* we *need* and ***when*** we *need* it? After all, *looking* around the world, it's obvious ***most*** of the *gods* in which people have *placed* their *faith,* have not only *let **them*** *down*, but seem to literally *hate* those that *adore* and/ or ***worship*** them!

In fact, even in our *wealthy **Western*** *nations*, we see ***bad*** *things* occurring *regularly*. Our Christian nations still *suffer* many ***injustices*** and *maladies* as does the *rest* of the world, although maybe less *severe* as with the *starvation* and ***war*** *raging* in so much of the world. Bottom line, is there ***any*** "*god*" we can ***fully*** *trust*? Or, is the ***obvious*** *true*, they're all just ***hit*** and *miss* at best in their *provision* and ***protection***?

Considering our shockingly ***complex*** *creation*; such as the so-called "*simple* cell' that ***supposedly*** *created* itself, is *estimated* to have over 180,000 ***irreducible*** *complexities*. What that means, if only one of those 180,000 *parts* and *functions* do not come *together **exactly*** *right* and at the ***right*** *time*, it will ***not*** *work*! (Or live)

That brings us to the pre-*ponderant* question; did our Creator's, with *intelligence* we *can't **begin*** to *comprehend*, really *create* the *pinnacle* of Their creation, *mankind*, without an ***operations*** *manual*? In fact, would a car *manufacturer **sell*** *cars* without *showing* people *what* to *put* in the *fuel* tank and what *kind* and how much *oil* to use?

If we *foolish* humans are *smart* enough to *educate* people on how to *use* and **care** for *products* **we** *create*, would not the Creator's, who are *billions* of times *smarter* than we, *leave **us** clueless*? Don't we need an **operations** manual to **outline** how to *live **healthy**, **prosperous***, and **happy** *lives*? And, if the Creator's **did** *give* us an *operations **manual**, what* and **where** *is **it**?* After all, most of us take very **good** *care* of our *pets,* and we can be sure we are *much **more*** than just *pets* to our Creator's.

Well, the *only* **operations** manual even *coming **close*** to **that** *goal* of *teaching* us *how* to be *healthy **happy*** and *prosperous*, is of course, the *Bible*, at least the **Torah** section. But, how do *we **know*** we can *trust **it**?* Well, showing its **supernatural** *origin, embedded* within the *original* **Hebrew** *text* is what is *called* the " **Torah** *code*" where every **49th** *letter* all through **Genesis** and **Exodus** spells *"Torah"* **without** *fail.* Then, **Numbers** and **Deuteronomy** also *spell* it **without** *fail,* only *backwards*!

Then most shocking of all, is the book of **Leviticus**, in the *middle,* where every **7th** letter, **spells** the *Name* of the **Father** Creator *"YHWH"* **without** *fail!* It seems the two books before **Leviticus** and the two *after,* spelling *"Torah"* or **instructions**, are *like **arrows** pointing* to that **middle** *book* proclaiming our *Creator's* **Father's** *Name* and Torah!

Bottom line, *embedding* those *codes* thousands of years ago, while *maintaining* a coherent (sensible) text, is virtually *impossible* even with modern *supercomputers*! That *reality* shows without a doubt, a **supernatural** hand in its *compilation*! But, the real *proof* is how the *promises* for *following* those *Torah* **guidelines** are *unfailing.*

The *problem* with the *gods* of **this** *world* is they are *not* the **true** *Creator gods* and although **able** to *perform* **some** *supernatural* acts, and *answer* **occasional** *prayers* (even *supernaturally*) *cannot* be *trusted* to **be** *there, when* and *how* we **need** *them*!

Those angelic *beings* (called *watchers* and/or *defected* angels) and their **demon** spawn, **give** just *enough* to *gain* some *trust* and **worship**, but have *no* true **benevolent** interest in us. In fact, they have *deliberately* **hidden** the true Creator's (by *hiding* their Names) *from* us via their *translators*!

But, our Creator's are *faithful* in Their *plans* for us and have **not** *abandoned* or *forgotten* us. They've simply given us *free-**moral**-agency* and a *time* **frame** for us to **freely** choose to *follow* their **behavior** instructions and to then *fully* **honor** and **trust** them. In fact, that's the *point* of this *essay*. We are *free* to place our **faith** in *anyone* or *anything* we *choose*, but will *reap* the *consequences* of **those** *choices* either way!

Bottom line, *true* **faith** and *trust* is to have an **intimate** relationship with the *ones* or *things* in which we **place** our *faith*. It's that **intimacy** that *erases* **all** *doubts*! Only then can we truly *please* our Creator's. They **need** our **complete** *trust* as we see in **Hebrews** 11. "*Without* **faith** (true faith) *it's* **impossible to please Him**" (our Creator) that is, to *harbor* the **slightest** *doubts* of *what* they *can* and "*will*" **do** for *us*.

Again, to have that *kind* of *faith*, **requires** a very **intimate** relationship with YHWH and being *filled* with **His** *Spirit* (and mind). Yes, the Creator's *promises* are *real*, but **conditional**. We have to do **our** part "*first*"! That *part* is *outlined* in the "*Torah*"!

To end this *study*, and referring *back* to the scripture *referenced* in the beginning of this study "**Hebrews** 11, does just giving **lip** *service* to **our** *faith* **suffice**, or do we need *that* **faith** to be **tested**? Well, all *through* the scriptures we *find* our **patriarchs'** *faith*, from *Noah* to *Joseph* being **majorly** *tested*! In fact, the Israelites were **required** to *pass* the **faith** test before being *allowed* into the *Promised* Land! (Which most failed)

Will we be able to *enter* the *new **Promised** Land* (Eden) *without **our** faith* being *severely **tested*** also? Again, *most* of the *older* generation of Israel miserably *failed **that** test* and were *condemned* to ***die*** in the *wilderness*! Seems *harsh*, but it shows just how *important **true** faith* in our Creator *Father* (YHWH) and His *promises **is***!

Chapter 29

Feast Outline and Meanings

Probably the most *important* teaching of the Bible is the *Creator's* **ordained** *Feasts* and *their* **meanings**. Simply put, their extreme importance is they were (and are) *physical* **rehearsals** (teachings) of *coming* **spiritual** *events* (fulfillments) which *outline* and *teach* us (humanity) *what* our Creator is *doing,* **with** and *for us*!

Without these Festival *teachings*, humanity is like *half* **blind** *children* stumbling through an *endless* forest on a *moonless* night! Of course, it's the *demons* and their (dragon) *leader* who *hate* the Creator YHWH and His *human* creation; **convincing** Christianity (and humanity) those Feasts are *burdens* and *foolishness* to be **discarded** and even *despised*!

The *truth* is, those **Feasts** *outlined* in **Leviticus** 23 (the heart of the Torah) are **more** *precious* than **all** the *riches* in the world! In fact, those *Sabbaths* are *literal* **invitations** from our Creator's to come *feast* **with** Them. Yes, they are *actual* Feasts, both *physical* and *spiritual*, with special *food* and drink. But more importantly, they are *celebrations* of *what* YHWH **has** done and **is** doing **with** and *for* His Children!

Of one *thing* we can be sure, those *Feasts* (with Him) also come with *gifts* for those who **honor Him** with the *acceptance to* His *invitations*! Just *imagine*; **what** could be *greater* than *receiving* an *invitation* to **attend** a *literal* **Feast** with the *Sovereign* of the universe!? Certainly, it's *nothing* to be taken *lightly*!

What then are those *Feasts* and *what* do they *mean*? To understand, we must first realize they are *divided* into **two** *seasons*; **spring** and **fall**. Actually they are literal *pictures* and **rehearsals** of *two* **harvests** (seasons) of *people*! The two *harvests* apparently span a period of 7-8 thousand years; probably the time *span* required to spawn the *number* of **children** our Creator's have in mind for *Their* **Family.**

After all, Their family is *what* **this** *existence* is all about! It's *not* about reverent **worship** as the *pagans* would have us *believe*, but *love*! We were created *"free"* **moral** *agents* to **choose** to **love, honor,** and **respect** our *Creators* **first** and our *fellow* man *second*. Upon *making* that *choice*, it's only **real** if **fought** *for!* Only by **battling** *adversaries* (demon forces) does that **decision** to *love, honor,* and *respect* YHWH and our fellow humans become truly *authentic!*

On the other hand, we were *created* **physical** so if we choose **not** to *love, honor, respect* YHWH and our *fellow* human, we simply **die** and *return* to the *dust* from which we were *created!* Those who **choose** *love* (outlined in the Torah-Ten Commandments) and spend their lives *fighting* for that choice, will be *qualified* to *enter* our Creator's *eternal* **family** where He and His *children* will live *together* for *eternity,* that is, without *fighting,* **bickering,** and *strife* in general!

The *first* Feast of the **Spring** *Harvest* then, called the *"First-fruit"* (priestly) *harvest*, is *"**Passover**"*. As we see in **Exodus,** *Passover* was the *"death angel's"* (Mastema) *"**passing over**"* the *"**firstborn**"* of the *Israelites* after they *placed* the *blood* of a **lamb** on their **door** *post*. Unlike the teaching of **Christianity,** it was **only** the *firstborn* who would have *died* without that *blood!* That *rehearsal* **played** *out* in **real** time in the *first* century when the *"Lamb"* picturing the **Hebrew** Messiah Yahshua, shed His *blood* to **save** the *spiritual* **first** born of Israel!

In the Torah, we see the *first-**born** belonged* to *YHWH* and were to *serve* in the Temple as *priests* unless *redeemed* (bought back) by the *parents*. That makes the *Spring* (first-fruit) *harvest,* Yahshua's **priesthood**. After all, the *Book* of **Hebrews** *proclaims* that Yahshua is the *"High Priest"* of *Israel.* (Not Gentiles)

Then, ***three** days **after** the *Passover,* they were to *celebrate* the **Wave- Sheaf;** a small *bundle* of **green** *barley* (grain) the Priests would *gather* and *wave* in the temple. It was *waved **down**, signifying death,* and then *up, signifying **resurrection**.* How amazing that after **three** *days,* not only did the *Messiah **emerge*** from the *grave,* but the *saints* of *old.* (Matt.27:52-53) That's *what* was meant by Yahshua *leading* the **captives** out of *captivity*! (Death) Those *saints* of *old* that rose from their *graves* in Jerusalem, were apparently the **24** *elders pictured* sitting *around* the *throne* in **Revelation** 7!

The wave-sheaf then *signaled* the *count-**down*** to the **<u>completion</u>** of the **spring** *harvest* starting the *next* day. The *first **seven*** of those days being *"unleavened"* picturing the *purging* of the *spirit* of **pride** and **replacing** it with the *spirit* of **humility** (and love)! Considering *Passover* and the *Wave- Sheaf* came to *fruition* in **real** *time,* and the Wave-Sheaf *beginning* the **countdown** to the **completion** of the *spring* harvest, did the *spring* harvest not **also** *come* to **fruition**? <u>Of course it did;</u> **fifty** *years* later.

Just because the **religious** *leaders* (Pharisees) *chose* to **omit** that *reality* from the NT scriptures, does not mean it *didn't **happen**!* After all, if it didn't, the *Messiah* was a *liar* and *deceiver*!

Growing up on a farm, it's common knowledge that when the *spring* harvest is **gathered**, the *fields* are *plowed **under*** (into darkness) for the **fall** *harvest* to be planted. Is it only a *coincidence* the centuries *following* the *first* century were called the *"Dark ages"*?

Somewhere during that *dark* time, the *seeds* of the **fall** *harvest* got *planted* and are now coming *up* **into** the **light** (truth). That *fall* harvest was *announced* by the *first* **fall** *Feast* called the "*Feast of Trumpets*". (Donald Trump) This *Feast* no doubt also **announces** the *commencement* of the *trumpet* **plagues** listed in **Revelation** 8-9.

The *Feast of Trumpets* announces the *beginning* of the *great* **humbling** (tribulation) that *culminates* in the *Day of* **Atonement** (repentance). It's in this great *humbling* the *prodigal* people (Israel) **return** to their Creator in *repentance* and consequently are *forgiven* and **taken** *back*!

It's during this ceremony the High Priest (Yahshua) selects a "**goat**" *to* **die** for the *sins* of Israel. This *goat* is described as a hairy *adult* **male;** an extremely *powerful* animal compared to the **docile** *Lamb* that *shed* it's blood for the *first-born*! (Priesthood) The Lamb (Yahshua) gained very *little* **attention** on the *world* scene, but we can be sure, the **whole** *world* is going to **know** about that *goat*!

Then, following the *Day of* **Atonement** (repentance and forgiveness) *begins* the exodus to the **New** *Promised Land*! The Promised Land in ancient times (Caanan) was simply a *type* of the **new** *Promised Land* that will eventually include the *entire* Earth!

But, until then, this **last** *Feast* is called the "*Feast of Tabernacles*" or "*temporary dwellings*". (Like a womb) It's a picture of *physical* humans being *supernaturally* **provided** *for* by the Creator for a time called "*The Millennium*" (thousand years) by Christianity.

The *seven* days of the Feast of Tabernacles, are then *followed* by a great **8th** *day,* which is apparently the "*day of the* **Gentiles**". The Bible gives us very little detail on that *day,* but it seems to be the Gentiles' *time* to *repent* and *come* to YHWH.

Chapter 30

False Apostles

Yahshua, the Hebrew Messiah *warned* His *disciples* in *many* places, of "*coming*" *false prophets*". These *false* prophets obviously would *include* *apostles* considering *apostle* means "*sent forth to proclaim*" "*announce,* and/ or *teach*". In fact, He *told* His *disciples* in **Matthew** 24:24 and **Mark** 13:22 that *false* "*anointed ones*" (christs) and *"false prophets that would deceive possibly even the elect"* would *come*! That was a *powerful* warning, but *did **it** happen*? We must keep in mind; Yahshua *gave* His disciples that **warning** to *their **faces,** personally.* (Privately-Matt.24:3) So, was He a *false* prophet?

Again, if Yahshua's *disciples never **encountered*** any *false* anointed **ones** (*apostles*) or *prophets,* how would that not have made a *deceiver* (false prophet)? Besides, if He was *speaking **over*** their **heads** to *some **generation** thousands* of years in the *future,* as the Churches teach, that also makes "*HIM*" a **deceiver** (false Messiah). After all, His Apostles believed He was *speaking **to*** *them* (personally) and *taught* He was **returning** in **their** *generation!*

Obviously, we can't accept Yahshua *lied* or *deceived* His *disciples,* so *where* were *those **false** prophets* and *false **anointed*** ones (Christs) He *told* His disciples *were **coming**!* That's a tough one, but we must keep in mind; *deceivers tell* mostly **truth** while *slipping **in** some lies* (poison) into their *teachings.* So, unless a person is *paying **close** attention,* they **will** be **deceived***!*

Sometimes, the ***greatest*** *deceptions* are the ones right *in **front** of **our*** *faces*, which make them the *most **difficult*** to *see* (like our noses)! But, there's *one* thing we can always ***rely*** *upon* to show the *truth*, it's a persons' *actions* (the proverbial ***fruit*** on *the **tree***). Unfortunately, to have someone *expose* the *truth* involving a *cherished **icon*** we've *harbored,* is extremely *difficult,* but it does set us *free*. In fact, President James **Garfield** once stated; "*The **truth** will **set** you **free**, but it will **make** you **miserable** first*"!

So, in reading this short dissertation it's *imperative* to keep in mind how the *translators* and *compilers* of the canon have ***manipulated*** *it,* by ***adding*** and ***subtracting*** *books **at will**,* like the 10 ***apocrypha*** *books* in the ***first*** *King James translation* of *1611*.

With that in mind, we can begin *examining* the *fruit* on the 13th' *tree* (apostle). Don't forget, **Revelation** 21:14 gives us a huge *clue* by clearly *stating* there are *only **12** apostles*; not *13* or *more*! But, that should come as ***no*** *surprise* when we dig a little and *discover* it was the Catholic (Universal) bishop *Athenatious* (fourth century CE) who *authorized* Paul's writings! (Bart Earman-Lost Christianites)

In fact, he did it in a letter to his parishioners in Alexandria Egypt, *instructing* them on the ***proper*** *keeping* of *Easter,* which of course, is a very ***pagan*** *rite*! (Ishtar-Easter was the *goddess* of *fertility*)

That said, we must remember our *introduction* to *Saul* (Paul) was his *participation* in the ***stoning*** of *Steven,* not to mention his *persecution* of the saints. With that in mind, can a *leopard* really *change* its spots?

There's a common *strategy* in *war* used all through *history*; if an enemy is too *strong* for a *frontal* assault, a better strategy is to ***pretend to be one*** *of them* and ***destroy*** *them* from the ***inside***! (Infiltration-spies-5th column) That in mind, can we ***honestly*** *believe* Saul's ***demon*** *puppet masters,* the ones ***using*** *him* to ***arrest*** and ***murder*** the saints, were not *aware* of this ***crafty*** *strategy?*

No doubt, the *demons are* the **authors** of that extremely *effective* **covert** *strategy* in the *first* place! (Art of War-Sun Tsu) In fact, our leaders are *currently* **employing** that very *method* to bring *down* the US and all *modern* **Western** *nations*!

Looking a little further, we see Yahshua **personally** *chose* His *disciples,* and **Hebrews** 13:8 (and Mal.3:6) tells us "*He* (or YHWH) *does not change*". So, did He really *change* His *method* of choosing an apostle by **blinding** Saul on the road to Damascus, in *spite* of that scripture in **Hebrews**? Here's a clue; **who** is the **one** who **blinds** (*deceives*)?! Did Yahshua also *change,* by *not* including His 12 *anointed* Apostles as He spent years *teaching* Saul in the *wilderness;* that is with **no witnesses**?

There are **red** *flags* everywhere, but let's look a little closer at Saul's **personal** *actions* and *teachings.* One *huge* **red** *flag is* the fact Saul "**nowhere**" *teaches* the *things Yahshua* **taught** His *12* in sermons like **Matthew** 5&6! Did Yahshua really *send* Saul to *teach* **different** *things* than His *12*? Well, the common *justification* is his supposedly being *sent* to the *gentiles* who are **not** *under* the *law* of Moses.

But, shockingly, we have Saul's *own* admonition in speaking to the Romans that he was *converting* them with "*his lies*" (Rom.3:7)! Is *using* **lies** to *convert* ("*con*"vert) really an *acceptable* **way** to *behave* and *teach*? Besides, **Revelation** 21:8 tells us "*all **liars** with have **their place** in the lake that **burns** with **fire**"*!

Speaking of *lies,* we also have Saul (Paul) **misquoting** *scripture* (more lying) in **Romans** 3:10, where he says; "*As it is written, there is **none** **righteous**; no not one*"! But, we find **Hebrews** listing *dozens* of them in chapter 11, beginning with "*righteous*" Able! So much for that being *true*! Actually, Paul was telling the *truth* about "*it is **written**"* considering he was *misquoting* **Psalms** 14:1-3 where it states "*The **fool** has **said** in his heart*'- (v.3) "*there is **none who does good**; no not one*".

Saul's *lying antics* get even more manifest with his *confrontation* of *Peter* in **Acts** 11:2-3. We know Saul was among "*those of the circumscion*" getting *in* Peter's *face*, because of his **braging** about *it* to the *Galatians* (Gal. 2:11-14). But, if we read the *entire* account in **Acts**, we find Peter was **justified** in his *actions* with the *vision* of the *sheet* of *animals*, while Paul was **not**!

After all, Saul was a *young* man with Peter being at least 20 years his *senior* as well as a *Chief* Apostle (of Yahshua's 12)! Paul showed **zero** *respect* and did what **no** *honorable* or *righteous* person would ever have done; *publicly* **correcting** his *spiritual* (and physical) **elder** *Peter*!

Probably the greatest *proof* of **who** and/or *what* Saul was, was the *message* given to the *congregation* at **Ephesus**. The Ephesians were *commended* in **Revelation** 2:2 for *discerning* **false** apostles and **exposing** *them* as **liars**.

Then, in **II Timothy** 4:16, we find Paul lamenting how *no one* **stood** *with him* and all *forsook* him (apparently forcing him to *leave* in a *hurry*) in his *trip* to **Ephesus**! In fact, he had to send Tychicus back to *retrieve* his "*cloak" books*" and "*parchments*" which he apparently was *forced* to *leave* in his *hasty* **exit**! (v.12&13)

Considering Paul's *lying* again, how interesting how he *laments* to the *Romans* in chapter 7 (verses 14-24) how he *does* the **things** he *does* **not** *want* **to** *do* (sin) and **doesn't** do the *righteous* things he *knows* **he** *should* (wants to) *do*.

On top of that, how *hypocritical* for him then to *reprimand* his *congregation* in *Corinth* (chap. 5 and 11 of I Cor.) for their **unrighteous** *behavior*, which he himself *admits* to being *guilty*! The glaring *white* **elephant** in the room here is; "**if**" Paul and his *congregations* were *filled* with YHWH's **Spirit** of **righteousness** and **power** (and life) he obviously would have had **control** over his *own* **unrighteous** *behavior*!

Is it any wonder *why* he had to *invent* a *philosophy* of being "*saved*" (from death) by this *so-called* "**grace**" versus **righteous** *behavior*? You will *notice* that **NONE** of Yahshua's 12 apostles talked **that** *way;* in fact, *their* teachings were just *the* **opposite;** *all* **about** *behavior*! (See James)

I will wind down this mini *study* with a couple of those statements of Saul's in **Romans** 7, beginning with verse 18; "*For in me* <u>*nothing good dwells--*</u>". But, how could he say that if he were *filled* with *YHWH's* **Spirit** of **righteousness** and **life**, as he *insinuates*? Obviously he **wasn't** filled with YHWH's *Spirit* of *righteousness*!

He goes on to lament in **Romans** 7:24; "*O wretched man that I am! Who will **deliver me** from this **body of death**"*. Of course, YHWH's *Spirit* of *righteousness* and **Life** would *deliver* him if he were actually *filled* with that Spirit versus the *spirit* of *death*!

Again, if Paul *knew Yahshua's* **teachings** and was *filled* with *YHWH's* **Spirit** of **Life**, he would **never** have *posed* such a **ridiculous** *question*! In fact, isn't that the very reason Christianity *loves* Paul so much, because they, also being *void* of YHWH's Spirit of *righteousness* and *life*, are in the same **sinking** *ship* of **unrighteous** *behavior* and **death** as their favorite *Apostle*, Paul?

To conclude this chapter, we must keep in mind how the *compilers* of the Bible Canon's were notorious for *including* and *removing* books. As mentioned earlier, a good example is the **apocrypha** *books* included in the LXX in 270 BCE which were part of the first **King James translation** (1611) but were then taken out of the *later* King James *editions*.

To say YHWH *inspired* them to be *taken* **out** means He obviously *made* a **mistake** *inspiring* them to be put in, right? Again; Yahshua *told* His disciples **false ones would** *come* and be so **deceptive** as to **deceive** even the **elect**!!! Paul (Saul) fits the bill *perfectly*!

Chapter 31

Fear Porn

A new *term* has of late *emerged,* and become common *"fear porn"*. Honestly, I don't know *what **fear*** and *pornography* have in common, except they both *evoke* very **powerful** *emotions*, but someone, *somewhere* made the *connection* stick, to become the *popular* saying. Maybe it's because *fear* has now become a *major **issue*** in our *current **world*** and *state* of *affairs*, which of course, is **nothing** new. In fact, not long ago, *fear,* such as *nuclear **war*** breaking out, was a big *thing.*

Now we're being *inundated* with *new **fear** "porn"* called "**man-made** *global **warming***" (*climate* change). Of course, just as the *images* in *pornography* are not real, neither is "**man-**made" **global** *warming*. But, it's taken seriously *enough* to **allow** *governments* to *implement* **extreme** *regulations*, which are *causing* the *prices* of virtually *everything* to *escalate* and at the *expense* of **many** of our *freedoms*.

Considering **loss** of *freedoms*, look *what* the *attack* on the *trade* towers in NY City did. We cannot now *go* to an *airport* and *buy* a ticket without showing our *IDs* and having our *name* **run** through some **criminal** *data* base. Then, we are *forced* to stand in long **security** *lines* as if we're all *suicide* bombers. Unfortunately, we **allowed** this to be **done** *to* **us** in the *name* of *fear*! But, *what* are we *afraid* **of**, *really*? Is it *really* a *fear* of people who want to *board* and *blow* **up** *airplanes*? Just how often has **that** *happened* anyway?

Honestly, we are far more likely to be *killed* crossing a street, than to get *blown* **up** in an airplane. Besides, who's to say the *plane* we're **on** after going **through** all the **security** *checks* won't get *shot* **down** by one of those **same** ones that would have *done* it internally?

After all, most nations in the world, including many **terror** *states*, now have those kinds of *missiles;* even *remote* **drones** to *deliver* them! Suddenly, *fear* of a *hijacking* becomes a rather *irrational* **joke**! But, instead, of **quelling** *fears*, our governments and *medias* have been exponentially **multiplying** *fear* using a *virus* that has less than **one** *percent* chance of *killing anyone*, especially *healthy* people!

Unfortunately, *fear*, makes life very *uncomfortable* and adds such *unnecessary* **stress**. In fact, I once knew a woman who was *afraid* of so **many** *things*, it made spending time with her literally *agonizing*! Needless to say, her *obsessive* **fear** made being *friends* impossible.

Fearful people *cannot* have *many*, if *any* friends, with *one* **prominent** *reason* being *fear* makes *people* **unpredictable,** and all *relationships* need a large degree of *predictability*!

That said, let's *dissect* this *concept* of *fear* in an *attempt* to understand *what* it **really** is. Isn't *fear* the **worry** that *things* are not *going* to *go* **well** with us in some *way,* or the *worry* we will be *harmed* in some way or even *die*? Of course, there are *rational* fears that involve simple **common** *sense*, such as not *hand* **feeding** a wild *grizzly* bear! By simply invoking **common** *sense* and *logic,* **most** worries suddenly *evaporate*.

What about issues we have little *control* over, like getting the *flu?* Are those **legitimate** *reasons* to be *fearful?* Is being *afraid* of *what* "**might**" *happen* really a **legitimate** *fear?* But, *what is gained* in *fearing* **something** we **cannot** *control?* One thing's for sure, **irrational** *fear* is a very *senseless* and **destructive** *emotion,* if **allowed** to go very *far.* It *reduces* people to *living* **in** what *amounts* to **prisons**; *prisons* of our own *minds!*

Again, using *fear* (mostly irrational) has *resulted* in the *loss* of **most** of our *freedoms.* Allowing the *communist* **globalists** to *shut* **down** *businesses,* **restrict** our *movements,* wear **useless** *masks,* and *take* **untested** *vaccines,* and have **forfeited** our *constitution.* In fact, even our precious *Bill* of **Rights** is now also *null* and void. They are *not* openly *voicing* **that** *truth,* but their *actions* **proclaim** it quite **loudly**! Again, fear is an *extremely* **powerful** *tool,* especially for *destruction!*

With that in mind, *what* does our Creator and the Bible tell us *about* **fear?** First of all, I **John** 4:18 tells us "*perfect* **love** *casts* **out** *all fear*"! Fear is literally the **opposite** of *love.* With that in mind, let's look at a couple *examples* of how the Creator *treated* **fearless** *people.* One *example* is some young Jewish men who had become *captive* **slaves** in Babylon.

King Nebecanezzer had a statue made of himself to which everyone was to *bow* when commanded. Well, these brave *young* men *refused,* knowing it would possibly *result* in their *death.* Their refusal resulted in being *thrown* into a **super** *heated* **furnace** that even *killed* the *guards* throwing them in. But the fire did **not** *touch* **them**! Bottom line, those young *men* put *trust* in their *God* above *their* **own** *lives.* For that, they were greatly *rewarded.* We find the same *story* with Daniel who was *thrown* into a *pit* of **hungry** *lions* for *trusting* His God (YHWH)!

Again, His trust in His *God* was **more** *important* than his *life!* In fact, we have an even better *example* of how YHWH views *fear* in what *happened* to the *Israelites* in the *desert.*

When they *arrived* at the *promised* land, *twelve* spies were sent in to *inspect* the country. But, *ten* of the *twelve*, returned *full* of **fear** concerning the *giants* there. Only two, Joshua and Caleb, were *unafraid*. Due to **that** *fear,* most of the people over 20 were *sentenced* to **wander** the desert *until* **dead,** except apparently, Joshua and Caleb, which speaks *volumes* as to how our Creator **views** *fear*.

That said, the chief *agenda* of our new *one* **world** government is to *reduce* the *population* to **half** a *billion.* Using the *fear* of an *almost* **harmless** *virus,* has frightened most people into *accepting* a mostly **lethal** *injection.* Of course, it's supposedly being a vaccine is just a bald faced *lie!*

Just like the **fearful** *Israelites,* **fear** is going to *kill* **most** of the **worlds** *population!* At least the *Israelites* had a **somewhat** legitimate **fear,** considering the *man-**eating*** *giants,* but to take an untested *injection* for an *almost* **non-lethal** *virus,* is beyond shocking!

What it really boils down to, is a lack of **faith** and *trust.* **Hebrews** 11:6 tells us; "*Without faith, it's "IMPOSSIBLE" to please Him*! What that scripture is *telling* us is; if we *cannot* **fully** *trust* our Creator, that is, *have* **no** *fear,* we are *worthless* to Him! Fear is a *giant* **stone** *wall* between Him and us! In fact, *how* would we as *parents* feel if our children didn't *trust* us to *feed* them, *protect* them, *provide* for them?

Obviously, *trust* is the *most* important *element* between *children* and their *parents,* not to mention **all** relationships! Again, **trust** is *essential* for **any** *relationship* to *work,* and since our Creator's are *creating* an *eternal* family, that **primary** *ingredient* of **complete** *trust* is **essential.**

In fact, we find a list of people who are to be *thrown* into a lake of fire that *burns* the entire Earth. How interesting, the one on *top* of the *list* is "*the fearful*". Fear will literally keep us **out** of that **eternal** *family* to be **burned**! Again, perfect *love* casts *out* **all** *fear!*

Chapter 32

Follow Your Heart (or not)

One of the admonitions we hear virtually everywhere, in movies and on TV, is to "*follow your **heart***". In fact, a large number of *movies* and TV *shows* openly **condemn** the idea of *listening* to our **head** versus our *heart*. Supporting that rhetoric also, are many *songs*. That in mind, just *where's* that *advise* **originating**? Is it **good** *advice* or **bad**, and *how* do we **know**?

Personally, I've *never* trusted my heart, because I know my *feelings* about *something* or *someone* can *sometimes* **change** *overnight*. For *example*, how many **toys**, and *things* we felt we just could **not** *live* without *ended up* in the yard *sale* or *junkyard*?

How about the *cars* and *furniture* we *could* not **live** *without*? Or maybe that **beautiful** *house*? And let's **not** *forget* our *loves*? How many people did we have *crushes* on in *school* or **high** *school* we thought we *die* without? But we *lived* anyway, and upon meeting them *later* in *life*, were left *asking*; "**What** *was I* **thinking**"? The bottom line; we were **not** *thinking*, we were simply *following* the *prompting* of our **hearts**!

Well, it all *becomes* very *clear* if we use the *scriptures* (Torah) to *instruct* us beginning with **Jeremiah** 17:9. This is a most *enlightening* scripture; "*The* **heart** *is* **deceitful** *above* **all** *things and desperately* **wicked;** *who can know it*?" Wow, what a *mouthful!* It goes against virtually everything we *hear* and are being *indoctrinated* with! But, there's more. **Proverbs** 16:5 states; "*Everyone who is* **proud** *in* **heart** *is an* **abomination** *to YHWH*" with verse 18 *echoing*; "**Pride** *goes* **before** **destruction**"! In fact, *transgenderism* is **following** *ones* **heart**!

Obviously, there's a *connection* between the *heart* and **pride**. Do you suppose it's because the **heart** is *where* the *spirit of* **pride** *resides*? Heart, by the way, is a *biblical* **metaphor** for the *seat* of our **emotions;** although, it's said the **heart** *literally* contains a large *percentage* of **brain** cells, which is why many *emotions* are *felt* in our *hearts*!

At any rate, one *part* of our brain *deals* in **logic** while the *other* (the heart side) deals in *emotions*. Unfortunately, *emotions* can **turn** on a *dime*. A good *example* is a child (and bi-polar adults) who can be *laughing* one minute and *crying* (or screaming) the next! There's **no** *logic* to *emotions*, they are just **feelings** with no actual *substance*. They mostly go *flying* **through** our *hearts, rarely* sticking *around* for *too* long!

The bottom line is; the *educated* **logical** side of our *minds* needs to keep a *leash* on our *emotions* (heart) although *many* (of the heart) *emotions* are certainly **not** *bad,* if *expressed* for the **right** *reason* and at the **right** *time.*

But, if we *allow* our *emotions* to *lead* and **rule** us, we are *completely* **unpredictable;** like a *rowboat* on the open *ocean* (all *over* the place). Unfortunately, *relationships* **require** a large *degree* of **predictability** to *work.* When we **can't** *trust* a *friend* or *mate* to be **predictable** (to one degree or another) that *friendship* and/or *marriage* is usually doomed to *fail.*

Again, one of the chief *foundations* of any relationship is "**predictability**" or "*trust*"! We cannot have a **real** relationship with someone who is **unpredictable** and *untrustworthy*. That's why YHWH in **Isaiah** 44:8 (last part) declares that He is "*The Rock*" (*and that there is no other*). See, the great *thing* about a *huge* **rock** is it does **not** *move* **or** *change*. We can always *count* on a massive *Rock* to be *where* it is *supposed* to *be*!

The "*Rock*" is the perfect *description* for YHWH considering He tells us He *does* **not** *change* (Mal.3:6) and **cannot** *lie*! (Heb.6:18) Another extremely important *truth* in reference to the "*heart*" of **Jeremiah** 17:9 (pun intended) is how the *evil* ones **manipulate** *us*. They are **not** *allowed* to *physically* mess with us physically (unless we give them permission) but they **are** *allowed* to "*tempt*" (influence) us with *emotions*. You see, *all* they *need* to **influence** us to **miss**-*behave*, is to simply *invoke* the **right** *feelings* (emotion) at exactly the *right* time.

If they *infuse* us with such *feelings* as **fear, lust, jealousy, greed, anger, hate** and/or **rage**, they can get us to do *most* **anything**! Using those *emotions* they can *influence* people to **lie, steal,** comment **adultery**, and even **murder**. Again, the *medium* with which they *utilize* those emotional **tools** is the **heart**!

You see, when Eve and Adam *chose* the *dragon* over YHWH, they gave it *permission* to *fill* every human **heart** with their "**foul**" spirit. That *foul* **spirit** is "*pride*" which is *why* it always comes "*before* (leads to) *destruction*" (death)! How interesting; *winged* creatures to this day, are called "*foul*"! A prime *example* of *murder* being *promoted* by the "*emotions*" of *lust* and *selfishness* is the *slaughter* of over 1.4 billion *unborn* **children.**

That *emotion* of **selfishness** and/or lust, *promotes* **fornication**, and *adultery,* and even elevates **sodomy** to something "**good**"! How amazing, the *sodomites* (gays) *label* themselves as **proud**!

Emotions are also being *used* to *flood* (invade) our country with our *enemies,* by **evoking** the *misplaced* **emotion** of *sympathy*; that *these* **illegal** foreign nationals (migrants) are just **poor** *refugees* looking for a *better* life. Unfortunately, many, if not most, are *military* age young men the **globalists** are *planning* to use as *soldiers* in their *coming* **civil** war.

The *emotions* of **rage** and *pride* are currently being *utilized* to *stir* up **rioting** and *civil* **unrest** against *authority* and *police,* with the *lie* of **supposed** mistreatment of *minorities* (non-Israelites) to ultimately *foment* that all out *civil* **war**! (And WW111) In fact, anyone paying *attention* has *noticed* that most of our leaders (globalists) are just *itching* for *it*!

In fact, there's a general move to *exterminate* our nationalist (X) *president* as well as those who *support* and/or *supported* him. Also being targeted are *conservatives* in general, those that support **gun** *ownership,* *believe* and *teach* the Bible, *anti-abortionists* (right to life) *anti-sodomites,* and of course, what the left calls *right-wing* **racists***,* which *includes* **all** *Caucasian* people (now the **new** *Jews*)!

But, just as there are *evil* emotions, which we must **not** *allow* to *control* us, there are *good* emotions we "**need**" to *exercise.* Those **emotions** are **thankfulness**, **peace**, **love**, and **joy**. Even the *emotions* of *anger* (against injustice) *jealousy* (of family) and *hate* (of evil) can be used for *good,* but, it takes *great* **maturity** to *control* and *exercise* those emotions *properly.* That's *what "growing up"* **spiritually** is all *about.*

YHWH *gave* us *emotions* because they are *important* to *relationships,* although there's a fine line between being *controlled* **by** them and us *controlling* them. Our *emotions* are a large *part* of what make us *unique* and give us our *particular* personalities.

Again, probably the main reasons for being *created **physical*** is to learn to *control* our *emotions* and use them for *good*. After all, YHWH cannot and *will **not** sentence* His children to an **eternity** of *bickering* and *fighting* like the *pagan **gods*** do! His family is going to be one of *peace*, **love**, and *joy* for **eternity**!

Chapter 33

What is Family?

When we look around this creation we see something *unique*, which is *family*. None of the *animal* kingdom has *family* like humans. Yes, *some* animals and birds do *mate* for *life*, but it's certainly **not** the *same*. If, as so many *teach* and *believe*, humans (and animals) are simply a *product* of *evolution* and *chance*, why the **major** *difference*?

If we *accept* the idea of Creator's would they not have had *more* in mind *with* the creation of **human** kind? After all, if we are to *accept* the Bible (Genesis) we are told the Creator's *created* us *after* **their** kind (male and female). Sadly the *current* **trend** is to *relegate* the Bible to ancient *myth* and *legend*. Unfortunately, another *passage* (Hosea 6:4) tells us "*His* (the Creator's people) *are destroyed for lack of knowledge*". One thing's for sure, the world is being *destroyed* and we can be *sure* it's due to **lack** of "**true**" knowledge!

Lies and *lying* are the *prevailing* **norms** these days, which ever *direction* we look! In fact, the first century *Messiah* (Yahshua) told the **religious** leaders (Jewish Pharisees) that they were of their *father* the *devil*, whom He also said was the *original* liar! A little known truth is, the first *15* **popes** were *Jewish*!! (Rabbi Randy Weiss)

Is anything *different* today, whether we look at *politics*, **religion**, or *science*, for that matter? Of course, one of the greatest *moves* these days is the *destruction* of **traditional** marriage and *family*! Just *what* or **who** is *behind* this *movement*? That's a *no-brainer* **question** to *anyone* who has been around very long. History shows us the *family* has **always** *been* the foundation of any **strong** *nation*.

Destroy the *family* and the *entire* **nation** *crumbles* into *ruin*, which is exactly what's *happening* to our modern *Western* nations. Interestingly, the modern *Western* nations are virtually across the board *modern* **Israelites**. After all, YHWH (Creator Father's Name) told His people He would *"sift His people through the Gentile* **nations** *like grain through a sieve, but that* **not one seed** *would* **fall** *to the ground"*! After all, what *kind* of *god* **looses** his *people* anyway?

One of the chief *problems* is *time*! That may sound *strange*, but people have *short* memories and II **Peter** 3:8 tells us *"***one day** *in the* **spirit** *realm is like a* **thousand** *years in the* **physical***"*! So, for YHWH's people to *forget* Him and His *plan* for **us** (knowledge of) after a *few* **thousand** years is very *understandable*.

But again, we can be sure He has **not** *forgotten us* as we did Him! After all, His **week**-*long* **plan** in His realm is *thousands* of *years* to us. We can be sure He has **not** *forgotten* or *abandoned* His **plans** for His *people*, and/or *children*! He *"does not change"* (His plans) or *forget* as He tells us in **Malachi** 3:6.

If it isn't obvious (like to me) the whole *purpose* of **our** *existence* is because YHWH and His *Wife* (Hokma) are *creating* an **eternal** *family* for *themselves* as is shown us in **Proverbs** 8 and 9. Since **real** *love* cannot be *forced* or *coerced*, we were *created* (unlike the angels) *physical* to *choose* to *love*, **respect**, and *honor* our Spirit *Parents* **first** and then *each* **other** *second*. But, in order for our **righteous** *choices* to be *real*, they need to **fought** *for*, which is *where adversaries* (demonic beings) were *necessary*! (Necessary evil)

One thing's for *sure*, our Creators *cannot* and **will** *not* have an **eternal** *family* that is *bickering* and *fighting*, which means if we do *not* **choose** to *love*, **respect** and *honor* our *Creator's* **first** (first four commandments) and each *other* (last six) second, we simply *return* to **dust** *from* which we were *created!*

The bottom line is, *family* is a **spiritual** entity. It is quite literally a **sacred** *union!* In fact, family is **so** *important* to our Creator's, **adultery** was *punishable* by **death** in the **Torah** *instructions!* *Marriage* and *family* are not just some *human* **game** we *play!*

Just because we've been *allowed* to **adulterate** *marriage* and **family** due to our *free* **moral** *agency*, does *not* make it *unimportant!* We can be sure, *marriage* and *family* will be set *back* on the **correct** *course* very soon after the hellacost (judgment) that has been currently *decreed* upon the *world*.

All those *hundreds* of *millions* of *babies* **murdered** over the last 50 years **belong** *to* our *Creator's* and were intended to be a part of our Creator's family and we can be *sure* those **innocent** *little* **lives** *will* be vindicated!! Proof is found in **what** happened to Egypt after *throwing* the babies in the river and king Herod *murdering* the **baby** boys in the *first* century. In *both* cases *Egypt* and *Judaea* were all but **erased** from the Earth.

The book of **Jublees** (once a part of the OT) has the *Angel* of *YHWH* telling Moses that *1000* **Egyptian** lives were *required* for **every** *baby* thrown into the river. No doubt, since YHWH *"does not change"* that same *degree* given Egypt *applied* to **Judea** in the *first* century.

Due to that *destruction* of YHWH's *family*, we are about to *see* most of the worlds **population** *destroyed*. This will primarily *accomplished* by the brown *dwarf* **solar** system called *"Nemesis"* which will be arriving soon. *Nemesis*, by the way, means *"just instrument of punishment"*!

Chapter 34

The Four Horsemen Ride!

A very interesting and rather *hotly* **debated** set of *scriptures* are of the *four* **horsemen** of **Revelation** 6. Beginning in verse 3, we read; "*I* (John) *looked and beheld, a* **white** *horse and he who* **sat** *on it had a* **bow** *and a crown was* **given** *to him and he went out* **conquering** *and* <u>to **conquer**</u>."

There are *myriads* of *interpretations* of this scripture, but *one* thing's for sure, the *context* shows it to be the *end* of *the*, or **an age**. What is so amazing is; we no longer have to *guess* at **when**, but only to look *around* and *see* **what** *is* or has *been* **happening**! How amazing also is that these *horses* and *riders* are called the **four** *horsemen* of the *apocalypse.*

Most people be*lieve* "*apocalypse*" means the *end* of the *world*, but that's **not** *what* it means at all! *Apocalypse* is the simply the Greek word for "*revelation*" meaning "*to* **reveal**"! Most think **Revelation** is a book of *riddles*, **hyperbole** and/or *metaphor,* but again, it means just the *opposite,* which is "*to* **reveal**" or "*expose*"! (The truth)

That said, and *backing* up, an **honest** look at **Revelation** shows the *first* **three** *books* were *letters* of *warning* (and teaching) the *truth* of the Messiah's **eminent** *return* to *congregations* in **Asia** *Minor* in the **first** *century*. The next couple chapters, give us a *peek* at what was *happening* in heaven right *after* the *first* century (spring harvest of humans). Chapter *six* then jumps forward to the *end* of **another** *age*, which, brought together with *other* prophecies and the **current** *world* **condition**, can only be *now*!

With that in mind, let's *examine* that *first* **horse** and *rider* and *what* it "*reveals*" to us! First, the *white* horse *denotes* **goodness** or at least **perceived** goodness. For instance, *doctors* (who mostly wear white) whom most people view as *saviors*, are actually *hit* and *miss* at best! Then in 2020, a *virus* was *unleashed,* which those **white** *clad* **doctors** *told* us the *masks* (also primarily white) would *save* us, which of course, they did *not*. Then we were told their *injections* would **definitely** *save* us.

Well, **recent** *history* **showed** those *both* to be *falsehoods*. Again, fitting with the *context* of those horsemen, **not** being **good** *things*, it all becomes perfectly *clear*! Those who *released* the **virus**, *used* **it** to **take** control and literally **conquer** *most* of the world! With that in mind, how interesting the virus was called "*crown*" (corona) which the conquering *rider wore*. It also had a *bow*, which *implies* the **shooting** of *arrows*! Do the *injections* they were *forcing* people to take, not **perfectly** picture **arrows**?

The *prophecy* tells us, that *horse* and *rider* went out to *conquer*, and using that **crown**, *nullified* our *constitutional* **rights**, such as *freedom* of **religion**, not to mention **freedom of speech** (symbolized by the masks)! Not only did they *force* churches to *close* their *doors*, but many *businesses* as well.

They also *stopped* **public** *gatherings* and again *disallowed* **free** *speech* especially when anyone stood *up* with a *cure* for the *virus*. At this point, it seems the **only** *freedom* **we** have **left** is to say "*how* **high**" when they say *jump*! For all *practical* purposes, we *have* **been** conquered*!

Now that *much* of the *population* of the **Western** *world* has come to realize *our **freedoms*** are all but *gone*, the *second* horse (the *fiery **red*** one) becomes obvious! Verse 4 of **Revelation** 6, tells us this *rider* of the **red** *horse* is *given* a **sword** to **take** *peace **from*** the world! In fact, in 2023, we saw *that* horse had already *begun **its** ride fomenting* not only **world** war as well! ***civil*** *wars.*

Naturally, ***war*** ushers in a whole *host* of **evils**, which the third, **black** horse, *chronicles.* The ***fruits*** of *war,* are obviously ***famine***, and *disease.* It is *estimated* that *war,* along *with* the *Nemesis **solar** system* coming *through,* that *three-**fourths*** of the *worlds* **population** will be *decimated*!

That brings us to the *final* horse to *ride,* which is the *green* (wrongly translated "*pale*") horse. This ***final** horse,* is **death**, which again is *estimated* to be most of the **worlds** *population.* That's *interesting* in that the *book* of **Jubilees** (once a part of the OT) shows a *conversation* between Moses and the *Angel* of YHWH, that He was *requiring* the *lives* of **1000** *Egyptians* for every *Israelite **baby** thrown* into the *Nile*!

That *decimation* of ***Egyptian** population* occurred about 100 years after they began **drowning** the *babies,* which again *shows* just how ***important*** those *babies* are to our Creators. If we're *inclined* to *think **what** happened* to the Egyptians was simply *because* they were *pagans,* guess again.

We need only jump *forward* to the ***first** century* where king Herod *ordered* all the ***baby** boys* two years and younger to be *murdered* because of a *prophecy* he *heard* of a *king* that had been *born,* to *replace* him!

About 80 years later, after a *three **year** siege,* and *slaughtering* everyone *inside*, Jerusalem was completely *leveled* by Emperor *Vespasian*!

Considering these were YHWH's own **chosen** *people,* tells us He is **not** a *respecter* of *persons*! But then, all *babies* (human) technically *belong* to the *Creators* and they obviously don't take *our **slaughtering*** of them *lightly*!

We can be sure, after *murdering* a **billion** and a half *babies* (in the womb) we can be sure the *world* is going to **pay,** and pay *dearly*!

Chapter 35

Good Made Evil and Evil Made Good

I don't think there's a more shockingly *prophetic* scripture to come to *fruition* than the prophecy in **Isaiah** 5:20; "*they would* (will) *call evil good and good evil*"! It seems the list of *evils* **called** good and *good* **things** *called evil* has become shockingly long. In fact, it seems the whole world had been turned **upside** down and *backwards*. That said, let's look at a short *list* of *things* the *world* **calls** "*good*" and the Bible **calls** "*evil*".

The *first* and more *obvious* is "*pride*". The scriptures plainly tell us **pride** is **evil** and "*comes* **before** (brings) *destruction*". (Prov. 16; 5&18) It also tells us **pride** is a *barrier* **between** *us* and *YHWH*. "*YHWH* **walks** *with the* **humble**" (*opposite* of *proud*-Isa.57:15) and "**resists** (shuns) *the* **proud**" yet everywhere we turn we *see* and are *prompted* to *tell* our *loved* ones how "*proud*" we are of them!

According to the Torah, that would be *pronouncing* a **curse** upon them! We are also told to *take* "**pride**" in our *work*, our *dress*, our *country*; etc. The "**idea**" those *promotions* present, is *not* a *bad* thing, but "**pride** or *proud*" is certainly **NOT** the *correct* **word** with which to **bless** *someone* or our *nation*; it's *a* **curse**! Impressed, *delighted* and/or *happy* would be the more *correct* words.

Again, the evil spirits *ruling* this world have *subtly* **replaced** the **correct** *words* with their own **evil** *substitutes* (replacements). We now hear people, especially young people, using words like "*sick*" and "*bad*" for *something* **perceived** *good*. How "*sick*" is that? (Pun intended) Since when did "*bad*" *and* "sick" become "*good*" versus the "**bad**" they always *were*? Interesting *question*, but *how* was our world *coerced* into **switching** so many "*evil*" words to *good*?

Well, if the *parents*, **teachers**, *elders*, and *leaders* were *doing* their *job*, they would have **stopped** this *corruption* and **adulteration** of *language* **before** it went so *far*! Words are **no** *trivial* matter; in fact, in *words* are the *power* of **blessings** and **cursings**! We are told in *scripture* we will *held* **accountable** for "*every word we speak*"!

It's *obvious* to *anyone* paying *attention* the demonic *powers* **ruling** this *world* are *leading* a *hapless* and **foolish** *humanity* further and *further* from the *truth* and **reality**! By *applying* the **opposite** *meanings* to *words*, we have not only *been* **dumbed** *down literally*, but are *becoming* **insane**!

Yes, the *powers* that *be* are literally **stealing** *our* **sanity** and **common** *sense* **bit** *by* **bit** with their *promotion* of every sort of *evil* as the "**new**" *good*. In fact, it's become *difficult* to find a *young* person who hasn't been *led* to *believe* **traditional** (*monogamous*) *marriage* is **good** and that **sodomy** (*homosexual* relations) is *evil*. Even **murdering** of our *unborn* **babies** is now considered a "*good*" thing!?

Another *evil* for *good* trend is *lack* of **self** *responsibility*. We see it *promoted* virtually everywhere we are too *stupid* to *think* **for** *ourselves* and be *responsible* for our **own** *actions*. Unfortunately, a *large* percentage of people, really have become *too* **dumbed** *down* to **think** *for* **themselves**, primarily through the *promotion* of a **victim** *mentality*; that *every* **bad** *thing* we do (or are) is *someone* **else's** *fault*.

That *attitude* has *reduced* us too *little* more than **slaves,** giving the *government* **free** rein to **pass** *endless* **freedom** *robbing* **legislation**. Bottom line, *refusing* to **accept** *responsibility* for our *actions* and *words,* gives *others* the **permission** to **control** *us, a* downfall that's come through *pride,* **selfishness** and *greed*!

With that in mind, just how on Earth (pun intended) did we ever get so *far* **down** this *astonishing* **path** to **evil** and *destruction?* Well, it *all* **began** with the demons *prompting* **religious** leaders to *change* the **true** *Names* from which come *health,* **wealth**, and *blessings,* to *evil* names, bringing *instead,* **destruction.**

That *destructive* **trend** began with some *Rabbi decreeing* the **true** *Name* of our Creator with just too *"holy"* to be *used* by the *average* person and was to *only* be *used* by the *religious* **leaders** in *religious* ceremonies. But that's **not** *what* our Creator **commanded.**

There are *dozens* of scriptures *"commanding"* the *"***praising***"* and *proclamation* of our *Creator's* **personal** *Name,* YHWH (Yahweh). That was our *first* major *mistake,* considering **all** (true) *blessings* come from Him and the *"Glorifying"* (honoring) of *His* **Name**!

I know from *personal* **experience**, *making* a *commitment* to *embrace* and **honor** His **correct** and *"Set Apart"* (exclusive) *Name* is the **door** from which all *understanding* and *blessings* **flow**! It's not just *hyperbole* but *"***real***"* *beyond* human *reasoning*! YHWH *literally "***is***"* understanding, **truth,** and **love**!

How shocking the translators were demonically *persuaded* to **replace** the *all* **powerful** *Name* of *YHWH* with *"The Lord"*. Unfortunately, *the lord* (Baal) is one of the *chief* **enemies** of YHWH and **His** *people.* "Baal" is a Canaanite god the Hebrews *adopted,* meaning *"lord"* and (slave) *"master"*. YHWH plainly *proclaims* that *dishonoring* His *Set* **Apart** *Name* (exclusive) like *calling* Him *"the Lord"* (Baal) *brings* a **curse** (Mal.2). And, one of the greatest *curses* is that of *little* or **false** *understanding*!

Adding *insult* to *injury*, the *apostle* (wanna-be) Paul apparently *began* the *practice* of using a **generic Greek substitute** for the **Hebrew Messiah** as his *designation*. It seems Paul's *fear* of **retribution** (punishment) for the *"blotting out"* law, **prompted** it.

You see, one of the *penalties* for **blasphemy** for which Yahshua was *crucified* (by the Jews) came with the *blotting **out*** of His Name, which meant anyone *caught **saying*** or *writing* it would *receive* the **same fate** as the *name **blotted*** *out*. Obviously, the **true** *apostles* would *not* have *been **afraid*** of such a *decree*, clearly *demonstrating* Paul was **not** *one* of Yahshua's *twelve*. And of course, those who *commissioned* all the *other* NT books (passed orally) to be *written, exercised* Paul's **same** *fear*!

Looking at this world from a *physical* perspective, *what **hope*** is *there* of ever *turning* it **around**? Have we *passed* the *point* of **no** *return;* having *reached* the *inability* to once again view *evil* as **evil** and **good** as *"good"*? Well, I for one, don't see even the **slightest** *hope* of that *kind* of **reversal**, at least *by* humanity. It seems only a *catastrophic* and **devastating** *event,* which **destroys** *humanities* (especially modern Israel) **faith** and *trust* in their *pagan* and **false** *gods* (and themselves) would be *sufficient* to *accomplish* such a *task!* That's how it's always been in the past.

Well, it seems that very *terrifying* answer is *menacingly **approaching*** from the *wings*. It's the *"nemesis"* **solar** *system;* a *brown dwarf star* with some 4 *planets* in *tow.* As it soon slices through our *solar* system, it will doubtless *destroy* a **large** *portion* of humanity and certainly *bring* **humanity** to *its **knees**!*

As *horrible* as it sounds, it's *just **what's*** *needed* to **slow** this *train* of **evil** that humanity has become (especially modern Israel) to bring us to the *fulfillment* of the *"Day of Atonement"* when YHWH will *gather* His People to *His* new **Promised** *Land;* the **new** *Eden!* I pray *often* for the end of this **evil** *demonic* generation and the *arrival* of the *new!*

Well, when we *listen* to Christian teachings, we're told *good*, **righteous** *behavior* is *impossible,* which is *why* the "*law*" (Torah) was *done* **away** and *grace* was *given* instead. Is that *correct?* Unfortunately, that *teaching* **originates** with the **self-appointed** (false) *apostle* that *complained* how he **did** the *things* (evil-selfish) he *did* **not** want to *do* and **did** not **do** the (righteous) things he *wished* he could.

Interestingly, **none** of the *other* (12) Apostles of Yahshua talked **that** *way.* Why? What was the *difference?* Was it because they *received* the great *outpouring* of YHWH's Spirit of *life* in **Acts** 2? Remember, Paul was **not** *among* the 120 **receiving** that *outpouring!*

Bottom line; the *spirit* of *pride* **imbued** *us* by the dragon, is far too *powerful* for us to *overcome* (control) without **supernatural** *assistance;* which Paul obviously had **not** *received!*

Just *before* Yahshua *ascended,* He *promised* His 12; "*You will receive* *power when YHWH's* **Spirit** *comes* **upon** *you*-" (Acts 1:8) It's taught virtually across the board *the* **power** they *received* was the *ability* to **perform** *miracles.* No doubt that's also *true,* but there was a much more *important* **reason** for that *power!*

That's exactly what Paul was *alluding* to when he said he **did** the *things* he **didn't** *want* to *do* and *didn't* **do** the (good) *things* he **wanted.** Again, the reason the 12 apostles of Yahshua didn't *talk* like *Paul* is because they *had* **received** the **power** *needed* to **overcome** the *spirit* and **power** of the dragon! The dragon is a **supernatural** *creature* and only with *supernatural* **power** can we do *battle* and *overcome* the *dragon's* **spirit** of *pride,* **selfishness,** and *greed!*

Getting back to the *premise* of this study; what *determines* a person is *good* or not, is if we have the *Creator's* **Spirit** of **humility** and **love.** Without that Spirit, all people *fall* into the category of "*carnal*" that is, of the *spirit* of the *dragon* (tree of the knowledge of good and evil). Only after *embracing* the "*Tree of Life*" are we technically *good!*

To *embrace* the **Tree** of **Life**, we must first *give* our Creator the **Honor** "*due*" His **exclusive** *Name* (Names) and put away the **pagan** *gods* and *names*. Secondly we must **Honor** *Him* by *attending* His **Sacred** *celebrations* (His special anniversaries) with Him. That shows Him we *care* about **what** He's *done* and **is** *doing* for us.

YHWH also tells *us* those **celebrations** are a "*sign*" between *Him* and His *People*! (Ex. 31-Ez. 20) Considering those *special* celebrations (Sabbaths) are *rehearsals* of *His* **Plan** for mankind (His Children). There's **no** *way* we can *honestly* say *we* "*Love*" Him without *participating* (honoring Him) in His *special* **anniversaries** of *what* He has *done* and *what* He is *still* **going** to *do*!

To *end* this study, it's *imperative* to *understand* we **all** "*will*" **reap** the *fruits* of our *actions,* good or *bad*. But, unfortunately, we sometimes *fail* to **understand** the *depths* and **consequences** of *our* actions. A perfect Biblical *example* is the *story* of Job.

The account *opens* with the devil (adversary) *approaching* the Creator and being asked *where* he had *been* and *doing*. He was then *asked* if he had *seen* YHWH's *servant* Job, the *most* **righteous** *man* of the East? The devil *challenged* Job's *obedience* to YHWH's **special** *protection*. To *prove* that, the devil was *allowed* to *take* **all** his *possessions*, including his **ten** *children*. Talk about **bad** *things* happening to *good* people!!

Due to the *compliers* of the OT canon **failing** to *include* all the *original* books, like **Jasher** (meaning "*true account*") the *story* **behind** *Job* was *lost* leaving us *scratching* our heads as to "**why**" Job was *fated* to *suffer* all those **terrible** *things*!

In **Jasher**, we *discover* **Job** was one of Pharoah's *chief* **advisers** (along with Baalim) that Pharaoh brought in to *advise* him on *what* to do with the **mushrooming** *population* of *Israelites* in his country. We find it was **Jobs'** *advise* to have all the **baby** *Israelite* **boys** *thrown* in the river, which the Pharaoh *adopted*.

That *prompts* one to *ask*; **why** would a *righteous* man give such *terrible* (too us) *advise?* Well, *obviously*, Job did **not** *realize* the *Israelites* were *YHWH's* **chosen** *people*. All he *knew* is they were a *threat* to Egyptian *sovereignty*, to which he simply acted *logically.* But his *actions* make **obvious** the *reason* all his **10** *children* were all *killed!*

Chapter 36

What is *"Godly"*?

It's so *rare* to listen to a *preacher* or radio *minister* without *hearing* them *speak* of "**godly**" or "**being** *godly*" but *what* does that *mean; exactly?* On the surface, I think we can safely *assume* it means to "*be*" or "*act*" like "*God*". But, **who** or **what** is "*God*"? Is *God* a *reference* to the *Creator* (Father) God or *someone* (or something) **else**? Considering virtually all Christian denominations *believe* "*Jesus*" is *God;* maybe *He's* the *God* to which they're *referring?*

Well, unfortunately, if one does **not** *use* their **god's** name "*godly*" can be a *reference* to **any** *god*, right? After all, doesn't *everyone* **believe** that **their** *god* (gods) is the "**true**" one? So, if one *uses* the **generic** *term* "*god*" *how* can *we* **know** *who's* being *referenced?* Considering the **devil** is "*a*" *god*, how do we know *someone* making a *reference* to **being** *godly* or **acting** *godly*, isn't referring to *acting* **like** the *devil?*

Unfortunately, one of greatest *disservices* the translators (demonically motivated) did was to *change* and/or **remove** the *names* of the *gods* (angels-demons-Creator-Messiah). For instance, by taking out the *Creator's* **personal** *Name* (YHWH) which He *gave* to *"Moses"* and **replacing** it with the "*Lord*" almost 7000 times (in the OT alone) and "*God*" the whole book becomes *nonsensical* to one degree or another!

An excellent *example* is found in the *Book* of **Joel** (chap.1&2) where it speaks of "*The day of the Lord*". Since *Lord* simply denotes *authority*, or *one* **in** authority "lord" can be *virtually* **anyone**; from an *English* **lord**, to a *demon lord*, or even a *Messiah*. Which is it? Well, it could be *all* or *none* of *those*!

Another well *known* "*Day of the Lord*" *passage* is found in **Zechariah** 14, where "*the Lord*" comes and *stands* on the *Mount* of Olives; "*splitting it in two*". Is this "*Lord*" the **same** *Lord* as the *one* in **Joel**? How can we know unless the **true** *names* are *used*?

Unfortunately, because of the *demonic* **manipulation** of the *names*, mainstream Christianity *believes* "*The day of the Lord*" (for instance) is a reference to *Jesus,* but, how can we **know** without **actual** names? How can we *say* or *know* with *assurance* without the **actual** *name* being *used*?

Well, how *different* the **picture** *becomes* when we can go back to the *original* text and see t**he "Lord"** in the Old Testament is a *generic* **replacement** of the *true* Name of the **Creator "<u>YHWH</u>"** which was also the *name* of the *favorite* **Canaanite** *god* the Israelites were always getting in *trouble* for *worshipping*!

Wow, talk about *radically* **changing** the *text* and **picture** to *realize* it's *YHWH*, **the Father**, who is **coming** to *stand* on the **Mount of Olives** and *split* it in *two*! What a shock it is to most *Christians* and **their** *belief* the so- called "**Day of the Lord**" is actually "*The day of YHWH*" the Creator **Father**! He is also the *Father* of the **Hebrew** *Messiah*, who's *Name* **change** has caused another *massive* **deception** in *Christianity*!

What I'm referring to is the *changing* of the *Hebrew* **Messiah's** *Name* to the *generic* **title** *Jesus* (Greek word for savior). You see, the Hebrew Messiah's Name was *Yahshua* which *means* "*YHWH* (the Father) *is salvation*"!

That's *beyond* shocking to the average *Christian* to *realize* their *generic* **Greek** *messiah* is a **fake** and *fraud*; that *YHWH* is "**the** *Savior*" as **Isaiah** 43 (v.3&11) plainly *proclaims* and is the **one** who is **returning** to *save* His People!

So, *what* is "*godly*" in the Christian world? Considering the fact it's **not** a *reference* to *YHWH,* the *Savior,* or His **Firstborn** *Son* and *High* **Priest** *Yahshua,* you *decide*! But, we must bear in mind, **Revelation** 9 tells us the *devil* has "*deceived the whole world*"! Yes, that would be **all**, *not* just **part**!!

Chapter 37

God (s) of Death

In the Garden of Eden, Adam and Eve were *offered* **two** *choices*; one was *life* (the Tree of Life) and the other was *death* (Tree of Knowledge of Good and Evil). They were told they could **freely** *eat* of the *Tree of Life* and **never** *die*, but if they *partook* of the *other* (in the middle of the Garden) they *would* "*surely* **die**".

Well, we all *know* the *story*; they *chose* **badly** and yes, they *died*! Of course, they were *tricked* by the *promise* (lie); "*You* **won't** *surely* **die**—*you will be like the* **gods**". (Gen. 3:4) You see, *one* of the *attributes* of the (watcher angels) was that they were *immortal*, so it seemed to Adam and Eve that they couldn't *lose* here.

Unfortunately, Adam and Eve's **foolish** *choice* **opened** the *door* for the *watcher* **gods** to **rule** this *world*. And, of course, except for a **rare** *few*, most everyone has *embraced* that *Tree* (dragon) and its' *ways*, which *assured* a *life* **ending** in *death*.

Interestingly, the great *immortal **lie*** (*immortal* soul-we don't *die*, just *change* places) told in the Garden, is still taught by ***every*** *major* (and most minor) *religion* on Earth. In fact, it's the *one* and *only* thing upon which they ***all*** *agree*! Imagine that?! Why do you *suppose* that is? Well, here's a *clue*; all these *religions* belong to the god (gods) of this world! Of course, that god (gods) is the *god* of *death*! How amazing that virtually everywhere we *look* we **see** that god (gods) *proudly* **proclaiming** their *immortal **lie***.

How funny that *everyone* who *knows* the Garden *story* believes they are *smarter* than our *ancestral* parents; really? Well, a major *truism* everyone would be *wise* to *learn* and *remember*; "*There is **no-one** we **lie** to* (and about) **more** *than* **ourselves**"! Unfortunately, it's *due* to a little *thing* that also *occurred* in the Garden. Eve and Adam's foolish choice *opened* the door for the *god* of *death* (dragon) to *fill* us with its ***lying*** *spirit*; that is the *spirit* of ***pride*** and *death*.

It is written; "***Pride comes before destruction***" (death-Prov. 16:18). It is also *written*; "*YHWH* (The Tree of Life) ***dwells with*** (only) *the **contrite** and **humble** of spirit"*. (Is. 57:15) In fact, Yahshua (the Hebrew Messiah) and His Father YHWH are both called "*Life*". YHWH tells us by His *Prophets'* that He not only *hates* the ***death*** of the *righteous*, but the *sinner* as well! In other words, He *hates **death**, period*!

He told the *Israelites* at Mt. Sinai that He set before them "*life*" and "*death*" and to "*choose **life** and blessings*" not "***death** and cursings*". (Deut. 30) Unfortunately, very few have *chosen **life*** (Enoch, Elijah, Moses) until the *first* century. There, most of Yahshua's followers apparently *chose **life*** as He *advised* them in **John** 8:52; "*He who keeps my words will **never taste death**"*.

Unfortunately, those *left* behind after the *spring **harvest*** was *completed*, did a bang-up job *suppressing* that *part* of *history*. In fact, they (in Christianity) have *convinced* everyone that we are *required* to *physically* "*die once*" (Hebrews 9) which makes no absolutely ***no*** *sense* if we have ***immortal*** *souls* and go to *heaven* or *hell* when we *die* anyway!

Actually, it's the ***death*** *god* (gods) that *rules* this world, which have *con- vinced* everyone to *choose* (accept) *death* in leu of *life*. Again, they *first **accomplished*** *this* by the *immortal **soul*** *lie,* and secondly *convincing* everyone "*choosing **immortality***" is ***not*** an *option*; that we ***must*** *die*. After all, if we only ***change*** *places* (heaven) when we *die*, what's the *problem*?

In fact, one of the *common* sayings we *hear* in *Christian* circles is "*going home*" when we ***die***. (And go to heaven or hell) Considering **Isaiah** 5 tells us "*the **soul** that **sins;** it shall **die***"; not *live **forever*** in *heaven* or *hell* (*going home)* is just a ***lie*** to *encourage* people to ***accept*** *death* over *immortality*!

The ***death*** *god,* gods of *darkness,* who *rule* the *night* have *coerced* Christianity into literally ***worshiping*** *death*! They *decorate* their ***houses*** of *worship* with one of the most *horrific **death*** instruments ever *devised* by a ***deranged*** mind as if it were a *good* thing! They *hang* them on their walls, on their car *mirrors* and even *wear* them around their *necks* and *ears* as jewelry! Hopefully you *know* what I'm referring to; the *cross*. They have *convinced* themselves it's a *sign* of *life* (resurrection) but are only ***lying*** to themselves, not to mention the *rest* of us!

Other religions have also been *coerced* into worshipping the *god* (gods) of ***darkness***, such as the Jews. They begin their *worship* (Sabbaths) with the onset of *darkness*. And, who is the god (gods) of *darkness*? Well, that's a no-brainer; it is the *devil* and its *minions,* the *demons*! In the case of the Jews and Seventh-day Adventist's (and off-shoots) they have taken very *plain* scripture and completely perverted it to support their ***dark*** *belief* systems.

Of course, *what* I'm referring to, is the fact *"evening"* is listed before *"morning"* in **Genesis** one. But, the *plain* and *simple* **truth** *is*, the sun was *not* in the sky until the *fourth* day, which means there was **no** *evening* and *morning* as we view it in our *modern* sense.

The late Charles Missler brought this *issue* to *fore* by *pointing* out that very fact. He makes the *obvious* point *"ereb"* (evening) and *"boker"* (morning) had **different** *meanings* in *paleo* (ancient) Hebrew. It's a very **common** *phenomena*; even in English, how many words have *evolved* into two or more *different* **meanings**.

That said, in *paleo* Hebrew *ereb* and *boker* originally meant something along the lines of **decreasing** *chaos* (ereb) and **increasing** order (boker). But, unfortunately, **traditional** *beliefs* are the most *difficult* to **change** in spite of how **obvious** the *truth*!

The bottom line is, since before Adam and Eve, a *war* was *waging* between *good* and **evil**, *light* and **darkness**, the *devil* (s) and the Creator (of life)! That, *behind* the *curtains* **battle,** is obvious *everywhere* we look; at least to all *those* who *care* to **open** *their* **eyes** and *see*! The *light* side (Creator and His angels) want us to *choose* **light** (the righteous way) and *reap* **life** (immortality) while the **dark** side wants us to *choose* the *selfish* and **proud** *way* (darkness) and **reap** *death*!

To *close* this study, I will *leave* you with this *question* to *ponder*. If we have the right (ability) to *choose* **life**, but are *taught* we have *no* such *choice*, **what** is *going* to *happen*? Obviously, we **die** by *default*! After all, *choosing* **life** is a *choice*; and not just a **verbal** choice, but a *choice* of **how** we *live* and **behave**! Are we to *believe* our Loving Creator was so *derelict* as to *not* leave us with a *manual* on how to make **that** choice and *what* it *entails*? Well, He *did* and it's called *"The Torah"* meaning *"instruction"* (on living).

Chapter 38

History of the Universal Church

The *Catholic* (Universal) Church, which was the **first** *Christian* Church, has a very *interest* **Chapter 38** *ing* and shocking history! This study will *not* be an extremely *detailed* study, but just a general *overview*. In fact, some of this **cannot** be *found* in any *history* books.

It all started with the **first** *century Rabbis'* who were *told* by the **Hebrew** *Messiah* (Yahshua) they were "*of their father the devil*"! Backing up a bit, we find the *Pharisees,* such as Saul (Paul) seeking to *kill* the Messiah, which they finally *accomplished*. The Pharisees went on to **demonize** *Yahshua's* **Apostles** as *false* ones and *liars,* but after the *prophesied* **destruction** of Jerusalem came to *fruition* (after many *heavenly* signs) they *knew* they were in *trouble*.

At that point, the *Jewish* **Pharisees** knew they'ed *been* **exposed** as the *real* **false** ones. They attempted to *regain* the *trust* of the people in the *following* **centuries**, which they *did* to a large *degree*. But, by the *forth* century (CE) Roman *Emperor* **Constantine** was so *tired* of the *bickering* amongst the *religions* of his *empire* in 324, he ordered all of them to a **counsel** at *Nicea*, and **not** to *leave* (on pain of death) *without* having *created* a "**Universal**" religion that would make **everyone** *happy*. (Like the Pagans) Again "**Catholic**" is the *Latin* word for **universal**!

But, during that Nicean *council,* **half** the Jewish rabbi's *refused* to *change* their day of *worship* (Saturn's Day) to *Sunday* (day of the sun) and went back to **traditional** *Judaism.* The others went on to *found* **Christianity.** In fact, according to Bible *teacher* and *historian,* Randy Weiss, the first **15 popes** were *Jewish!* An obvious *sign* of the **Jewish** *origin* of the *Universal* Church is the *Yahmulke* (skull caps) the *Pope* and many *cardinals* still **wear.**

Considering the *founders* of *Christianity* were **predominately** *Jewish,* we see to this day the *Catholic* Church *structured* as the Jewish *Priests* at the *temple.* The Pope is the **new** *High* Priest and of course, the variety of Catholic *"orders" reflect* the many *orders* of *levitical* **priests** at the *temple,* only with the *Vatican* as the *new* temple!

As a bit of an aside, *offering* even *more* **proof,** is **John** 3 telling us the (Jewish) Messiah (Yahshua) *shed* His *blood* for the "*world*" which is a blatant *miss-translation.* (The least of possible meanings)

The Greek *word* for *world,* is "*Kosmos*" meaning "**order**". In fact, that's why we call the *heavens* "**Cosmos**" as they are very *orderly.* (They don't change) What **John** really *tells* us is Yahshua (the Hebrew Messiah) **died** for the (His) **Order.** What *Order?* Well, that would be the *Order* of His *Priesthoods,* which is *why* the *rest* of the world is still **dying.** Obviously, the *penalty* for *sin* has **not** *been* removed.

Let's address this "*new*" **religion** called "*Christianity*". First of all, it was first *initiated* by a *Pharisee* named *Saul* (Paul). Due to the "*blotting out*" *decree* on certain *crimes* such as **blasphemy,** which is the *excuse* the Pharisees used to *murder* the *Hebrew* Messiah (Yahshua) anyone *heard* **using** the **blotted** *out* **name** would *receive* the **same** *fate* as the one **blotted** *out.*

So Paul (Saul) being the **first** to *write* anything in the *first* century, naturally *feared* the *blotting* **out** degree and used a **substitute** for the **Messiah's** name and *title*. He *substituted* the **Hebrew** *Messiah's* Name with the *generic* Greek word for *savior* "*Iesous*" (Jesus).

He also *replaced* the *Hebrew* word for *Messiah* "*Maschoc*" with "*Christos*" (christ) the **Greek** *word* for "*anointed one*". Considering all the others *conscripting* to *pen,* the rest of the NT books, also *feared* the **blotting** *decree*, resulted in the *Hebrew* Messiah's Name being **transformed** into a **Greek** *one*!

Actually, with a little *investigating* of the **Greek** *Gods,* we *discover* they were **all** "*Christos*" (Christs). In fact, *Zeus* was the Olympian *anointed* to be "*Savior*" (of the Greeks) while his *brothers* (the rest of the Olympians) were all *anointed* as *Christs* as well. **Hades** was *anointed* to be the **Christ** of the *underworld;* **Poseidon** the *Christ* of the *sea,* and **Aries**, *Christ* of the *sky* and/or **war**.

In other words, *Christianity,* the *Mother* of which is the Catholic (Universal) Church is a very *pagan* **Greek** *religion,* again ironically *founded* by the Jewish *religious* **leaders,** which the Hebrew Messiah called "*sons of their father, the devil*"! That fact is quite *obvious* considering all the *paganism* incorporated at Nicea.

They *established* the *celebration* of **Saturnalia** on the *winter* **solstice** (end of December) which was also the *birthday* of not just *Saturn,* but **all** the **pagan** *gods*!

Christmas by the way, means to kill the **anointed** one (Messiah) *Christ* is the *Greek* word for *Messiah* and "*Mas*" (mass) is the *Latin* word meaning "*to kill*". It's the *root* of our *English* word "*massacre*"!

They also *instituted* the **forty** days of "*weeping for Tammuz*" (Horus who was also killed) which the *Universal* Church now calls *Lent*. Horus was the *reincarnation* of **Osiris,** the *husband* of *Ishtar*. Ishtar (Easter) *originated* the *practice* of *temple* **prostitution,** which is where the *rabbit* comes in; as a **fertility** *aid*. The *eggs originated* with her celebration of *Horus* coming to her from *heaven* in an *egg* (Easter egg) after *Osrius* was *killed* by his brother Set! Valentines day is also connected to that *major* **pagan** (sexual) *rite*.

Of course, the *daughters* of the *Universal* Church (Protestants) went a step *further* by *replacing* the *Torah* (instructions for righteous behavior) with *grace,* while also doing away with the *concept* of a spiritual *Priesthood*. They also further *reinforced* the **pagan** aspects of that original **Universal** *Church*.

Chapter 39

How Did the Hebrew Messiah get a Greek Name?

Maybe it's just *me* and/or the way I *think*, but am I the *only* one who always *wondered* how the **Hebrew Messiah had** or *got* a **Greek,** or at least a *Greek* **sounding** name? This question began to *plague* me from my teenage years, but unfortunately, I like most in Christianity, *bought* the *story* that the *Jews* (Hebrews) all **spoke** Greek in the *first* century and it was *normal* for the *Jews* to have **Greek** names.

This sort of made *sense*, but was *problematic* when so many scriptures *showed* how the *Pharisees* and *Sadducees* (religious leaders) would go to great *lengths* **not** to *associate* with and *have* **any** *dealing* with the *Greeks*. And, let's *not* forget; the *temple* and its courtyards were strictly **off** limits to the *Greeks*. That being the *case*, would they not have also had a *problem* with *someone* with a *Greek* name (Ieasus)?

These are very **legitimate** *questions* which the churches (Christianity) have never had any *"logical"* (or honest) *answers* for. Unfortunately, I **loved** *my* **church** and *refused* to *believe* they would *lie* (mislead) about such an *important* thing.

Considering these *questions*, we must keep in mind, the *Pharisees* and *Sadducees* considered the *Diaspora* (10 *displaced* and *scattered* Israelite tribes) *the **same*** as *Gentiles*. We must keep in mind; the Pharisees were "**extremely** *fanatic*" with the **clean** and **unclean** *laws*! The Torah (which the Messiah makes reference) makes it very clear if the *unclean* (Greek-gentile) **touches** the *clean*, it was the *clean* that became **unclean**, *not* the other way around! That said, wouldn't *having* an **unclean** *Greek* name be the same as being "**touched**" by the *unclean*?

With that in mind, we have *accounts* of the Messiah (supposedly with a Greek name) not only being **in** the **temple** courtyards, but *teaching* **in** the **temple** *itself*! Would the Pharisees *really* have *allowed a* **Hellenist** (a Hebrew with a Greek name) anywhere *near* the *temple*, let alone *teach* **in** *it*?

In fact, the **so-called** *Gentiles* the Apostle *Peter* was *judged* (by Paul) for *eating* with, were some of those **Israelite** *Diaspora*! Remember, Yahshua sent out His 70 *disciples* to go "**ONLY**" to the **lost** *sheep* (Diaspora) of the *house* of **Israel**! (Mat.15) So, these so-called *Gentiles* Paul and the other Pharisees with him *condemned* Peter for *eating* with, were **displaced** *Israelites not* **literal** *gentiles*. Still, YHWH had to *remove* Peter's doubts that He had *cleansed* those *scattered* tribes!!

Because of my *misplaced* trust in the Church and its *leaders*, I never *investigated* the **sacred** names for myself until after *asking* the **wrong** *questions*, which resulted in my no longer being *welcome* in *that* denomination. It was that *circumstance* that finally *propelled* me into looking into the **Sacred** *Names*!

To my utter *shock*, I *discovered* the **Hebrew** *Messiah* really did *have* a **Hebrew** *Name*! But then, this should have been a **no**-*brainer* considering the Messiah's "*coming*" had been *established* "*from the foundation of the world*" as **Revelation** 13:8 *proclaims*!

That said, would the Creator YHWH really **not** have *planned* from "***that*** *time*" to slso. *give* His *first-born* **Son** a very *special* (Set Apart-exclusive) **Hebrew** Name? Well, *He* **did** and it was not only a **Hebrew,** *Name* but one *proclaiming* His *Father,* **YHWH** as *Savior*! (Isa. 45:21) That special *Name* **planned** *"from the foundation of the world"* was **Yahshua**

Well, that brings us back to the *subject* of this mini-study; just how did *Christianity* manage to *pull* **off** such a *monstrous* **deception** (scandal) as **replacing** the **exclusive** (Set Apart-badly translated "*holy*") *Hebrew* Messiah's *true* "**YHWH given**" *Name* with a *Gentile* one; and not just *any* **Greek** name, but one **dedicated to Zeus,** no less!!

Well, the *answer* is very *simple* actually. You see, Yahshua was *hung* on the **tree** for the supposed *crime* of "*blasphemy*" which also came with the *punishment* of the "**blotting out**" of **His** *Name*! Blotting *out* was a *punishment* that traces back to the *Egyptians* (at least). (Dr. Olaf Hagee).

When someone *committed* a *crime* that *came* with a *blotting* **out** *sentence*, it meant if *anyone*, including *family,* were *caught* **using** the *name,* would *receive* the **same** *fate* as the person who's *name* had been **blotted** *out*, which in this case was *crucifixion*! Knowing that, we can certainly understand why *most* would *avoid using* **that** *name* like the *plague*!

Speaking the *name* in *private* with *family* and *close* **trusted** *friends* was *one* thing, but if one were to **write** *something* for the *public*, it was certainly a *suicide* venture! That brings us to *Paul*, who was the *only* one *writing* anything (NT) until about 50-60 BCE. (Professor Bart Earman)

Paul was a Pharisee and knew full *well* the *gravity* of *writing* the *Name* of the *crucified* and *blotted* out "*One*". Naturally, He *chose* a *Greek* **substitute** name "*Ieasus*" (savior). Unfortunately, that *substitute* had a very **different** *meaning*, which *completely* **changed** everything! (Omitted His Father) A major truth *was* **lost** due to the *changing* of the Hebrew Messiah's (Yahshua) Name to a **generic** *Greek one*!

Well, that *brings* up the *subject* of the 12 *Apostles* that Yahshua *appointed* and *sent;* were they *afraid* to **use Yahshua's Name** also? Surely they would not have been *afraid* to use the *Creator's* **given** *Messiah's* **Name**, would they? Well, according to Professor Bart Ehrman, a **leading** *expert* in 1st century Biblical *writings, none* of the *12* (or Yahshua) *ever* **wrote** anything.

That *fact* was probably due to the *reality* that *only* the Rabbi's and **university** *educated* **wealthy** (which the *disciples* were **not**) would have had the luxury of **learning** to *read* and *write*. Yahshua obviously knew *how* to *read* and *write* by the fact that He stood up and *read* in the *temple* and was also called "*Rabbi*" (teacher) but there is **zero** *evidence* He ever *wrote* **anything**. (For posterity)

Dr. Bart Ehrman also proves the books *dedicated* to some of the 12 Apostles, were all written by *Greek* **University** *educated* people and certainly **not** by *laymen* like the 12 *apostles*. The *language* and *writing* **styles** (university educated middle first century Greek) are a dead give- away.

It seems *what* was *written* was **passed** *orally* from those who *heard* first *hand* and then at some point *hired* a *Greek* **university** *educated* **scribe** to *write* it all down. Naturally, these writers were *not willing* to *risk* using the *blotted out* Name of Yahshua either.

The 64,000 dollar question then is; why would an Apostle (Paul) *recruited* by the **Hebrew** *Messiah* not *proclaim* His *true* Name **Yahshua**?? Well, it doesn't take much of a *study* to realize that *Paul* was one of those **false** ones that Yahshua *warned* His 12 **true** *disciples* about in **Matthew 24**! (But, that is another very fascinating study) Paul was much more interested in *preserving* his own *skin* than *proclaiming* the *true* **Hebrew** *Messiah*!

Chapter 40

Hokma (Chokma) Mother of Mankind!

A theme rather *predominate* in Bible scripture, is **marriage** and **family**. Those two are *lifted **up*** to a level of great *importance* when we see the *penalties* invoked for *disregarding* the **instructions** concerning them. For instance, **adultery** was *punishable* by **death**. That extreme *consequence* for *disregarding* the **sanctity** of *marriage* shows the extreme *importance* our Creators place upon the *institution*.

Even in our *current* society, although *diminished* somewhat from the *state* **once** *held,* **marriage** *fidelity* is still *upheld* by a *large* **portion** of *humanity.* Christianity is one *institution* **professing** to uphold *family* importance with phrases like "*Family of God*". Actually, that *phrase* is a loose reference to the "*Church*". Church is a translation of the Greek word "*Eccleccia*" which is actually a *misnomer* considering it *literally* **means** "*Called **out** individuals*" (not a group) a *calling **out*** of the *world.*

Considering the ***family*** *concept,* most Christians refer to the Creator as "*Father*". But, to be a *Father,* aren't **children** *required?* Of course, Christianity believes there is a *Son* called *Jesus.* Unfortunately, many also believe the *Father* and *Son* are "**one**" and the **same** *person.* This is obvious *nonsense* considering a *Son* **cannot** be his **own** *father* (and vise versa) but Christianity *insists* upon **promoting** such *nonsense.*

Another *common* teaching is a *Father* (Creator) and *Son* existed in the *beginning*. That idea *contributes* to the *concept* of a *spiritual **family***, but how can a *son exist **without*** a *mother?* Aren't children *formed* and *birthed* from a ***womb;*** that is, a ***mother's*** *womb?* To be a *son* and/or *children*, being *birthed* from a mothers' *womb* is a ***requirement***. To make a *case* for a *son* (or children) ***without*** a *mother* is *absurd;* they would simply be ***clones*** and/or *creations*!

So, *what* do we do with this *conundrum?* Either there was ***no** Father* and *Son* in the *beginning* or there ***was*** a ***mother;** we can't* have it ***both*** *ways!* With that in mind, we are told there's *no* mention of a ***spirit*** *Mother* in the Bible Scriptures, but is that *correct?* If true, the whole idea of a *father* and *son* in the beginning is *flushed*!

Well, to find the *truth*, prudence tells us to start at the *beginning*. **Genesis** 1 shows a *conversation* between at least ***two*** *persons*. We see it in the ***plural*** language; "*Let **us** make man in **our image** and in **our likeness***". It goes on to *say* of that ***plural*** entity "***they*** *created man both **male and female***" (in their image).

Again, many believe the *plural* language is referring to the *Father* and *Son*. But again, we can't have a *Father* and *Son **without*** a *Mother!* Besides, doesn't the fact *mankind* was created both *male* and *female* **demand** the ***two*** *creating* be ***male*** and ***female*** also? After all, it does say "*in **our image** and **likeness***"!

You say, the Bible doesn't support that conclusion anywhere, but, you'd be *wrong;* it does, very clearly! We find a ***female*** entity (Chokma-Hokma) very plainly, *addressing "**Her**" children* right there in **Proverbs**! **Proverbs** 8 uses very strong and ***clear*** *language* supporting the **Genesis** *account*. Unfortunately, the translators *buried* this shocking *truth* by ***hiding*** Her Name; *reducing **Her*** a mere aspect of *thought* and ***reasoning***. (Wisdom)

But "*wisdom*" is just a *function* of the mind, an *aspect* of **reason**, not a person. Interestingly, **Proverbs** 8 is all in the *feminine* text, and looking closely at "*Her*" words it's quite clear, *she* is not only a *Female* (woman) but a **Wife** and **Mother**.

In fact, we are told in **Proverbs** 8: 22, she was the "*first of YHWH's creations of old*"; apparently *before* the *Angels* and certainly **before** the *Earth* and *Mankind*! Also, it's **impossible** to *create* **wisdom**, without the one **creating** it *already* **being** wisdom (and/or wise) which makes such an action **redundant**!

Secondly, verse 30 (last part) tells us she *frolicked* (danced) and literally *flirted* with and *before* YHWH! An aspect of *thought* and **reasoning** certainly does *not* **frolic** and **flirt**! Also, in the first part of verse 30, she says She "*was **beside** Him as a master **craftsman** when He created the Earth*".

Right *there* is **proof** of *who* the *ones* **creating** man and *woman* in **their** image, were! But, the most amazing *thing* She says is; "*He who finds Me, finds **life** and **favor** with YHWH*". Actually, She was no doubt the "*Tree of Life*" in the *Garden* of *Eden*! The *truth* is *stranger* than *fiction*, but there's more!

Everything in this *physical* world is a *type* or **physical** *copy* of the *spirit* realm. The **physical** *woman* is a *copy* of the **Spirit** *Woman*. When a *woman* is in her *younger* years, she *ovulates* (produces eggs) and if they do not get *fertilized* by a male sperm, they're *flushed* out (with blood) and **die**.

But, if we are *fertilized*, they become a *fetus* in their **mothers** *womb* and are eventually *born*. Well, the **same** *thing* is *true* in the **spirit** realm only we (humans) are the *eggs* in our **Spirit** *Mother*. If we are *fertilized* by the Male's *sperm*, which is YHWH's *Spirit*, we become *fetus's* in our *Spirit* **Mother's** *womb*!

Then we're *born* **again** (from above) into **spirit** *bodies*! In fact, that's exactly *what* the *Hebrew* Messiah Yahshua was trying to tell *Nicodemus* about being "*born again*". (John 3) He said; "*That which is* ***born*** *of* ***flesh*** (us) *is* ***flesh***, *but that which is* ***born*** *of* ***Spirit*** *is* ***Spirit***". Being *born* of *Chokma*, is to literally be *born* **into** the **Spirit** *world* (like the wind) as **Spirit** *Children* of YHWH and Chokma!

If that understanding isn't enough, we find even more **eye-opening** *understanding* looking into the *meanings* of the *Hebrew* **letters** of **Her** *Name*. They are *Hei, Resh, Bet,* and *Hei.* Interestingly, the *first* and *last* letters (Hei) mean "**window**" and/or "*to* ***reveal***".

Considering Her many *admonitions* to "**listen to**" Her *words* and **instruction**, the letter "*Hei*" takes on **great** *meaning*. But *what* really *speaks* **volumes** is one of the **middle** *letters*. That letter is "*Bet*" which means "*suka*" "*tabernacle*" "*tent*" (small) "*dwelling*" and can also be *rendered* "**womb**"!

How interesting the letter *meaning* "*womb*" is right *there* in the *middle* of her *Name*! In the *celebration* of the *Feast* of **Tabernacles** the people were *instructed* to build *small* **temporary** *dwellings* called "*sukas*". These were *physical* **types** of *Choma's* **womb**.

There are at least *three* **prophecies** of a great *outpouring* of *YHWH*'s **Spirit** at the *beginning* of the *Millennium* (real fulfillment of Feast of Tabernacles). That means all those upon whom YHWH's Spirit is *poured*, are *now* **fertilized** *eggs* (fetuses).

Again, to be a *fetus*, we have to be **in** a **womb**. That *womb* is YHWH's *Wife*, our *Spirit* **Mother**. Then, after an apparent *50* **year** *gestation* **period**, we will then be *born* **of** *Spirit* into *their* **Spirit** *world* and *Family*; just what Yahshua told **Nicodemus** in **John** 3.

Chapter 41

HOW to SEE and OVERCOME our PRIDE

During my mid twenties, our minister gave a *sermon* on *pride*. I remember looking around room and thinking; "*I hope all you people are listening*"! Obviously, I myself had **no** *pride* or *problem* with it. Then our minister said something *strange*, which was we needed to *pray* that God would **show** *us* **our** *pride*. I thought to myself "*there's no point because I knew I didn't have* **any** *pride, or problem with it*". But, I thought I would *humor* the minister and *pray* **that** *prayer* anyway.

What a shock, to later have my *eyes* **opened** to the fact, I was not only *full* of *pride*, I was more like the "**king**" of *pride*, which I was completely *blind* too! That brings us to the big **question**; *why* was I *unable* to **see** my own **pride**? To *answer* that question, we need to *understand* **what** pride **is** and *where* it *originates*.

You may ask "*what does it matter*"? Why should we **care** or **worry** about *pride*? After all, we hear people telling family and others how "*proud*" they are of them, which seems like a **good** *thing*. We also hear about our *civic* and *national* **pride**. Are those things also *bad*? After all, they *seem* like *good* things, and are very much *encouraged*.

But, to *understand* **pride** (and its *source*) there really is only *one* book that **honestly** *addresses* it, the Bible. And considering we're told there *"pride comes before* (brings) *destruction"* (Prov. 16; 5&18) telling *loved* ones how *proud* we are of them is literally *pronouncing* a **curse** *upon* them. On top of that, we are also told *pride* is a **barrier** *between us* and *YHWH*. *"YHWH* **walks with** *the* **humble***"* (Isa.57:15) and *"resists* (shuns) *the proud"*!

Again, how can something **seemingly** *good*, bring *destruction* and *block* us from our Creator? Again, the only way to *answer* that question, is to understand the *source* of *pride* and **what** it *actually* is. As to the *source*, we have a chapter in the Bible book of **Job**, where a creature called *"Leviathan"* is *called* the *"king of the children of pride"*!

A close look at it's *descriptions*, we see it was *reptilian*, **immortal**, could **talk**, *fly*, had glowing *red* eyes. Not only that, it *breathed* **fire** and *smoke*! Actually, we could not find a more **perfect** *rendition* of the *proverbial* **dragon**! But, does the Bible tell us any *more* about *dragons*? Yes, it does, especially in **Revelation** 12.

Revelation 12 tells us of a *"war in heaven"* where a *leading* **angel** (arch-angel) *conscripted* a **third** of the *angels* to go to **war** *against* the *Creator* (YHWH). But, YHWH then sent His **chief** *angel* **Michael** to do *battle* against the *dragon* and its *cohorts*, which He *won*. The dragon was then *cast* to Earth and wound up in the *Garden* of **Eden** sporting a most **massive** *grudge*.

Actually, **Revelation** 12 is just *shedding* additional *details* on **Ezekiel**, 28 and 31, and **Isaiah** 14. They are all *different* renderings of a *beautiful* **creature** (angel) that became *vain* and **proud**, so much so, it **convinced** *itself* it *deserved* a **throne** with the Creator (or even above) and then was *laid* **low** in its attempts. (Is.14)

Jumping forward, and *meshing* all the *details*, we come to understand the "*Tree of the Knowledge of Good and Evil*" was this very **same** *creature* (*dragon*). After all, **Ezekiel** 31 shows us "*Trees*" are a *metaphor* for *powerful* **Spirit** *beings*. So, when Eve and Adam partook (embraced its way) of this *dragon* (serpent is a mistranslation) what they were really doing was *giving* that dragon *permission* to **infuse** *them* with "*its*" **spirit** *of* **pride**, which if we notice, was a **death** *sentence*. ("*You shall surely die*"- destruction)

The *opposite* side of this, is the **Tree** of **Life**. Remember, the Creator *admonishes* us He "*only **walks** with the **contrite** of heart*" (humble). Humility is the *opposite* of the **spirit** of *pride*, which nets us *life* (immortality) versus *death*. It was the *dragon* who *developed* the **spirit** of *pride* and **death** in the *first* place.

So now, our lives are all *about* the **same** *choice* Adam and Eve were *given* in the *Garden*; the "*Tree of the knowledge of good and evil*" (the *dragon* and *it's* **spirit** of **pride**) or the "*Tree of Life*" the Creator! We **must** *choose*, and will consequently be *given* our *choice*, **good** or *bad*!

Unfortunately, because Eve and Adam **opened** the *door* for the *dragon* to *fill* the descendants of Adam and Eve with *its* spirit of **death** (pride) by *choosing* the "*Tree of death*" (pride) we must first *recognize* that **spirit** of pride in us and **replace** it with the *Spirit* of **Life** (Humility). The **difficult** part of this is the *spirit* of **pride** is it's the *spirit* of the **liar**. Pride is *itself* a **lie**.

Pride *convinces* us we are all *manner* of **things** we are *not*; like how *generous*, **patient**, *loving*, **unselfish** etc. we are. It *hides* itself, but we can see its *fingerprints* everywhere in *our* **actions**. Every time we have an *evil* or **hurtful** *thought*, including *selfish* and/or *greedy* one, it's **evidence** of that *pride* **in** us.

Pride also *exposes* itself in our *attitudes* of *feeling* **superior**, or *more* **important** than others. Please understand, i'm not referring to the *different* **talents** we all have, but if those *talents* get us *believing* we are a **superior** *humans*, it's again, more *evidence* of *pride*. But, the most *difficult* part of *pride* is not just *seeing* it, but **rising** *above* (controlling) it. You see, *pride* is the *spirit* of *one* of the most *powerful* beings in the universe, and if we think we are *strong* enough to *defeat* it on our own, we are so *kidding* ourselves! In fact it's just more *conformation* of *pride*!

Bottom line: the only way to do *battle* again such a **powerful** *spirit* (and being) is to incorporate one **more** *powerful*. That *Spirit* of course, is the *Spirit* of our Creator (s) **humility**. But, the only *way* He is going to *imbue* us with **that** *power* is for us to fully **embrace** *Him* and His Torah of *Love*.

Only then can we *find* the *eyes* to **see** *pride* for *what* it really **is** and also find the *strength* to *control* it. Of course, that's also when we *find* **immortality**! (Tree of Life) As long as we're *dancing* to the tune of the **dragons** *spirit* of **pride**, we are on our *way* **down** (dying).

Chapter 42

Oh Hell!

Bible dictionaries, such as "*Strong's Exhaustive Concordance*" tells us *three* chief words (from the oldest texts) from which the **modern** *word* **"hell"** has been translated. The first is the *Hebrew* word "*sheol*" meaning "*grave*" or "*pit*" and secondly the Greek word "*hades*" (NT) which means "*place of the departed*" as well as "*grave*" or *underground*. There's also the **mythical** *tartarus*, supposedly a *part* of *hades*, basically *meaning* the **same** *thing*, but used only *once* in the NT.

And lastly, we have the Greek *transliteration* of the Hebrew word "*Hinnom*" or *Ge-Hinnom* (Greek *transliteration*). Ge-Hinnom was *a valley* just *outside* Jerusalem where the city *trash* was *dumped* and **burned**. In fact, *criminals,* **street** *people*, and those *without* family, were *burned* (upon death) *with* the *trash*. Of course, that fire was **always** *burning,* which is a *historical* fact very *influential* in developing *Dante's* (Christianity's) *concept* of *ever* **burning** "*hell*" fire.

The late Bible *historian* Earnest Martin, points out the word "*hell*" is simply an **old** *English* word for "*hole*"! In fact, for well over a *thousand* years "*hell*" was **a place** people **kept** their *potatoes* and *apples* during the *winter*. There's even a country named "*Hell-land*" which has been *anglicized* to the modern name "*Holland*". It was given that name because it's *below* sea level, or "*hell-land*"!

With those *definitions* in mind, let's address the ***white*** elephant in the room. How is it possible for Christianity, who *profess* to *believe* in a "*God*" of "***Mercy***" to *accept* people could be sent to a ***place*** of *torture*, not just for a *time*, but ***eternity***! And, for *committing* such *horrid* "***sins***" as ***not*** accepting Christianity's' *favorite* **Greek** god "*Jesus*"! Of course, that leaves one *wondering* about the millions (actually "*billions*") who *never* in *their* ***lives*** ever ***heard*** *that* ***name***, which actually didn't *exist* until after the 15th century CE!

That said, why on Earth would anyone *preach* and *expect* people to *accept* such a *grotesque* ***demagogue***? You would think any "*sane*" person would get as ***far*** *away* ***from*** such a *horrific* "***god***" as possible! In fact, such a *god* makes *dictators* such as *Lenin, Stalin, Hitler, Pol Pot* and others who ***tortured*** and ***slaughtered*** *millions*, look *like* ***saints***! I *gasp* in *amazement* to see the astonishing *lengths* Christian preachers will go to ***protect*** this ***twisted*** and ***hellish*** *belief* and the ***god*** *who* ***authored*** *it*!

The *truth* is; there's no *direct* scriptural *support* for such a *heinous* teaching. That fact *forces* those supporting it, to *resort* to *major* "***private*** *interpretation*"; like making the purely ***metaphoric*** language of "*parables*" such as *Lazarus and the* ***rich*** *man*, ***literal*** not to mention the *absurd* ***attempt*** to *justify* the "***Christian*** *hell*" using the "*immortal* ***maggots***" of **Mark** 9:46! ("*The worm does not die*")

Personally, I *refuse* to *accept* Christianity's *obscene* "***god*** *of* ***hell*** *fire*" and *choose* to *worship* a "***God*** *of mercy*" such as the ***one*** the scriptures *reveal* to us. In fact "***Mercy***" is *one* of His *Titles* as we see in **Psalms** 106:1.

We are told there in **Psalms**; "*Praise YHWH! Oh, give thanks to YHWH for He is* **good***! For* <u>*His* **mercy** *endures* **forever**</u>." (Not torture) What an *intrepid* statement considering Christianity's *conviction* He's the ***kind*** of God that ***tortures*** people for *eternity*! Again, how can *torturing* people ***for eternity*** in any *way, shape,* or *form* be *construed* as "***merciful***"?

In fact, according to the ***true*** *rendering* of scripture, YHWH's idea of *"death"* is simple *lights **out***, which is a ***trillion*** *times* more *merciful* than an *eternity* of **torture**! In fact ***"true loving mercy"*** is the whole *point* of YHWH's *plan* of *two* **resurrections**! He's the *Merciful* **God** of **second** *chances,* which everyone gets.

Another *problem* faced with Christianity's *teaching* of *"hell"* is with the ***sinless*** Messiah *going **there*** after He was *crucified.* We have a couple scriptures telling us He "*descended*"into the Earth and **led** the *captives* (in hell) out of *captivity.* (Ephesians 4:9) But, if the Christian *hell,* is *what* they claim, h*ow* is it a *perfect* (sinless) Messiah went *there* in the ***first*** *place*?

Notice what Yahshua told His disciples in **Matthew** 12:40, the only ***"sign"*** He would *give* them was He would be *"three days and nights in the heart of the Earth."* Isn't the *"heart of the Earth"* where *"hell"* is supposed to be? Again, in **Ephesians** 4:9 we find the *author* commenting on Yahshua's *leading* or having "*led **captivity** captive*" after *"first **descending** into **the lower parts** of the Earth?"* Again *"hell"*?

The answer to this *seemingly* **major** *problem,* that the *sinless* Hebrew Messiah went to *"hell"* is so *simple* when we *understand "hell"* or *"hades"* simply means *"grave"* or **in** the *ground,* which is the *tomb* where He *spent* **three** *days* and *nights.*

The reference to "*leading **captivity** captive*" is Yahshua's *leading* the **resurrection** of the *saints* (if old) in **Matthew** 27:52-53 out of their **imprisonment** of *death.* They were being *held "captive"* by *"**death**"* which was **overcome** by Yahshua's *death* and **resurrection**! Death could no longer *hold* them *captive* and they *rose* from their *"graves"* (not Dante's hell)!

One last thought; since virtually *all* religions, who *believe* in *"hell"* as a place of **torture**, *agree* on only **one** *aspect* of *hell*, that it's a *separation* from the Creator. But, if *"God"* is **omnipresent**, as Christianity **also** *teaches*, such a *separation* would be **impossible**; well, *impossible* except for under **one** *condition*; **literal** *death*! (Lights out) But then, that's what the scriptures on *death* (and hell) actually teach!

The bottom line; to not **reap** *death* (from the tree of the knowledge of good and evil *"Heylel"*) we need only *embrace* the *"Tree* of **Life"**. That would be our Creator's and their Torah *instructions* for **loving** *behavior*! Once we do that, every **tiny** *detail* of our lives will be taken care of, which *removes* any *reason* for *fretting* and/or *worrying*! What an amazing life *awaits* us if we **choose** *it*!

Chapter 43

Was the Hebrew Messiah Really Named "Jesus"?

This is a *subject* (truth) that *should* be a **no-brainer**, but has been *hidden* right in **front** of our *faces;* that is, was the **Hebrew** Messiah *named* or *called* Jesus? Besides "*Paul*" (Christianies' favorite apostle) *Jesus* is the most *well* **known** and used *name* in Christian circles, but is it the **correct** *name,* or a **replacement** of the *original?*

Unfortunately, most people simply *accept* the *name Jesus* **without** *question* and/or *research.* But the *origin* of the *name* **Jesus** is beyond *shocking* to the *average* Christian or Mormon, considering that *name* **didn't** *exist* before the 18th century CE!

As shocking as that *sounds,* **proof** is *abundant.* One proof inadvertently stumbled upon (a fluke) was *obtaining* a copy of the *first* **King** *James* Bible (1611) translation. What a shock to *discover* the most *famous* and *beloved* name in Christianity is *missing!* Yes, that's *right,* the name "*Jesus*" is **not** *found* in the **first** *King James* **translation**! Well, that's beyond shocking for the **average** *Christian,* but one need only *go* on *line* or to a library and *find* a 1611 King James *translation* to *see* for yourself the *Messiah's* Name there is "*Iesus*". (E-sus)

Most already *aware* of this, simply shrug *Iesus* off as being the **same name** as *Jesus*; only the *modern* **English** pronunciation. That may be *technically* true, but still leaves the *white-elephant-in-the-room* **problem** of the fact *Iesus* is a **Greek** *title* meaning "*savior*" and **not** a *name* at all. With that in *mind*, did the *well* **respected** (by the Pharisees) *Jewish* family, who went *into* the temple *regularly*, really *give* their son a **Greek** (Hellenist) *name* and/or *title*?

Considering Greeks were **not** *allowed* in or **anywhere** *near* the Temple and the Pharisees would *not* even *walk* on the *same* side of the street as a *Greek*; something's *very* **wrong** with this *picture*! It's like saying 1 plus 2 equals 5. It just doesn't add up! Obviously, *something* happened!

On top of the *problem* of the **Hebrew** *Messiah* supposedly having a **Greek** *name*, is the *teaching* "*God*" (His Father) is also a *name*, with "*The Lord*" (Baal-in Hebrew) His *title*! Considering that, who in their *right* mind can possibly and *honestly* believe it's *ok* for us "*nothing*" humans (in comparison) to "**change**" the *Name* of the Creator and/or His *first-born* Son? What *arrogant* **hubris**!

Considering we humans are called "*less than nothing*" in **Isaiah** 40:17, where on Earth do **we** *think* we have the *authority* to so *arrogantly* and blatantly *disrespect* our Creator by calling *Him* and His *first-born* **Son** by **whatever** *name* we feel, especially **pagan** ones? That's especially *absurd* considering **Revelation** 13:8 tells us His *coming* and *death* were *established* from **before** the *foundation* of the world! How can we possibly think His *Name's* **negotiable**.

Besides, most *names* in ancient times (especially *names* **given** by YHWH) were **instructive** and/or *prophetic*. Well, it shouldn't be surprising considering all the other *nonsense* Christians have been fed, such as celebrating the "*birthday*" of this *Jesus* on Dec.25 "*Christmas*". In fact, what a shock to look into the etymology of "*Christmas*" to find it literally means "*To **kill** the **Christ***" (Messiah)!

Another *glaring problem* is, in Greek *culture* (and most cultures-even ancient Israel) to *honor* someone, you would **attach** all or *part* of the name of your *favorite* god to their name. In Greece (and much of Rome) the most *favored* god was Zeus. To *honor* someone, they would then *attach* the last *two* letters of *Zeus* (us) to the name. That's the **actual** *reason* so many names in Greek *end* in *"us"* they're names *dedicated* to **Zeus**; Grecian's *favorite* **"anointed one"** (Christos-Christ).

The Greeks certainly weren't the *only* or *first* ones *dedicating* people and places to their *favorite* **pagan god.** In fact we find the ancient Israelites doing the **same** *thing* in the times of the kings by *attaching* "*Baal*" (the Lord) to many of their *names* and *towns*! (Nothing new under the sun) Again, how can it be *ok* to *rename* the **Hebrew** *Messiah* with a *name* or title **dedicated** to the **pagan god Zeus**?

Well, if you've concluded *changing* the Name the *Creator* (YHWH) **gave** His first-born Son *"before the foundation of the world"* (Rev. 13:8) especially a *gentile* name *dedicated* to a **pagan** god, there's no point of reading further. That would make you one of those whose *mind* is "**made up**" and doesn't want to be "*confused* **by the facts**" (Truth).

Also, that *position* shows no *love* or *respect* for our Creator *YHWH* either! On the other hand, if you care **why** and *how* YHWH's first-born Son's Name was *changed* to a gentile **Greek** name **dedicated** to a *pagan* god (title actually) just read on.

You see, the *truth* is **in** the true *original* Hebrew name "*Yahshua*" which means "*YHWH*" (Yahshua's Father) "*is **Savior***". (Isa. 43:3&11) For the demon spirits to *rob* us of one of the *greatest* **truths** of **all** time, all they had do was to *influence* (muse) the translators to *change* the Messiah's true **Hebrew** *Name* which again, *means* "**YHWH is salvation**" to the generic **Greek** (*Zeus dedicated*) name *meaning* "**savior**" *Iesus*! Right there is a **monstrous** *deviation* **from** Truth!

As for *how* Yahshua's Name was *changed* to the Greek *Iesus*, it's actually quite *easy* to understand. You see, the *excuse* the Pharisees used to *hang* Yahshua on the tree was the *charge* of **blasphemy**. All the way back to Egypt (and many cultures in-between) you will find the *penalty* for *blasphemy* was not only *death,* but the "**blotting** *out*" of one's *name*. That practice of *blotting* **out** names was still being *practiced* in the first century by the *Pharisees* and apparently the *Romans* as well.

What **blotting** *out* meant was that anyone *caught saying* (or writing) the Name of the one whose *name* was **blotted** *out,* would *receive* the **same** *fate*; in this case, *crucifixion*. So, naturally, the *writers* of the New Testament (**university** *educated* Greek scholars—not Yahshua or His twelve Apostles) dared not use the **blotted** *out* Name of Yahshua and *replaced* it with the **generic** *Greek* **word** for *savior* "**Iesus**". Due to that, *who* and **what** the *Savior* really **is** and **what** *salvation* is as well, became lost!

On the other hand, we can be sure, the *twelve* **true** *apostles*, being filled with YHWH's Spirit of "*truth*" and "**power**" used the **true** *Name!* It was the Apostle Paul who **first** *used* the **substitute** names and *those* Greek *scholars*, who had the **oral** *teachings* of the other 12 Apostles penned *later* (the latter half of the first century) *followed* his lead. Obviously, they were too *afraid* to use the **true** *name* either and the *substitute* stuck.

Chapter 44

The Problem With the Immortal Soul

It's an interesting *fact* that **every** *major* **religion** in the world all *agree* on only **one** *thing*; the **immortal** *soul*. That's rather strange considering they all *agree* on virtually *nothing* else. We'll get to the *origin* of **that** *belief* later in this paper, but first, let's look at some of the **obvious** *problems* with that **universal** *immortal* **soul** *tradition*.

There's a variety of *concepts* ranging from the idea **physical** *humans* were originally *created* **spirit,** to humans being *created* **physical** and then **becoming** *spirit* again. That said, let's examine being created **spirit** (or as angels) and then **becoming** *physical*. This is a *belief* of many **native** *Americans* as well as a few of the *Christian* denominations.

Of course, the most obvious *problem* that leaves one *scratching* their *head,* is **why** *become* **physical** after being created *spirit?* That seems rather *backwards* and redundant! If *created* **spirit,** why not *simply* **stay** *spirit?* Isn't being *spirit* and going to heaven the **ultimate** *goal* to be *attained* in life?

That said, some say the *reason* for *spirits* becoming *physical* is to *learn* **lessons** that can only be *learned* by *becoming* **mortal.** But, if that's true, why not be created *physical* **first** and **then** *become* **spirit** after *learning* whatever *lessons* **needing** to be *learned?* It seems *someone* is certainly getting the *cart* **before** the *horse.* Becoming *physical* after already having the **ultimate** spirit *existence,* seems *redundant* at best.

That *begs* another *question*, why would a **spirit** *being* be willing to *give* **up** being *spirit* (immortal) to become *mortal* in the *first* place? Why on Earth would a *spirit* **choose** to become *flesh* and have to deal with **mortal** *issues* such as *sickness* and *aging,* etc.? Or, maybe the *first* created *spirit* beings are *forced* to become *physical* by a **higher** *power;* like a *punishment* for **bad** *behavior*? Of course, that eliminates *free-**moral-**agency*! But, one thing's for sure, the *Bible* **doesn't** *teach* **any** of *that*!

The Bible *teaches* those created *spirit* (angels) **stay** *spirit*. It also *teaches* that *mortal* (physical) people do **not** *become* **spirit** *when* they *die*. In fact, the scriptures tell us; "*The dead know nothing at all*". (Ecc. 9:5) In fact, the *theme* of the entire Bible is *life* **versus** *death*! It *nowhere* teaches we *graduate* and simply *change* **places** when we *die*!

Since the Bible doesn't teach *any* of **those** *concepts*, just **where** do they *originate*? Were they simply *invented* by someone along the *line* until *finally* **accepted** as *truth*? One *truth* I've learned in all my years, is **nothing** *comes* **from** *nowhere*, or *us*! Everything we *know* and *believe* was **given** to *us* by *someone*. (Or something) In fact, according to a once *Biblical* book, The **Book** of **Enoch**, *all* **knowledge** was (is) given by the **spirit** *realm*, both *good* and *evil*.

In fact, in the *Garden* of *Eden*, the *evil* tree was called; "*The tree of the* **knowledge** *of* **good** *and* **evil**". Of course "*tree*" there is a *metaphor* for an **angelic** *being*. That being is called there; "*The* **craftiest** *of all the* **beasts** *of the field*". Further in-depth study shows that *crafty* **creature** was an *actual* **dragon**! But, one thing's for sure, virtually *all* human *knowledge*, both *good* and *evil*, come from **this** *creature* and its *co-horts*!

In fact, according to legend, *Zeus* one of the dragon's *cohorts*, supposedly *spawned 9 nymphs* that were sent out *into* humanity to *teach*. They are to this day called "*muses*" the ones that *supposedly* **inspire** *writers*!

At any rate, the Garden of Eden is exactly where the *concept* of the **immortal** soul **originated**. When *confronted* by the *beast*, Eve told the *dragon* the Creator had told them to **not** partake of its *fruit* "*lest they die*"!

But how interesting the dragons *reply*! It told Eve; "*You will **not** surly die, but be **like** the **gods**"*. Of course, the "**gods**" *referred* to *here* are the **immortal** *angelic* **watchers** (Guardian angels) who are also the **source** of all the worlds' *religions*. That's the reason they all *embrace* that *immortal* **soul** lie! By *convincing* humanity we simply *change* **places** when we (don't) *die*, **death** *ceases* to be a *terrible* thing; unless one goes to the proverbial "*hell*" instead. Sadly, though, *hell* would be a **necessary** *evil* if one actually *possesses* an *immortal* soul!

You see, the *Creator* (YHWH) is called the *God* of **mercy** who *sits* on the **mercy** seat. How does *torturing* someone for *eternity*, for anything, let alone for simply *never* **hearing** the *name* "**Jesus**" as many churches teach, *fit* **anywhere** near the *concept* of **mercy**? Well, it doesn't!

But, if *death* does not mean literal **lights** *out* (no consciousness) then this **torturous** *hell* becomes a *necessary* **evil** to *deter* **bad** *behavior*!

If **death** *actually* means *dead*, the Christian **hell** becomes *completely* **redundant**! Besides, let's be honest; if we go to *heaven* when we *die*, then wouldn't **killing** *someone* be doing *them* a *huge* **favor**? After all, it would be *freeing* them from the *confines* of this *physical* and very *often* **painful** *existence*. But, if we go to *heaven* when we *die*, that would mean *murder* is a **good** *thing*, right! Hmmm?

That's how *absurd* the *idea* of an **immortal** *soul*, and going to *heaven* when we *die*, is! But, that's exactly what the *evil* ones that **hate** *humanity* want us to *believe*! If *automatically* go to *heaven* when we **die**, *who* **needs** a *God* to *resurrect* us to **spirit** *life*?

Again, that **belief** *system* basically **eliminates** the **need** for a *god*! But, if becoming spirit (immortal) is *contingent* upon **righteous** *behavior*, suddenly it all begins to make **real** *sense*, unlike the **worlds** *religions'* **nonsensical** *teachings*!

Chapter 45

Immanuel *"God with us"*

In **Matthew** 1 we find a very interesting *scripture* that doesn't seem to *fit* with the *common* Christian *teachings*. We find in verses 20-23, where an *Angel* came to Joseph in a *dream* and told him *not* to be *afraid* to take Mary for his wife because that which was *conceived* in her was **of** the *Creator's* **Spirit**. But, *what* is really strange is verse 22-23 where it states; "*Now all this was done that it might be fulfilled which was spoken by God* (YHWH) *through the prophet, saying:* **"Behold, a virgin shall be with child and bear a Son, and they shall call His name Immanuel,** *which is translated "God with us"*.

Verse 23 tells us they would *call* his name "*Immanuel*" but, how many Christian *denominations* call the *Hebrew* **Messiah** *Immanuel*? Are there any? If so, there are very *few*! How is it everyone instead *calls* Him *Jesus*? Other than this scripture, we **don't** find Him being called *Immanuel* **anywhere** in the New Testament. Why is that, when **Matthew** 1:23 seems to be such a clear *prophecy* of what the Messiah's *Name* would *be* when He was born? All we can say is "*Houston, we have a* **problem**"!

One *common* **explanation** to *justify* that *conundrum* is He **was** *God* and after His *birth, God* literally was *with* them. In fact, that's one of the scriptures supposedly *proving* the *first* **century** *Messiah* was in fact *"God"*. But, that still doesn't *explain* how He *came* to **acquire** the Name *"Jesus"* instead.

The best way to *resolve* such a *conundrum* is to go as far *back* as possible to see *what* we can *uncover*. After all, the *oldest* scriptures are always the *closest* to the *truth*.

That said, we notice verse 23 of **Matthew** 1, is in *italics*, which means it's a *quote* from a *different* book and was later *inserted* into this text. Verse 22 gives us a clue as to where that *quote* came *from* with the words "*Now all this was done that it might be **fulfilled** which was **spoken** by **God*** (YHWH) *through the prophet*".

So, *what* prophet *prophesied* the Messiah's Name would be *"Immanuel"*? Well, most bibles have that scripture in the margin, which is **Isaiah** 7. So, naturally, the place to go to hopefully *discover* the truth is **Isaiah** 7. Turning there, we find that *prophecy* in verse 14, where it states; "*Therefore YHWH* (miss-translated *"the Lord"*) *Himself will* **give** **you** (King Ahaz) *a sign:*

The sign given King Ahaz then was; *Behold, the **virgin** shall conceive and bear a **son** and shall call his name **Immanuel**"* which seems quite *straight* forward, but we need to dig a little *deeper*. First of all, the Hebrew word *"virgin"* also means *"maiden"*. So, *how* can we be sure *"virgin"* is the **correct** translation?

Well, if we go *back* a few verses, we find the **one** for whom the *sign* was *intended,* and it was **not** *Joseph*! The *context* of this *prophecy* is a *problem* King **Ahaz** of *Judah* was *experiencing*. He was being squeezed between *Israel* (the northern tribes) and the *Assyrians*. (About to be attacked) He then *inquired* of the prophet *Isaiah* for *advise* and/or *help* from YHWH.

YHWH, through *Isaiah,* told Ahaz all would be well, Ahaz still had *doubts.* YHWH then told him if he would not *believe* Judah would be *delivered,* it would ***not*** happen. (V.9) He then told Ahaz to ask for a "***sign***" to *prove* ***what*** He had *told* him was *true.* Unfortunately, Ahaz thought ***asking*** for a *sign* would be *testing* YHWH and *refused.* So, YHWH said He would give Ahaz a *sign* anyway. That's when that ***sign*** *quoted* in **Matthew** 1, was given.

YHWH went on to *tell* Ahaz in verse 16, that *before* the *child* (born of a young maiden) was old enough to *choose between* ***good*** and *evil,* the *two* ***kings*** of whom Ahaz was *afraid,* would be ***dethroned*** and that the ***new*** king of Assyria would be focusing upon *Israel* and ***not*** *Judah.* Of course, that's exactly *what* happened. The *northern* tribes of Israel were subsequently *conquered* by Assyria a couple years later and taken *captive,* but *Judah* was *spared.*

Bottom line; ***that*** *prophecy* had ***nothing*** what-so-ever to *do* with the ***first*** century *Messiah* and was *only* given for *Ahaz,* king of *Judah* (about the 11th century BCE). Apparently, some *scribe* writing or *copying* the book of **Matthew,** *believed* the *prophecy* of **Isaiah** 14:7 where "*maiden*" was *miss- translated* "*virgin*" (in the Septuagint) had to be about the ***immaculate*** conception and *birth* of the ***Hebrew*** *Messiah,* which is completely *ridiculous* when the context of **Isaiah** 14 is fully read.

Chapter 46

Jacob's Stargate!

In **Genesis** we find a couple very *strange* stories (accounts) involving *Jacob*. (Father of the Israelites) The first is a *night **vision*** of a *ladder **to** heaven* with angels *ascending* and *descending* in chapter 28 (v.12-17). This is a very ***strange** vision* which begs the *question*; why was Jacob *having* this ***ladder** vision*? Obviously, someone was ***showing** him **something***, but *what*; and again, *why*? Was it God feeling *sorry* for Jacob considering he was using a *rock* (stone of Scone?) for a *pillow*? Personally I don't know how anyone could sleep with a ***stone*** for a *pillow*? But that's just me!

With all the *ministers* and preachers I've heard talk about *Jacobs **vision***, I can't remember any of them *coming **to*** any *meaningful* conclusions other than it was God *promising* Jacob He would ***bless** all* peoples ***through** him* and his *offspring*. That conclusion *seems* obvious, but again, what's the point of Jacob ***seeing*** the *ladder*?

Besides, *why* do the *angels **need*** a *ladder* to get *up* to *heaven* or *down* to Earth; don't they have the *ability* to ***fly***? I suppose we can conclude the *ladder* is simply a *metaphor* for the *way* angels *access* Earth from *Heaven* and vice-versa, but it sure ***doesn't** fit* with anything else we *find* in the Bible or with *traditional* teachings.

Whatever the *true explanation*, it's interesting to read in the **Book of Enoch,** how 200 angels (watchers) *descended* (from heaven?) and *procreated* with humanity. The Bible only *briefly* references *this* event in **Genesis** 6, but these beings set *themselves* up as **gods** and **kings** (and teachers) to *rule* the world. (Before the flood)

That in mind, was Jacob's *night* **vision** of the angels *ascending* and **descending** showing him the *watchers* **ability** to *come* and **go** from the *place* or *dimension* they *live* (heaven)? Was the *place* Jacob slept and had his *vision* a *literal* **portal** (star-gate) from where the *watcher* (angels) *descend* and *ascend* from Earth, like Mt. *Hermon*? (Where the Watchers descended)

Interestingly, the Book of Enoch (chap.) details how the Creator *ordered* His **righteous** Watchers to arrest and *imprison* those 200 and then *flood* the world to **drown** all their **nephilim** *offspring*. According to **Genesis** 6;9, apparently only *Noah* and his *sons* were **genetically** *uncorrupted* by those *watcher* **animals**.

We can be sure YHWH is *not* looking for **angel** (animal) *human* **highbred** *children*. No doubt, YHWH wants His children's to have the *pure* DNA He gave *Adam* and Eve. That all makes sense except for the fact the *nephlim* (giants and *half* **animal** highbreds) show up in Canaan *after* the flood. In fact, the Bible lists about a half dozen **Canaanite** *tribes* of **giants** (or mingled giants).

Obviously, **more** *watchers* came through a *portal* of some sort to once **again** *procreate* with humanity after the flood. With that in mind, can there be any doubt why YHWH *instructed* Israel to *destroy* them as YHWH did when He sent the **global** *flood* a *thousand* years before?

Getting back to Jacobs *vision,* it was obviously a *picture* of YHWH's **watchers** (angels) *coming* and *going* from Heaven (YHWH's realm) to Earth, which begs another question; was the *reason* for *showing* Jacob the *vision* because his *descendants* would be *given* that *land* where the **watchers** had *returned* and would **again** need *eradicating?*

Was the **ladder** *vision* as simple as *showing* Jacob **what** was *coming* so he could *educate* his *sons* and *grandsons?* We may never know, for sure, but it's something to consider. With that in mind, another strange event occurred with Jacob; his **wrestling** *match* with the *angel.*

According to the *account,* Jacob *believed* **this** *being* to be an *angel* of *YHWH,* but was it? In that account, Jacob *demands* a *blessing* from the *angel* and *wrestles* with him *all* night for it. Interestlngly,

Ephesians 6:12 tells us "*We wrestle not against flesh and blood but principalities—wicked spirits in heavenly places*"! So, instead of *blessing* Jacob, the angel *announced* that *dawn* was nigh and that *it* **had** *to* **leave.** But Jacob *refused* to let it go, so the angel *dislocated* his **hip.** So much for the *blessing*!?

This episode raises even more interesting and *obvious* questions. Why did *this* **angel** *have* to *leave* **before** *daylight* **came?** Did it simply not want to be *seen* by *anyone* else, or was it some kind of **creature** of the **night** *unable* to **tolerate** the *light* of *day* (like a vampire)?

Again, we may never know, but the question remains as to *why* this being came to Jacob in the *first* place. What were its intentions? Obviously, it *didn't* come to *bless* Jacob as **Jacob** *wanted;* unless *having* **his** *hip* **displaced** was a *blessing*?! (Apparently permanent displacement)

Maybe, this *angel's* actual *purpose* for *coming,* was to *bestow* a **new** *name* on *Jacob,* considering that's *exactly* **what** it *did?* With that in mind, how bizarre to *look* at the *new* **name** Jacob was *given.*

But before *looking* at that *name*, we must *keep* in mind "*Jacob*" meant **supplanter**, or *deceiver*. Of course, he fully lived up to **his** name after *deceiving* his father for *Esau's* **blessing** and the way he *manipulated* his uncle *Laban*! But then, Laban was not exactly a *pillar* of **virtue** *himself!*

Well, I like you, probably was *taught* Israel was a **good** *name*, but is it? We were told (in the account) it *means* "*he who wrestles with el*" (elohim). According to Unger's Bible *dictionary* (false god section) *el-elohim* was the *name* of the *father* **god** of the *Canaanites*! Wow, what a *revelation* that is!

What is even more shocking is to see the **three** names picked up in the *name* "**Israel**"! The first is "**Is**" which is the short *version* of the goddess "**Isis**" also known as "**Ashera**" *Astarte, Ishtar* (Easter) one of the chief **pagan** *deities* the Israelites were *continually* getting *into* **trouble** *for* **worshipping** in the phalic **groves** *built* in her *honor*.

The *second* name *encapsulated* in the name *Israel is* "**Ra**"! Ra (Ray) was a *pagan* **nephilim** *deity* of Egypt! He had a **human** *body* with a **Jackals'** *head!* He was one of the more well-known *rulers* and *gods* of *Eqypt!*

Last, but not least, was the *one* mentioned *first;* "**EL**". Again, *el-elohim* was the **father** *god* of the *Canaanites*. Archeologists have **unearthed** *statues* of that Canaanite *god* with his name "*el-elohim*" *inscribed!* I personally saw a *picture* of one in a copy of Biblical Archeology Magazine!

This may all sound nonsensical and a bit of a stretch, but we must keep one fact in *mind*. *YHWH* **uses** *names* as *prophecies* all through scripture like *Methuselah*, which was a **prophecy** of the *flood;* "*When I die, it will come*" which is *exactly* **what** *happened!* *Is-ra-el* was quite literally *a* **prophecy** of *three* of the *chief* **pagan** *gods* the *descendants* of Jacob would "*contend with*" (*wrestle* and *worship*)!

Chapter 47

Killer Guilt

There's an *entity* causing *major **trouble*** on our planet but *talked* about very *little* (except in *law* circles). That is the *issue* of **guilt**. Interestingly, very few are ever *willing **to** admit **any** guilt*, regardless of how *guilty* they are! In fact, very few ending up in **prison** *believe* they are *guilty*. The overarching *question* is "*why*"? Why is **admitting** our *guilt*, even when *obvious*, so **difficult**? Just *what* is the *source* of **that** *denial*?

Unfortunately, most never give the *issue* a second thought, let alone *any* real *amount* of *reflection*. That's a *sad **truth***, but in my *observations*, it's *one* of the most **destructive** *forces* in *every* society. Guilt is like a **living** *creature* that **hides** in *all* of us to one degree or another, but *never **goes** away* unless we make a *conscience* effort to eradicate it.

One *thing* really *opening* my mind to *guilt* was *seeing* a **new** *age* type **holistic** doctor, who had **combined** *Western* and *Eastern* **medical** *practices* to *attain* a shocking *new* level of understanding and **skill**. She had literally *discovered* a way to *tap **into*** the **sub-conscience** *mind*, simply with *touch*. And no, it was **not** *occult* or **magic**. You see, our *sub- conscience* mind **controls** the **mechanical** *aspects* of our bodies, such as *heartbeat* and *breathing*, along with a *thousand **other*** *duties*. It utilizes a *minute **flow*** of *electricity* to stay in *communication* with **all** *parts* of our bodies. (Like 7 hertz)

That *electrical **current** courses* all *though* our *bodies,* ***flowing*** *in* and *out* on an unseen *path.* She *explained* that when something *disrupts* that *electrical **flow**, communication* with the sub-*conscience* is *interrupted* and the mind *no **longer** knows* what's *happening.* Obviously it cannot ***repair*** a *problem* (like cancer) it does not ***know** about,* leaving the cancer to *metastasize* until it *kills* the ***whole** body.*

It was the *Chinese* that supposedly first *discovered* this shocking *truth* and ***learned*** to ***hot-wire*** *peoples **sub-conscience** minds* using *acupuncture.* Using that *method,* they could *re-**establish** communication* and *instruct* the body to go and *repair* the *problem.* The amazing *thing* is, this doctor *learned* how to *tap* into the *sub-conscience* just using ***touch.***

In fact, in *doing **it*** with me, she was able to *tell* me *everything* about myself, even *childhood* things I ***never** told **anyone**!* She explained how our sub-conscience *records* every *tiny **detail*** of our lives, even in the *womb!* One of the things she *addressed* was my *severe **allergy*** to *cats* which I also didn't tell her I *had.*

My cat *allergy* made no sense considering I grew up with as many as *30* cats on the farm. What she *explained* next was so bizarre that I *refused* to *believe* it, but eventually decided to *give* her the *benefit* of the doubt. She told me I had a ***traumatic** experience* with a cat, for which my sub- *conscience* was *punishing* me, *believing* me *guilty.* She said that our sub- conscience *stores* every ***trauma*** we *experience* until we are able ***deal*** with *it* with our ***conscience*** mind.

Well, after digging into my childhood, I remembered an *incident* where I was *milking* a cow and was *squirting* some juvenile *kittens* with milk. Suddenly the cow shifted her weight and *stepped* on the *head* of one of the kitties. Being a 70 lb little boy, it took me, what seemed to be *forever* to get the cow to *shift* her *weight,* but it was too late. Technically, the death of that kitty was *not* my fault, but my sub-conscience would none-the-less *remind* me of my *guilt* every time I went *near cats.*

So, the doctor told me, *what* I needed to do is **convince** my *sub-conscience* it was *not* my fault. She said it would take some time, which it did, and to my amazement, the *allergy* completely *disappeared!*

Another *problem* I had to deal with, starting when I was a little *boy*, was not being able to fall *sleep*. After going to this *holistic* doctor, and now in my mid thirties, I remembered being *molested* by one of the *farm* hands.

It finally *sank **in*** that it was my sub-conscience that would ***not** allow* me to go to *sleep*, because that apparently was when I was *molested!* He left for a couple year and upon *returning* tried to do it *again*. Being a little older by this time I went *crazy*. He *quit* and *left*, but that residual *guilt* unfortunately, made my life a *nightmare* by not being able to sleep.

This gets me to the subject of this *essay*. Most people are *plagued* with *guilt* which they, many times, are simpley ***not** aware* of, as I wasn't! How many people were *molested* as *babies* and young children, with **no** *memory* of it, but carry around *myriads* of **negative** *ramifications*. Having **guilt** *issues* we are not aware of is **one** thing, but what about those we **are** *aware* of? Are we to *accept* that *guilt* we are **aware** *of* has no *negative* consequences?

If the **unknown** *guilt* **causes** such *problems*, how can **known** *guilt* cause any less? Well, the *truth* is, it *does*. So, obviously the *simplest* **solution** is to **unload** that *guilt*.

It's simple if the *guilt* we *harbor* is the *mistreatment* of someone. All we need to do is *apologize!* Unfortunately, in most cases we **lie** to *ourselves* about **being** *guilty* and try to *ignore* and/or *forget* the *indiscretion*. But, our *sub-conscience* certainly *does* **not** *forget!*

We even have *Biblical* **instructions** on this *issue*. We are told in **Matthew** 18 to go to that person and *confess*, that is **apologize**, or *attempt* to *convince* the *other* side to *apologize*. Being **unwilling** to *apologize* usually means the *end* of the *relationship*. How many *children* and *parents*, **siblings**, and *friends* become *lifelong* **enemies** simply because the **guilty** *party* is *unwilling* (or unable) to *talk* and/ or *apologize*?

The *answer* to all this is simple! It is a very **little** *understood* thing called *pride*! We are told "*pride goes before destruction*". But where does **pride** *originate*? We find the answer in **Ezekiel** 28, where this *perfectly* **created** *creature* (dragon) became *vain* and *proud* and *launched* a **war** against the Creator (Isaiah 14 & Revelation 12) and lost.

It was the one that was *metaphorically* called "*The tree of the knowledge of good and evil*" in the *Garden* of *Eden*, By *partaking* of **that** *tree* (its way of living) that creature was *allowed* to *fill* **all humanity** with *its* **spirit**, which is *pride*. And, of course, that *pride* is an **insane** *spirit* which leads to all kinds of *relationship* and *health* **problems**, leading ultimately to *death*!

Again, in *unloading* our **destructive** *guilt*, that *cannot* be done *physically* (like with a person) we are told we can go *directly* to our Creator to *ask* for *forgiveness*, which our Creator tells us He is *faithful* to *give*, that is, **if** our *repentance* is *honest*!

Can you *imagine* a world where *everyone* **treats** *others* with **respect** and *honor* and are *quick* to *apologize* for inadvertent **wrongs** *committed*? What a world it will be! In fact, in order to be in our Creator's family, that's *what* is **required** of us. Our Creator's will *not* and *cannot* **sentence** their *children* to an *eternity* of *bickering*, **fighting** and general *misery*! They simply will not do it! We must *learn* to show *honor* and **respect** here or *return* to the *dirt* from *whence* we *came*!

Chapter 48

A Lot Like Now

In ancient times, there *existed* **two** *cities* in a *lush* area of what is *now* the **dead** sea. It seems those *cities* had become so *degenerate* and **immoral**, the Creator *decided* they *needed* to be **destroyed**. The problem was, in Sodom lived the *nephew* of the most *righteous* in the land. So, the Creator sent His *Angel* to this *righteous* man, **Abraham** to **warn** him of the *impending* **doom** of those *cities*.

But, Abraham *begged* the Angel to *spare* them in *spite* of their **evil** *behavior* because there just had to be *some* **righteous** *people* there. Shockingly, the angel of YHWH *agreed* if even *50* **righteous** could be *found*, the cities would be *spared*. But Abraham continued to *argue* for the *sparing* of the *city* if only *45* could be *found,* to which the Angel also *agreed*. Abraham continued to *bargain* with Him until He agreed to **spare** *Sodom* and Gomorrah for the sake of *only* **ten** *righteous*!

But alas, *not* even **ten** *righteous* could be *found*. In fact, the only **one** considered **righteous** *enough* to *save* was Abraham's *nephew* **Lot** and his *family*. So YHWH sent *two* angels to Sodom to **see** *Lot,* who being one the *elders* of the city, was found *sitting* at the *gate*. Before the angels even had a chance to *tell* Lot **why** they were *there,* he *insisted* they come to **his** *house* for an *evening* **feast** and to *spend* the **night**.

Word got around to the towns *people* who then *came* and *demanded* Lot turn the *men **out** to **them**,* that is, to *sodomize.* In fact, that's *where* we get the word "*sodomy*" which our nation is *quickly **becoming**.* According to the story, *Lot* even *offered* the *men* his ***virgin** daughters* which the *men* of the town *refused!* We are utterly *shocked* by such *behavior,* but as a nation, how *different* are we ***now,** really?*

How did those people *become* so *degenerate* as to ***think*** sodomy, or ***homosexual*** *behavior* (rape, as well as homosexual marriage) was an ***acceptable*** *behavior?* How shocking how the men of *those* cities had become so *decadent* they were not even interested in Lot's *virgin* daughters!

In fact, we've gone a couple steps further in the *promotion* of ***women*** having *sex* with *women* as well! In fact, our present ***degenerate*** *condition* would have been absolutely *unbelievable* and ***unacceptable*** just 50 years ago!

It's gotten so bad, those standing *against* such ***irreverent*** *behavior* have become the *perceived **evil** ones*!? Well, understanding how they *degenerated* to such a degree back then, we can understand how we in this *modern* age have *followed* the ***same*** *pattern!* There is *nothing **new** under* the sun as *spoke* the *wise* man!

Of course, along with the modern *promotion* of such *illogical **bizarre** behavior* (common sense with the "*plumbing*" clearly showing the truth) has come the *slaughter* of well *over* a *billion babies!* How on Earth, could we *sink* so ***low?*** In fact, the *applauded murdering* of our babies is apparently even worse than the ***immoral*** *sexual behavior* in the eyes of our Creators. We find that *truth* brought out in the total *destruction* of ancient *Egypt.* (And Jerusalem)

In the *ancient* writings, we find very **little** *evidence* of *irreverent* **sexual** *behavior*, in Egypt, but yet they were almost completely *obliterated* with the *plagues* of **Exodus**. We find the *reason* in a book, which was once a part of the *OT* canon, **Jubilees**.

There, we find a *conversation* between the *Angel* of *YHWH* and Moses, telling him YHWH was going to *require* the lives of *1000* Egyptians for every **one** of the **baby** *boys* thrown in the *river*!

We can conclude that only *happened* because the *Egyptians* were *pagans* (many gods) but if we *jump* ahead to the *first* century we find the *same* **punishment** *happened* to *Jerusalem* in 70 AD, only a couple decades *sooner* than Egypt. There, King Herod had *heard* a *prophecy* of a *king* that had been *born* to **replace** him, and *deduced* if he had all the baby boys 2 years and younger *murdered*, this one *born* to be his *replacement* would be *eliminated*.

Consequently, 70 years later Jerusalem was also *devastated*! In fact, so *decimated* Cesar Vespasian stood *overlooking* the city and *marveled* how you *could* **never** *tell* a *city* had ever been there! (Josephus) Obviously, YHWH is not a *respecter* of *persons* but *behavior*, after all, the Jews were His *own* chosen people. It's said; those who do **not** *pay* **attention** to *history* (even ancient) are *doomed* to **repeat** it!

II Peter 3 tells us *one* day in the **spirit** *realm* is *equivalent* to 1000 of *our* years. That means the *devastation* of Egypt was only *a **few** days* ago in the *spirit* realm, and the *destruction* of Jerusalem, just *a* **couple** *days* ago!

With that in mind, have our Creators really *changed* since a **couple** *days* ago, even though **Malachi** 3 tells us YHWH does **not** *change*? Are we really going to **dodge** that **monstrous** *bullet* (i.e.cannon ball) for the *murdering* of 1 and 1/4 billion *babies* in the last 60 years? The answer to that is such a *no-brainer*! In fact, the *instrument* of that **punishment** *is* **on** *its* **way**.

That "*instrument of just punishment*" called "***Nemisis***" (Websters dictionary) is our *binary **twin** solar **system*** that comes through every 3600 years. It will *arrive* in full *force* shortly. It seems we have *shaved* off another *decade* from the first century (only about 60 years) no doubt due to our *rabid **promotion*** of *sodomy* hand in hand with the *murder* of so many of the **Creator's** *children*! If we think its all *going **unnoticed***, we are in for the most *shockingly **rude*** *awakening* ever!

But thankfully, a *promise found* in **Revelation** 12, of a *place* of **protection,** *insuring* we will not we *wiped **off*** the face of the Earth, although the *experts* (like NASA) expect only about 1/3 to 1/4 of humanity will *survive* to *begin* the **new** *millennial* age!

Getting back to the *title* of this piece "***Lot Like Now***" it's a *play* on words showing we are in the ***same*** *position* of *eminent **demise***, just as *Sodom* and *Gomorrah* in the days of Lot! How willing are we going to be to *leave* the *comfort* of our ***familiar*** *societies* to *flee* to a *place* of **safety**, like Lot? Interestingly, Lot and his family had to all but be ***dragged*** *out* of Sodom. In fact, even after getting out, Lot's wife just couldn't quite break the *bond* she had *with* the place and was apparently *transformed* into *salt*.

Chapter 49

What is Life?

The title of this study may seem like a total **no-*brainer***, after all, doesn't everyone know *what **life*** is? Well, the hundreds of millions of **aborted** babies give that conclusion a *radically* different spin! We're *told* those *babies* have **no** *life* until they take their *first* breath; or is it until they are a *year* or *two* old! Unfortunately they keep changing their minds!

How about the *animal* kingdom? In fact, many people *refuse* to **eat meat** because it was a **living** *creature*. How ironic that many of those *same* people that have **deified** animals have **no** *problem* **murdering** *unborn* **babies**!?

What about *plants*? Are plants not *also* **living** *things*? But, if we can't **eat** *plants*, because they are **living** *things*, we all *die*! And of course, *animals* **eat** *plants* (dead or alive) and many *eat* each *other*. Personally, I only eat **vegan** meat! (Animals that only eat grass)! If nothing else, our modern world has certainly become a **quivering** *mass* of **nonsense**! They say the *first* **casualty** of *war* is **truth**, but in our society, another *casualty* seems to be *logic*! Where has it *gone*! Can it be *retrieved*?

Maybe our idea of **what** *life* is, is the *problem*? There are those that *believe* **all** *things* have some kind of *living* **essence**, which of course, gives us an even bigger *headache*! I suppose some *credence* can be *given* that idea considering all *atoms* are in **motion**, as if they are *alive*.

The scientist who *discovered* **quantum** *physics* (Max plank) concluded that *everything* that *exists* is made of *digital* (quantum) *bursts* of *photons* and *what* we *see* and feel is *simply* an **illusion** created by **electrical** *energy* (forces) in the *atoms*. That *reality* was so *disturbing* he *committed* **suicide**. Bottom line, science is only *guessing* at **what** that sustaining *energy* **is** or *where* it's *originating*.

For *example*, it completely shocked the *scientists* in the **two** *slit* (light) *experiment*, to see that the **measured** *results* with *photons* were *different* when being *physically* **observed** while *measured*!! The photons literally *behave* as if they are *aware*!! (Alive) Bottom line, *humanity* and *science* really has no clue what *life* and/or *energy* is and **where** it *originates*.

That *opens* the door to another *relevant* question; is *life* in **other** *dimensions* the *same* as ours? After all, science has *concluded* there are at least 10. What's interesting is we have a very **little** *understood* book that is **all** *about* **life** *versus* **death**.

Unfortunately, most people *don't* understand *death* anymore than they *understand* **life**, which is a *sad* state of *affairs* that doesn't *need* to be! Even though *life* is *impossible* for our *finite* **little** minds to fully *comprehend*, **death** it's actually very *simple*. It's simply the **cessation** of *life*, and/or *energy*. That *battle between* **life** and *death* began in the Biblical *Garden* of *Eden*.

There, we find the *Tree* of *Life* and the *Tree* of the *Knowledge* of *Good* and *Evil*, ie. the *tree* of **death**! But, the *only* way we can *begin* to **understand** *life*, is to understand there **is** a *Creator*, who is the *giver* and/or *creator* of **life** (energy). That's something we simply can't *begin* to *wrap* our *puny* brains around and are forced *accept* on *faith*. Unfortunately, most of *humanity* is totally *unwilling* to *accept* such a *being*, because it *reduces* us to **nothing** in *comparison*!

To conclude our *life* and/*death* is in a vastly **superior beings' hands** is simply too much for most. Even though humankind cannot create life (from nothing) we can **choose** *not to die* (immortality) means we must also *choose* the **giver** of *life* (Creator) which so many are unwilling to do. Actually, the reason for that is the **god** of *death* is **whispering** in everyone's *ear* that we *don't* **want** to *choose* **immortality**!!

The bottom line is, *life* is a **supernatural** (spiritual) *thing* that is well **beyond** *us*! We are like *ants* trying to *understand* the *beings* **observing** us! We can't begin too. The only way to *understand*, is to go into *that* world (dimension) which, by the way, the Bible tells us we eventually *can*, if we so *desire*! We can literally be *born* into that *spirit* world (other dimension) if we simply do the **little** asked us!

The most *difficult* issue to *accept* is that we are simply a **physical** *construct* (like a stage set) in a **spirit** *world*. (Other dimensional) We are like puppets *dancing* on *strings*. Until we understand that *reality* and *how* to **cut** *those* **strings**, we're *doomed* to *being* **only** *puppets*. Little children watch *puppet* shows and *believe* those *puppets* to be *real*, but eventually come to understand they are just *dolls* **controlled** by *strings*.

We humans are just the *same*, only on the **next** level up, only *alive* and controlled with **invisible** *strings*. But, by watching all the **illogical** *behavior* of humanity, those **strings** *become* quite **visible**!

It's like science understanding *atoms* (which are too small to be seen) by *viewing* their *effects* (tracks). But *atoms* are obvious by everything we *see*, and *touch*. With that in mind, the Creator's *fingerprints* are **everywhere** if we will only *open* our *minds* and *hearts* to the concept! We *see* and **know** the *Creators* by their shockingly **complex** Creation and occasionally, a *supernatural* **event**.

Millions of *those* are *witnessed* yearly, but most are bizarrely *rationalized* away! I have *experienced* **hundreds** of these *myself*! I *know* without the **slightest** *doubt* how **real** the **spirit** *world* is and how we can *interact* with it!! That's **real** *life*!

Chapter 50

Proud Leavening

Growing up in a Messianic Jewish Church, a lot of *attention* given to *something* few people give a **second** *thought* to, unless you're a *baker*; "*leavening*". Of course, the Jewish community was also quite aware of this *substance* as well, considering one of the spring *Feasts* is *centered* upon it. That *Biblical* **High** *Feast*, is the *Feast of* **Unleavened** *Bread*. (A part of Passover) It's a very *strange-**sounding*** religious *Festival* to the *average* person and even to *those* who *observe* and supposedly *understand* it.

In fact, I was one of *those*. We were told *leavening* **represented** *sin* and by putting it *out* of our *houses* and **not** *eating* it for Passover *week*, pictured *putting **sin** out* of our lives. The big *problem* was; after a week, we went back to eating it! (leavening products). If we put away sin (leaving) and got it "*out*" of our *lives*, how is it we *bring it **back** in*? Am I the only *one* who **sees** a *problem* with this *metaphor* **celebrated** by the Feast of *Unleavened* Bread? I know I'm *not* the **brightest** *bulb* in the *fixture*, but after putting **sin** out of our *lives*, shouldn't we, umm, **keep** it *out?*

Well, *private* interpretation and the *inability* to **see** the **big** picture allows to *rear* its **ugly** head again. After all, to *metaphorically* put *sin* **out** of our *lives* and then go *back* **into** it after a week *renders* the whole picture completely *nonsensical*. No wonder so many have *discarded* the *whole* **thing** as *absurd*. So, *what's* the answer? Well, if we pay *attention* to other scriptures; those *connected* as well as some that seem to have **no** *relation* (big picture) the Bible *makes* the **truth** *obvious*!

First, we have to step back and *establish* some of the *big picture* framework for any of this to *make* sense, which of course, means we have to go back to the *beginning*; **Genesis**. There we *find* the couple in the Garden being given a *choice*; to choose "*life*" (YHWH) symbolized by the "*Tree of Life*" or "*death*" symbolized by the "*Tree of the Knowledge of Good and Evil*" which was simply the *embracing* of the **false** *god*; the *reptilian* "*Nachash*" (angelic dragon).

If we also *incorporate* the *theme* of New Testament into the mix, it becomes clear that the **two** *choices* given in the Garden were actually *two* **spirits**; one the *Spirit of Life* (Love) and the other, the **spirit** *of selfishness* (pride) *and* **death**. To add a little more *framework* to the **big** picture, we find Israel (YHWH's chosen descendants of Adam and Eve) enslaved in Egypt; a glaring example of the *consequences* of the *choice* to *follow* the "*creature*".

The Dragons' *tree,* was the one *of choosing for one's* **self** *what is good* and/or *evil"*. That of course, was in *contrast* to choosin g the Creator YHWH's **living** *instructions* (Torah) and *immortality*.

While in Egypt, the Egyptians *taught* the *Israelites* to *worship* every kind of **animal**. (Pagan gods) But YHWH *demonstrated* He was *master* over the *animal* (creature) *gods* by the *plagues* (each plague *involved* the destruction of an **animal** god and its *power*).

YHWH *lead* them (His people) *out* of their *enslavement* in the **Dragon's** Kingdom, into *freedom*, represented by the **lack** of *leavening* (in their rush to leave, they didn't have time to leaven their bread). But, once there, He asked them to do *something* very *strange*; offer up <u>two **leavened** loaves</u> of *bread* (Lev. 23:17) on the *Feast of Firstfruits*, which was the *celebration* of the *spring* **Firstfruit** harvest.

The *implication* is *clear*; the **leavened** *loaves* represent two *entities* (whose identity is another study) ascending to *Heaven* (YHWH's Realm). But, the crazy thing is; why arethey are *leavened*! Doesn't that mean the *loaves* offered are **full** of *sin*? Ahh, Houston, we have a problem!?

In checking the *original* (and many other translations) "*leavened*" in that verse is *not a mistranslation*. So, what gives? Again, the *truth* is found in the beginning! You see, Adam and Eve *didn't* **choose** *death* so much as choosing the **Spirit** that *leads* to **death** and *destruction*!

That *Spirit* of the *Nachash* was **pride**! (See Ezekiel 28:12-17 and Ezekiel 31) In *looking* up all the scriptures on *pride*, we *discover* we *cannot* **walk** with YHWH (life) *filled* with **pride**, which brings *destruction* and *death*! (Proverbs 16:18)

The truth is, **all** *evil* and *sin* (selfishness) are **rooted** in *pride*. On the other hand; *love* and *righteousness* (leading to immortality) are *rooted* in **humility**! Pride (death) and **humility** (life) are *diametrically* **opposites** of each other.

Pride always *prompts* us to *believe* every kind of **falsehood** *imaginable*, especially about our own "*self*" *righteousness* and **value**! It puffs us up with *lies* (air) to make us *look* and **feel** like something we're *not*. That's why **Jeremiah** 17:9 tells us the "*heart is deceitful above all things*"; because our *hearts* are (from conception) filled with the *spirit* of *pride*!

Now, if we take those basic *bits* of understanding and *attach* them to the *spring* **Feasts**, it's easy to understand how *leavening* is certainly a *picture* of *pride*. In fact, our entire *purpose* for our **physical** *existence* is to come to see our *inner* **pride** and *purge* it. But, at the same time, I'm sure you've *heard*; "Nature **abhors a vacuum**".

You see, once we've been brought to *see* our (devils spirit) *pride* for **what** *it* **is** and *clean* it out, *something* has to **replace** it. Otherwise, we're like the *parable* Yahshua told His disciples about *casting* out a *demon* (pride) **out** of the *house*; if we don't *fill* it with **something** *else*, the *demons* (spirit of the animals) *will* **come** *back* with a *vengeance*! (Matt.12:43)

Well, what to *fill* the "**clean** *house*" (our hearts after cleaning out pride) is a real *no-brainer*! We must **fill** that *void* left with *humility* and the Spirit of YHWH! YHWH's **Spirit** coming to *dwell* in us is also a *type* of *leavening*; what the *two* **leavened** loaves that were *offered* on the Feast of *Firstfruits* were *leavened* with; YHWH's Spirit of *Humility* and *Life*!

Chapter 51

Liar, Liar, Lips on Fire

One of the *fastest* **growing** *problems* in our modern *society* is little *problem* called "**lying**". It seems to have become the *norm*, whether it's *politics* or the *news*. In fact, a popular *joke* is; we *know* a **politician** is *lying* because his *lips* are *moving*! We *laugh* about that, but there's more *truth* there than most are *willing* **to** *admit*. After all, how could we **tolerate** *leaders* that **lie** to us? But unfortunately, they always mix just enough *truth* to *make* the *lies* **almost** believable.

Plus, it's easy to *conclude* the political *party* we don't *belong* to, is the *one* **lying**; after all, **our** *party wouldn't* **lie**. But just "**who**" is it that's *lying*? Could it be **us** *lying* to *ourselves* about *who* and **what** we *are* **willing** to *believe*? In my observation, I have come to *understand* there's *no* **one** we *lie* to more than *ourselves*! That said, let's look at who *else* out there is **obviously** *lying*.

One of the most *respected* institutions of **truth** *relied* **upon** is, of course, the *media*. In fact, one of the *chief* **reasons** for the *creation* of the *media* was to **expose** *lying* **politicians**! They were to be the **watchdogs** of the *government*; to keep our *politicians* from **selling** *us* **out** on the **world** and/ or *local* stage. Unfortunately, instead of *keeping* our *politicians* and *government* **honest**, they've *turned* to **protecting** *the* very **liars** they were to *expose*! In fact, one of our *newest* **sayings** is "**fake** (lying) *news*"!

Just how on Earth did *that* happen? Well, the short of it is, the *globalists* have literally **bought** *us* with their *Federal* **Reserve** system using the support of all the *worlds'* major *medias,* of course. So, rather than giving us **honest** *news* to keep us *informed* as to what's really *transpiring* (here and in the world) they have become *globalist* (socialist-communist) **propaganda** machines. How's that *possible,* you may ask? Well, it all goes back to the world's *golden* **operating** *rule*; "*He who has the* **gold,** *makes the* **rules**"! That, of course, is the *twin* brother of the *other* one; "**Power** *corrupts and* **absolute power** *corrupts* **absolutely**"!

A little **real** *truth?* Both those *sayings* are **absolutely** *correct,* in spite of our willingness to *accept* them or not! Both are *proof* of our *human* **condition.** *Greed* and *power* **run** the *world!* Money **delivers** *power* and **power** *births* **control.** Anyone who *concludes* otherwise is a *complete* **fool.** In fact, a very well known radio host once quipped; "*Is it possible for a man* (or woman) *to go to Washington and not become corrupt*"?

Well, the answer to the *radio* **host's** *question* was a *profound* "**no**"! In fact, the only *power* **greater** than **human** *nature* (selfishness, greed, and pride) is the Creator's *essence* (Spirit)! On the other hand, the Creator's *Spirit* is *Love,* **Humility,** and *Truth.* And *what* we call "*human nature*" is actually *pride*; the *nature* (spirit) of the *rebellious* watchers (defected angels).

When Eve and Adam *partook* of the *Tree of the knowledge of good and evil,* it gave the *dragon* (not a serpent) **permission** to *fill* all humanity with *its'* **lying** *spirit* of *pride.*

In fact, the Hebrew *Messiah* tells us, the devil (dragon) was the **original** *liar* and the "*author of lies*". Considering the *devil* is the **god** of this *world,* is it any wonder why **lying** has *become* the *norm?* In fact, one of the *communist* dictators (Hitler?) once *quipped*; "*If you* **want** *people to* **believe** *you,* **tell** *them a* **lie**!" And how *true!* Because we are filled from *birth* with the *spirit* of the *liar,* we *naturally* **identify** *with* the **lie** before the *truth!*

The *"natural" man* has *an **aversion*** to *truth and* will *embrace* the *lie* over the *truth* virtually *every* time! That should come as **no** *surprise* considering, the ***first** thing* most people *teach* their children is the **lie** a *red* clad *fat* man living at the *North* pole delivers *billions* of presents in *one* night in his ***flying** reindeer* and *sleigh*! And let's not forget the *bunny* that **lays** *colored* eggs and the *fairy* that pays good *money* for *used* teeth!

How ironic how we begin our children's lives *teaching* those *falsehoods* (lies) and then spend the next 10-15 years *teaching* them **lying** is *bad*! What *insanity*! That said, do we really think the *lies **stop*** once we become adults? Or, do they *simply **grow** larger*?

Considering a related note concerning *babies* and *lies*; are we really to *accept* a baby in the womb is **not** *human*? But then, in the *past* people were *taught* (and believed to an extent) that **Native** *Americans*, *Blacks* and *Jews* were *not* human either! Another connected *lie* is that ***abortion*** is about *woman's **health***.

The *facts* are, ***post** abortion **multiplies*** a woman's risk of *cancers* as well as their chances of becoming an *alcoholic* or ***drug** addict,* and least ***doubling** their **suicide** rates*! Isn't the *lie* that babies in the *womb* are **not** human, the ***same** lie* told that *resulted* in the *slaughter* of some **6** *million* ***Jews***?

That in mind, the ***latest** propaganda* is the *white **caucasian** people* (not just Jews) are **now** *responsible* for the ***worlds** evils* (just as the Jews were *accused*) that ***Caucasians** stole* all their *wealth* from the poor *muslims* and *blacks,* not to mention *slaves*. Again, has anything *changed*, or have the *lies* just gotten *larger*?

How about the *idea* (lie) that *reducing* man-made ***carbon*** will *reduce **global** warming*, considering *carbon* is one of the *chief **foods*** for *plants,* which do the *most* to keep the planet ***from** overheating*! On top of that, plants *need* the *carbon* to *live* and *produce* our ***oxygen***! The *more* we *reduce **carbon***, the more we *reduce **plant** proliferation* and *our **oxygen,*** which we need to *live* and be *healthy*!

Another *outrageous* **lie** is we can *solve* the *problem* of world *poverty* by *taking* **down** our *borders* and letting all the *poor* and *diseased* of the *world* **flood** in. It's like a *drowning* person that pulls their *rescuer* **under** the water as he tries to *save* them.

And then, there's the *all*-time *big* **lie** that *socialism* (communism) is the *answer* to humanities *problems*. The *truth* is, **socialism** *removes* the incentive to *work* and creates *myriads* of **maladies** such as *alcoholism* and **drug** *addiction* while reducing the *population* to abject **poverty** due to *reduction* of **productivity** and *creativity*.

Communism (socialism) also *strips* people of most of their *personal* **rights** and *freedoms*. The most recent *example* of what *socialism* **does** was Venezuela. It was once one of the most *prosperous* countries in South America, but is now largely *starving*.

Considering *communism,* another astounding *lie* is our government *hates* it. In fact, one of the political *parties* greatest **insults** is to call their *opponents* "*Nazis*". But, anyone who *knows* about *Hitler,* knows he was a *socialist*. In fact, "*Nazi*" is the German *acronym* for "<u>*National* **Socialist** *Party*</u>"! Unfortunately, America also has a *national* **socialist** *party,* only now they call themselves *Democrats*, who openly *admit* being *socialists* (Nazis).

Another *monster* **lie** is our **twin** *sun* (and planets) is *not* about to **pass** *through* our system, bringing all *hell* with it! Our wonderful *leaders* are hoping it will *kill* **most** of us after they *dive* into their *underground* **bunkers** and *cities*! (They want to reduce the population to 500 million!)

Chapter 52

Liberty and Consequence

The United States was *founded* upon the idea of *liberty*; **freedom** to *practice* our *religion* **where**-ever and **when-ever** desired. The US was also *founded* upon the idea of the *freedom* of **property** *ownership* and the *ability* to *do* **with** the land as **we** *see* **fit** as well. Hundreds of *thousands* gave **their** *lives* to *provide* us those *freedoms*. In fact, one of our better known *founders*, Patrick Henry loudly *proclaimed*; "**Give me liberty or give me death**"! **Without** *liberty*, **life** was **not** *worth* **living** for that man!

That's a slogan *embraced* by so many **freedom** *loving* people, that *literally* **gave** their *lives* to *achieve*. Are *we* willing to *forsake* our *lives* for **that** *freedom* also? It sure *didn't* **ring** *true* with the *covid* scam!! With that, our **constitution** and *bill* of **rights** were *stripped* from us! Why were most so *unwilling* to **fight** them and *die* to **keep** from losing those *freedoms*. Unfortunately, it was a little *thing* called "**fear**"!

A scripture tells us it's "*the truth makes us free*" but they were *lying* to us like *rugs,* which is *why* they were *able* to **steal** our *freedoms*! Whether or not we *believe* it, **keeping** our *liberty* came with a **steep** *price* tag. As history shows, nations have, virtually across the board, gone *through* the *process* of *great* **sacrifice** (war in the *beginning)* to *shed* whatever *bondage* they *found* themselves to *achieve* **freedom**.

Freedom brings *prosperity,* which unfortunately *breeds* **complacency**, which leads to general **unthankfulness**. That *unthankfulness* then leads to **unproductively**, *poverty,* **societal** *collapse* and finally re-*subjugation*. We are now *currently* in that re-*subjugation* phase.

We have seen our **beloved** nation go down that *same* road. We are *facing* the emanate **collapse** of *everything,* since we **allowed** our *enemies* to *come* **to** *power.* How did that *happen*? Well, that brings us *back* to that *scripture* referenced *earlier;* "*the* **truth** *will* **make us free**".

What *truth* is that? Is it not **who** our *leaders* really **are** and *what* they are *doing*? Well, that's a large *part* of it, but *how* is it we **allowed** them into *power* in the *first* place? Sun Tsu advised; "*Keep your* **friends** *close, but your* **enemies** *closer.* Unfortunately, we didn't, which *allowed* our *leaders* **steal** our *freedoms*! What then is the **real** *source* of our *personal* and *national* **blindness**? A scripture, II **Thessalonians** 2:10, clues us in.

There we find an *ominous* warning; those who **reject** the *truth* are **given** *over* "*to strong* **delusion** *and the* **lie**". This is *all* a **spiritual** *issue.* You see, there are two main *powers* in the **spirit** *world,* the *liars* and the **truth** *tellers.*

In fact, it's stated the Creator (Yahweh) and His Son *literally* **are** *truth.* So, if we *reject* their *teachings* (*truth*) we are *supernaturally* **blinded**. And, with *blindness* comes *destruction.* **Hosea** 6:4 tells us the Creator's people are "**destroyed for lack of knowledge**". What *knowledge* is that? Well, there are many *aspects* to *knowledge,* but the *foundation* of all **true** *knowledge* is the Creator's *Torah* (instruction) *of* Love.

Of course, Torah means *instruction*; instruction on *how* **to** *live* and *behave,* which primarily is *how* to **love**, *honor,* and **respect** our Creator's *first* and each *other* second. The Creator's are creating an *eternal* family and will *not sentence* their *eternal* children to an *eternity* of **bickering**, *fighting,* and general *discontent.*

They simply *will* **not** do that. Their *eternal* **family** will be *one* of *peace* and *happiness*. In fact, when we **disrespect** and/or *dishonor* our Creator's in *some* **way**, it's a **sin**! Of course, *disrespecting* each *other* is **also** a *sin*! But, we are told in I **John**, those who are *born* from *above*, that is *of* **spirit** "*cannot sin*"!

What that means is, once we've set our minds to *loving*, **respecting**, and *honoring* our Creator's *first,* and each *other* second, and spending our *lives fighting* **for** that *choice*, we are *on* our *way*.

But, *words* **are** *cheap* and the *decision* to **love**, *honor*, and **respect** our Creator's and *each* **other**, has to be **fought** *for* in order to be *real*! When we spend our *physical* lives *fighting* for that *choice* and **way** of *living*, we are now ready to *join* our Creator's *family*! (Simple)

Our Creator's are incredibly *patient*, long-suffering, and *merciful*, but they can only *allow* people to go *down* so far before they are *forced* to **step** *in* and *reset* things. Unfortunately, getting *set* **right** (punishment) is a very *painful* but a **necessary** *process*! That's precisely where we *currently* **find** ourselves. After the *murder* of over a billion of the **Creator's** *babies*, and the *destruction* of "**Their** *institution*" of **marriage** and *family*, its **correction** *time*.

That *reset* is *coming* in the *form* of a *binary* **twin** *sun* and its half dozen *planets* in tow, which is about to *slice* through the *center* of our solar system. All *hell* is literally going to **rain** *down* to *destroy* much of the Earth and its *inhabitants*. But, how *poetically* **just** to *understand* its name is "*Nemisis*" which according to Webster's dictionary means "*A just instrument of punishment*"! How perfectly *poetic*!

Even though the *leaders* of the *Western* nations have valiantly *attempted* to *bury* that *truth*, our Creator has *promised* to *never* do **anything** without *first* **warning** His people. (Amos 3) That *warning* has *gone* **out**, but unfortunately *most* have *refused* to *believe* it or have simply **ignored** it. But, there is a *remnant* group of people called "*the woman*" in **Revelation** 12, who will be *whisked* **away** to a *place* **of** *safety* for 3 and 1/2 years.

According to the **heavenly** *signs*, such as the **Revelation** 12 "*sign of the woman in heaven*" (virgo) the *solar* **eclipses**, and also the *Bible* **time** *line* (feasts) the *arrival* of *Nemisis* is **imminent**. In fact, the approximate **arrival** *date* is late *spring*, or early *summer* of *2024*. It also seems *Michael* the arch-angel has a *book* with the *names* of those *destined* to be *saved* at that time. (Daniel 12)

Bottom line, with *great* **liberty**, comes **great** *responsibility*. Unfortunately we as a *nation* have *neglected* that **righteous** *responsibility*, and now *must* **pay** the **price**. The *blood* of those *innocent* babies so viciously *murdered*, is **screaming** to *heaven* for *vindication*! Well "*vengeance is mine says the Creator*" He is *about* to liberally *dish* **it** out on a mostly *ignorant* and guilty world.

Sadly, it's **too** *late* for **our** *nation* as a *whole* and the *world*, but personally, it's not too late to *return* to and *embrace* our Creators. Our Father Creator (**YHWH**) tells us in **Malachi** 1:6 that we are *cursed* for **not** *giving* **Him** the **Honor** due His **exclusive** *Name*. So, the *place* to *begin* is to *repent* for not *giving* His **true** *Name* the **honor** *due* and then to *return* to His *Torah* **instructions** (and true Sabbaths). After all, He tells the *sign* **between** *Him* and **His** *people* will be *His* **Sabbaths**! Only then can we *expect* His **mercy**, *protection*, and *provision*! (Exodus 12 & Ezekiel 20)

Chapter 53

Love Is

When younger, I remember a very popular *poster*, called "*Love **is***" which listed dozens of *things* about *love*, such as "*love is a warm puppy*" or a "*beautiful **sunset***" and many other **warm** fuzzy *thoughts* and *pictures*. No doubt *love* can be *connected* to all those *things* in *some **way*** or *another*, but *what* is **true** (real) *love* anyway? Many others say **real** "*love*" is that ***feeling*** people get when they "*fall **in** love*" but is that *warm **fuzzy** feeling*, **true** *love*, or is **real** *love a* much **deeper** *emotion*?

With that in mind, how many *people*, for instance, see an *outfit* of *clothes* and exclaim; "*I love it*" only to buy it and *quit wearing* it a year or two later? How about that *house* or *car* people *fall* in **love** *with* only to *sell* or become **junk** a few years *down* the road. Obviously, these *feelings* of love **feel** quite *real*, but are quite *shallow* at best!

How about **relationship** *love*, is it any *different* from the *feeling* people *acquire* for those *non-living* things? In fact, how many people get *married* (or live together) because they *believe* they have *found **true*** love. But then, how *true* is **that** *love* when over 60% at some point *decide* they have *fallen **out*** of *love* and go their **separate** *ways*. Again, was that **real** *love*, or *something **else***? Of course, if you were to *ask* them in the *beginning*, most, if not all, would tell you **that** *love* they were *feeling* was **very** *real!*

So, what *happens* to that supposedly *very* **real** *love* most people get *together* with? If it goes *away* so *easily* and *sometimes* **quickly**, *how can* it be *real?* Well, one *type* of *feeling* people **call** *love* is simple *lust*. Lust *masquerades*, as *love*, but, it's very *fleeting*. When most people *fall* in *love* with something (or someone) it's *nothing* but the *feeling* of **desire** or *lust*, or again, that closely related to *lust*; **infatuation**. Let's not forget **Jeremiah** 17:9; "*The* **heart** *is* **deceitful** *above* **all** *things*"!

These *feelings* are *natural* and **normal**, but It's *what* we **do** *with* **them** that *makes* the *difference*. Lust is based in *selfishness* and *greed* and rarely can be *turned* **into** *anything* more. Another *natural* attraction **related** to *lust* is *infatuation*. But, that *temporary* feeling of *love* is *very* **necessary** to bring people *together*.

In fact, **most** *relationships* would *never happen* without that **spark** of *attraction* called *infatuation*. Again, my **personal** *feeling* is we were **purposely** *created* with that *type* of **love** *attraction* to be the **foundation** for **true** *love*. But, unless that *feeling's* **fed**, it will **die** *out* like a **camp** *fire*.

If we stop *feeding* a fire *wood*, it goes out rather quickly. Real *true* love is not only a *choice* with a **feeling** attached, but an **action**. If people don't understand that, their *relationship* is most likely to *end*; that is, unless it morphs into a *selfish* **need**. Many relationships that stay *together* is simply out of "*need*".

If we look to the *Bible* for the *meanings* (or types) of *love*, we find at least *four* **different** types. The *first* is the *Greek* word "*Philao*" which means **family** or "**brotherly** *love*". In fact, a city in Pennsylvania, *Philadelphia*, means "*city of* **brotherly** *love*". Everyone knows **that** *type* of *love* for a **sibling** and/or *friend*.

Another type of *love* listed in the Bible is "*staros*" which is the *kind* of *love* a *mother* or *father* has for their child. This is a kind of *possessive* or *selfish* love, because a *parent* automatically has a *level* of *love* for their child, considering it' s literally their **own** *flesh* and *blood*. Of course, we all *automatically* **love** *ourselves* whether we are able to **admit** *it* or not. This *kind* of *love* can *rarely*, if ever, be will *felt* for **another** *child* that's **not** our own *flesh* and *blood!*

A *third* word for *love* is "*eros*" which is "*amores*" or **sexual** love. That's a very *powerful* **feeling** *fueled* by *hormones*; primarily *testosterone*. Unfortunately this *important* type of *love* is also the *drive* that causes much *trouble* for people. It's a very important part of marriage, but *uncontrolled,* these **testosterone** driven **feelings** *destroy* so many *marriages* and *homes*. But, it can be *controlled,* though it doesn't *seem* like it sometimes.

Finally, the most **important** *word* for *love* in the scriptures is "*agape*". Agape is a **selfless** *love* while all the others all *involve* some element of *selfishness*. Agape can be *applied* to *marriage*, but it's primarily the *feeling* that's *developed* by doing **unselfish** *good* for others. It can also be a *mate*, but it can be *anyone*. I have *personally* **tested** this *phenomena* and *found* it to be quite *real*.

When we *unselfishly* give our *time* and *resources* to *someone*, without **expecting** any *thing* in **return**, we are literally *giving* someone else a *piece* of **ourselves**. Unfortunately, much modern *rhetoric* tries to *sell* us, we have to *love* **ourselves** *before* we can *love* **anyone** *else*. But, the truth is, there is *no-one* we *love* **more** than *ourselves*.

When people *tell* us they **hate** *themselves*, what they are *saying* is they *hate* some *issue* or *problem* they have with *themselves*, which, by the way, usually comes from **too** *much* **self-love,** like *drug* **addicts** or *alcoholics!*

Another *reason* people tell us they *hate* **themselves**, is because of the *image* they *believe* others *have* of them. (Like being fat or ugly) If it's an *image* they *hate*, they **kid** *themselves* that it's *themselves* they **actually** *hate*. Bottom line, when some people (especially narcissists) perceive **others** *don't* **love** them the **way** *they* **love** themselves, it breeds *self- loathing* and a type of *hate*, which is really just a *false* feeling.

It's *written* in the scriptures, we are to "*love our Creator with **all** our heart, soul, and **mind**, and **others** as we **love ourselves***". We **all** have a *love* for ourselves because it's **ourselves** we are most *interested* in *taking* **care** *of*. You see, *we **all** wear* the *clothes* **we** like (in our price range) and *eat* the *foods* **we** *like*, unless we are trying to *lose* weight or *something*. We also *wear* **our** *hair* the way **we** *like* and the *shoes* **we** *like*! And, if someone tells us they **don't** *like* our *hair,* clothes, or *shoes*, it's upsetting.

But, if we *really* **hated** ourselves, we would **not** *eat* the *foods* we *like* or *drink* the *drinks* we like. In fact, *eating* **healthy** and **not** *overeating* (or drinking) would be no problem! We would **only** *wear clothes* we could *afford* that **other** *people* **like**. In fact, we would only *marry* for **utilitarian** *reasons* like to *aid* the *population*, or just because someone *else* **loves** us not the other way around.

Actually, there's **nothing** *wrong* with *liking* or **loving**, ourselves. After all, we were created this way. If we didn't *love* **ourselves**, we would **not** be *happy* and would eventually *die* **out** as a *species*! Our Creator's want us to be *happy* and to *enjoy* the *things* they bless us with. But, the *happiest* we can be is to **love** *them* and each other as we *love* **ourselves**!

Chapter 54

The Long Dark Night

A word we see used all through the Bible is "*darkness*". We first see it first *used* in the beginning of **Genesis** where the Creator "***divided the darkness from the light***". Apparently, at that point, *darkness* had *enveloped* **everything** and the Creator(s) was *restoring* "*light*" to the *planet*. In **Genesis** 1:3-5 He *divided* the *light* from the *darkness, calling* the "*light day*" and the "*darkness night*" which began a *competition* between those **two** entities throughout the *course* of the Bible (and history). Interestingly, our 24 hour day is currently a **mix** of *those* **two**. (Like good and evil *mixed*)

Genesis tells us that *before* Adam and Eve partook of the "*Tree of the Knowledge of "Good" and "Evil"* there was **no** *night* or **darkness**. (Book of Eden) Night only *became* a *reality* (for them) "*after*" they were *put* **out** of the Garden. And, that **mix** of "**good**" and "**evil**" (day and night) has been the *norm* in this *world* ever *since*. Again, Adam and Eve had only *light* (day) *synonymous* with *life* in the *Garden,* while **darkness** *is synonymous* with **evil***,* as we will *see*.

Day (light) is *good* because it is the *time* we can be *productive* and able to *enjoy* **life** considering **nothing** can be *accomplished* in *darkness,* although *these* days we have *developed* **artificial** light which gives us more *light* time to enjoy *life,* even though we still need to *sleep.* Night is *when* most people "*sleep*" which interestingly is also a scriptural *metaphor* for **death**. We find many scriptures calling *death* "*sleeping*". What a coincidence *death* and **darkness** are *bedfellows;* **darkness** brings *death* (sleep)!

In **Genesis** 1:15-16, we find the *sun* being *placed* in the sky to "*rule*" the *day,* while the "*stars rule the night*". With **that** *thought* in mind, all *through* the scriptures (especially the New Testament) we find **evil** and **death** *synonymous* with **darkness,** and *righteousness* and **life** referred to as *light!* In fact, the Hebrew Messiah in many places *proclaimed* He *was* the "*light*" and "*Life*" not to mention "*the way*" that is, to *life* (light) and YHWH. That said, how interesting "*sun*" (light) and "*Son*" (of YHWH) have the same verbal *pronunciation* and carry the same **basic** *concept,* that **light** *equals* **life**!

I'm certainly *not* advocating *sun* **worship** as many of the *pagans* have *done* throughout history (and many still do). I'm just making the **connection** between the *light* and *life.* Without the *sun* (& Son) everything would *die*!

Is this *picture painted* for us, with the Messiah as *light* and **life,** mere *coincidence,* or an incredibly **profound** *teaching*? Again and on the *other* side of the coin, **Genesis** 1 (14) states the "*stars*" **rule** the *night*; in other words; they are the **lords** of the **darkness**!

Interestingly, one of the Biblical references to the *angels* is "*stars*" as we see declared in **Job** 38:7; "*the morning stars sang together*" at the *creation* of the Earth. We can *shurg* that off to *metaphor* except **Revelation** 9 tells us a "*star*" *fell* from heaven having the *key* to the *bottomless* **pit**. (Also darkness) That "*star*" is obviously *not* a reference to a giant ball of *burning* hydrogen but an *angel* (watcher-messenger).

We also have the book of **Enoch** telling us of 200 watchers (guardian angels) which he also calls **stars**, *defected* to Earth and *established* themselves as **gods** and **kings**. In fact "*Malak*" the primary *word* used for "*angel*" in the Bible, is also the most oft word *used* **for** "*King*"! In other worlds, those *angels* are apparently the *origin* of the entire *concept* of a **king**!

We must not forget, YHWH strongly *condemned* the *idea* of His people *demanding* a **king** rather than His **Prophet** (teacher-guide) *Samuel*! Also in **Enoch** (chapter 84) we find *watchers* refereed to as *stars*. Enoch makes it very clear how these *watchers* (stars) **destroyed** *humanity* and the *Earth*! Again those **stars** *placed* in the *heavens* were to "**rule** *the* **night**" which again, is *metaphor* for **darkness**, *evil*, and **death.**

Considering all the **evils** *rampant* in the world, we can be sure, its due to the *stars* (*watchers angels*) *ruling* the world since the *Garden* of Eden. In fact, it was the *war* between *YHWH* and the *dragon* (Cherub) that *destroyed* the Earth and *brought* it into **darkness** (*tohew* and *bohew*— empty and void) before Adam and Eve. We find that prevailing *condition* in **Jeremiah** 4:23-26 and *again* in **Genesis** 1:2.

Again, Yahshua (the Hebrew Messiah) stated many times He *was* the "*Light*" (truth) and the "*Life*" (immortality) not to mention the "*Way*" to *light* and *life*. Considering that *truth*, after **departing** for *heaven* in the *first* century, is it any wonder those times were called "*The* **dark** *ages*"? After *returning* for His Disciples (priesthood) as He *promised* them (in **their** *generation*) the *light* **departed** this *world*, but was *slated* to **return.** (Rev.19-22)

In the meantime, since the *first* century, this world has been in *spiritual* **darkness;** literally **ruled** by those *stars* of **darkness** (evil *angels* and demons). What a coincidence the scriptures *teach* us *evil* **loves** and *hides* in *darkness*! What a **dark** *mess* this *world* **is** due to that fact! We *hear* and *see* **lies** and/or *half-truths* virtually *everywhere*!

But, **morning** is *coming* and as it's written "*darkness must flee*" (the *light*)! We are *entering* the *age* of true en**light**enment; the *dawning* of a whole new era of **wonderment** and *righteousness*; an age of **no death**, **disease**, *poverty*, **war**, or **evil** in general! (See The Grand Trans-dimensional Delusion) Of course, it starts *small* (like a tiny seed) and *grows* into a *giant* tree; providing *shade* and *protection,* eventually for the *entire* world.

Interestingly, **Revelation** 22 tells us the "**New** *Earth*" will **not** have any **night** (darkness)**.** That of course, is after being *restored* from the *burning* of the *rebellious* watchers and their **demon** *offspring* in "*the lake of fire*".

We can only *speculate* how "**no** *night*" is *possible* under our current *configuration* on a *round* Earth, but of one *thing* we can be sure, the age of **no** *evil* (darkness) is almost upon us! What a *wonderful* age of "*light*" we have to look *forward* too. In fact, **Isaiah** 58:8 (and other scriptures) tells us YHWH's *light* will "*break forth* (and come) *in the **morning***"!

That's exactly right, considering *He* **is** *light* (Righteousness) and the *arrival* of his Spirit will literally be the *dawning* of a *new* **day** (Millenium)! Let us *diligently* **pray** for the **end** of the *long* **night** and the *arrival* of the **dawn**; the *dawn* of a brand *new* and **beautiful** *age,* which thankfully, is *dawning* just *over* the *horizon*!

Chapter 55

Metal Man

In **Daniel** 2, we find the *account* of *Nebuchadnezzar* having had a really *strange* and **impressive** *dream*. But, the dream *troubled* him, probably by being so *vivid*. So, he *assembled* his *wise* men and *soothsayers* to *interpret* it. But, Nebuchadnezzar was no *fool* and **knew** if he *told* his soothsayers the *dream*, they could just pull any *interpretation* out of their *rear* ends and he would have no *way* of *knowing* if it was true.

To *solve* the *problem*, he told them, under *pain* of **death**, if they could *not **first** tell **him*** the dream, they and their families *heads* would *roll* and their houses would be turned into **manure** *piles*! Obviously, they were quite concerned with this *conundrum* and only saw **one** *way* out; to *consult* the *prophet* Daniel. They knew *Daniel* had a **great** God (YHWH) that did **amazing** *things* for him such as **interpreting** *dreams*. Daniel and his *friends* were no doubt also *concerned*, considering they could also *participate* in the *head-**rolling*** event.

So, Daniel asked his *Jewish* friends to *fast* and **pray** with him for an *answer* from YHWH which they *received*. Wisely, Daniel was very *careful* to give all the *credit* to His God and *proceeded* to tell Nebuchadnezzar the *dream*. It was of a *monstrous* metal **statue** of a man with a *head* and *crown* of **gold**, which was *Nebuchadnezzar* and his **Babylonian** empire. The statue also had a *chest* and *arms* made of **silver**, which was a *succeeding* **kingdom** that would *arise* **after** *Nebuchadnezzar* (the *Medo-Persian* empire).

Moving down the statue, the *belly* was *another* **metal**, a little *harder* than *gold* and *silver*; **brass**. The *brass* **kingdom**, turned out to be the **Greek** empire under Alexander after he **defeated** *Darius* the *Persian*. Then, finally were the **legs** *of* **iron** with *feet* **mixed** with *clay*. That *hardest* (cruelest and longest) of *kingdoms* was the **Roman** *empire* that rose up *against* the *Greeks* in about 150 BCE, finally *conquering* them. Interestingly, the dream showed the entire *statue* destroyed by a *stone* **from** heaven, which **crushed** the *feet*.

You, as have I, probably heard *numerous* **renditions** of **what** the **different** metals **mean** and *meant*. The most common of which was the *worth* of the kingdom being directly *connected* with the *qualities* and **value** of the *metal*. The *other* is the *strength* of the *metals* showing the *size* and **power** of the *kingdom*.

Good cases can be made for these *conclusions*, but there's still **one** more I've **never** *heard* espoused, which is; *each* of the metals *represent* the **power** and **quality** of the **spirit** *Prince* (watcher) *guiding* and **watching** *over each* of these *kingdoms,* as we see *pointed* **out** in **Daniel** 10.

With that in mind, the *strength* of each of the *metals* could very well be an *insight* into the *strength* and *purity* of the **angelic** *prince* of the nations **Daniel** 10 notes. Again, the Babylonian *head* was a **single** *empire,* like the head.

The the *chest* and *arms* of silver were the *two* parts of Medo-Persian empire. The belly was also *singular*, as was the *Greek* empire. The **Roman empire**, then, represented by the two *legs,* showed it also was *split* into **two** *parts*; the East (Byzantium) and the West (Rome). Considering the *Roman* empire *collapsed* in the **fifth** *century* CE, leaves people *scratching* their heads as to the **ten** *toes*. What were they?

And, why were they a *mix* of **iron and clay**? Again, the *iron* representing the Roman empire is *fitting* considering *iron* can be a symbol of both *strength* and *size*. After all, Rome was the *longest* lasting and *largest* of the *four* consecutive *kingdoms*, but again, what were the *ten* **toes**?

Most (if not all I've heard) say the *ten* toes are the *ten* **horns** mentioned a couple times in **Daniel** and **Revelation**, but the Roman *empire* **fell** in the *fifth* century CE. Those clinging to the idea the **ten** *toes* being *smashed* is still a *future* event, claim the *Vatican* is *still* the **Roman** *empire* **revived**.

But, of course, none of that *fits* with the statue, considering the *Vatican* does **not** have *ten* parts. Plus, all the *parts* of that statue representing those *kingdoms* were *contiguous* until *all* are <u>*destroyed* **together**</u>. The *gold*, **head**, *arms* and **chest** of *silver*, **belly** of *brass*, and **legs** of *iron* were still **one** *entity* until the *stone* from heaven **destroys** them <u>**all**</u> at the <u>**same** *time*</u>.

That said, how can they *still* be all *"one"* **complete** *statue* after the *Persians* **destroyed** *Babylon,* the *head* of gold? How is it the head of the statue was not cut off after Babylon fell? Plus, when the *Greeks* **conquered** the *Persians*, which were the *chest* and *arms* of *silver*, the chest and arms did **not** *disappear* either.

Finally the *Romans* **legs** of **iron**, *brought* **down** the *Greek* (belly) empire but the *belly* of *brass* was **still** *there*! Considering the *first* **three** *metals* (parts) were already *destroyed* **before** the **legs** of *iron* even existed, all I can say to that is; *"Houston, we have a problem"*! This picture is just **not** *figuring* or making any *sense*! So, what are we *missing*?

Well, there's another *theory*. That *theory* is the *metals* are a reference to the *immortal* **spirit** *guides* (watcher princes) of **those** nations. After their *physical* nations were *conquered*, the **immortal** spirit *princes* are **still** *here*! But, if true, are we to *conclude* those **immortal** *entities* are **not** still *involved* with modern *peoples*; only nations that are no longer are **world** *ruling*?

After all, *modern* **Babylon** is *Iraq*, while *modern* **Persia** is *Iran*. Of course, *Greece* and *Rome* (Italy) are **still** *here* as well! How can we conclude, the giant *metal* man is not *destroyed* until the **spirit** *princes* that *comprise* it, are also *destroyed*?

With that *idea* in mind, just *when* are the *components* of this giant *metal* man *destroyed*, and by *whom*? Well, **Daniel** 2 tells us the *entire* statue will be *destroyed* by "*A stone cut out of a mountain without hands*". Most of Christianity tells us that *stone* is "*Jesus*" but that of course, is pure *nonsensical* **speculation**. Jesus did **not** *destroy* the *Roman* empire. When the *Hebrew* Messiah *came* in the *first* century (the one they call Jesus) the *Roman* Empire was at its *Zenith*. It was **not** *destroyed* until some *500* **years** *later*.

Well, **Revelation** 20 tells how a *fire* (lake of fire?) comes *down* from *heaven* and *devours* all *nations* that are *left* and apparently their **spirit** *princes*, which no doubt includes the *metaphoric* **metals** as well. For some reason, **Revelation** 19 does not say anything about a *stone*, but speaks of one riding on a **white** *horse* with a **Name He alone** *knows* with His *heavenly* **army**.

How can we conclude that stone is any other than YHWH who is called the "*Rock*" in **Isaiah** 44 (v. 8) with that *new* **Name no one** but *He knows*? If that *One* on the *white* horse were YHWH's *Son*, that *Name* would have been **given Him** by His *Father*, right? Regardless, YHWH certainly would have *known* it!

Chapter 56

Man of Sin?

In the books of **Daniel** and **Revelation** we find a reference to *someone* called "*The man of sin*". The big *question* is; just *who* or *what* is this so- called "*man of sin*"? Over the years, I have heard so many *preachers* **attempt** to *satisfy* that *question*. But, the **only** *answer* that even comes *close*, is **not** an *answer* at all, but simply *another* question. One of those *answers* is the "*false* **prophet**". So much for an *answer*, considering *no-one* **knows** *who* or *what* the **false** *prophet* is either.

Another *non-answer* is the "*Anti-Christ*". No one knows *who* (or *what*) that *person* or *entity* is either, although *most* preacher-teachers have *convinced* themselves they *do*. But, from *where* I stand, **none** of them have a *clue*! And, on top of the "*man of sin*" the "*false prophet*" and the "*Anti-Christ*" is "*the Beast*"! Who or *what* is that now?

Are the *false prophet,* the *man of sin* and the *Anti-Christ,* all the **same** *entity* or are they all *different*? Ask a *hundred* different **Bible** *teachers* and we will likely get a *hundred* **different** answers. Which one, if any, is *correct*? How can we *know*? Would the Creator really give a *prophecy* (revelation) through one of His *prophets* without *clueing* us in on who this *man* or **beast** is?

It's said; "*If you can **control history**, you can **control** the **present**; and if you **control** the **present**, you **control** the **future***"! What this *axiom* is *saying;* the *key* to **everything** is *history;* hence the other oft quoted axiom; "*If we **forget*** (or don't know) *our **history**, we are doomed to **repeat** it*"! Of course, the *reason* for that is *human* (pride) **nature** does **not** *change!* Unless we have *supernatural* help, we'll automatically *exhibit* the **same** *behavior* humanity **always** has. The *reason* for which is actually very *simple.*

In the Garden of Eden, Eve and Adam *chose* the *spirit* (tree) of **pride** (Tree of the Knowledge of Good and Evil) over the *Tree* of **Humility** (Life). That *spirit* of **pride** is the *spirit* of the **creatures** (beasts). **Genesis** 3 tells us the one (dragon) that *conned* Eve, was the "*craftiest of all the beasts of the field*". (Not snake)

And, of course, that **beast** was *one* of the **animal** kingdom. **Genesis** 1:26 tells us the *animals* were created "*after their kind*", which of course, was the only **existing** animal **kind**, the **angels**. The *physical* animals are just a *reflection* of their *spirit* (angelic) *kind*, just as *mankind* is a **physical** *reflection* of the *Creator's* **kind**.

With that in mind, have you ever *watched* the **animal** kingdom in *action?* Growing up on a farm, you *realize* very quickly that *animals* are *creatures* of **habit**. They are *programmed* to *act* a **certain** *way* and they **rarely** *deviate* from *that* **programing**. Cows and *sheep* will always *follow* their *exact* **same** routine. You can *depend* on it.

Another good *example*, are *birds;* they also exhibit very **programed** *behavior* as well; always *making* the **same** *kind* of *nest*, and singing the **same** *songs*, no matter how many *generations* of birds have **come** *before*. The only *thing* that *changes* is the *placement* of the nest. And, they *never* **change** their *songs* with the **rare** *exception* of a few that *mimic* other birds, such as the *mockingbird.*

Well, humanity is the *same* to a large *degree*. Due to the ***animal nature*** (dragons' spirit of pride) we are all *given* from ***before*** *birth*, we *follow* the similar *patterns*, just on a larger scale than *animals*, but *repetitive*, non-the- less. It seems that approximately every ***third*** *generation regresses* into ***complacency***, *unthankfulness*, and ***selfish*** *behavior*.

Of course, those *attitudes* come with a whole *plethora* of evils *beginning* with the *forgetting* of ***who*** or *what* our Creator's are. To *forget* Them is to also *forget* ***where*** all our *blessing* and *provisions* ***come***.

With that in mind let's get back to the *identity* of "*Man of Sin*" *Anti-Christ*" and the "*Beast*". A little known Biblical fact is the one called "*Serpent*" in the *Garden* was a ***crafty*** "***beast***" (dragon actually) The 200 watchers that *defected* and ***procreated*** with humans (Book of Enoch) were apparently ***also*** animals. Their offspring were the *animal-**human** high-breds* ***worshipped*** in *ancient* times.

According to Bible *Historian* Olaf Hagee and others, ***Cain*** (Quain) was one of the ***first*** *human-**animal** High-breds* to appear. Also, *Jewish* ***writings***, such as the Talmud (and others) *claim* he had ***glowing*** *skin*, ***horns*** and *grew* into a *giant*!

We then find in the Book of **Enoch**, a great flood was sent to *drown* the Nephilim (offspring of the Watchers) after *their **watcher** parents* were put in some sort of *dimensional **prison**.* After being drowned, the *immortal **spirits*** of the Nephilim *could **not** return* to their *angelic* parents and have *become* what we call ***ghosts***. Those, of course, are the *spirits* that ***possess*** *people* whenever *allowed*.

These ghosts are quite literally *what* are commonly referred to as "demons". It's their jumping from *one **body*** to *another* where the *concept* of "***reincarnaton***" originates. (Literally-"*new **meat** suit*")

Bible Historian Olaf Hagee traced the *movement* of Quain (Cain) from his *murdering* of Able and his being *banned* to the *East* (Nod-land of *wandering*). That land is modern day *India* (in-*nod*-ia—in the land of Nod) where *Hinduism* and the idea of *reincarnation* (demon spirits finding new bodies) *originated!* Quain (Cain) was eventually *killed* by Lamech (see the Book of Jasher) and apparently *reincarnated* in the *body* of **Nimrod**. After the death of *Nimrod* (apparently by Esau) re-appeared as the great *Osiris* in Egypt.

Interestingly, there was a *song* from the 60's called "**Quinn,** *the* **Mighty Eskimo**" that speaks of the **whole** *world* **jumping** for *joy* at his *coming* (return). Who ever *heard* of a "**mighty** *eskimo*"? But, as Dr. Olaf points out, all the "*Nick*" names (and words) *originated* from the root of "*Nachash*" which is the **Hebrew** *word* for the *dragon* (watcher-angel) that *deceived* Eve in the Garden.

With that in mind, who supposedly *lives* at the **North** pole and brings presents to the whole world in his ***flying*** reindeer and *sleigh*? Is it not *St.* "**Nick-laus**"? After all, part of the *lure* that *enticed* Eve was the *promise* of **gifts,** such as **knowledge** and **immortality**; to be *like* the *gods!* Just as Enoch tells us *those* Nachash (watchers) *gave* humanity so many *gifts* of **illicit** knowledge, that literally *destroyed* humanity!

With all this historical *knowledge* in mind, who better fits the *profile* of the the "*Man of Sin*" the "*Anti-Christ*" the "*False Prophet*" and the "**Beast**" than the **reincarnated Quain** (Nimrod-Osirus)? I personally have no doubt (my opinion) it will be *he* that causes the whole world to *jump* for **joy** and fulfill the roll of "*Man of Sin!*

Chapter 57

Michael, the Great Eagle

We find a very *strange* passage in **Exodus**, where the Creator *tells* His people He *brought* them **out** of Egypt "*on the wings of a great Eagle*"

Well, obviously, they didn't *ride* a **giant** eagle, so *what* does that scripture *mean*. Does that *great* **eagle** *exist* or is that passage simply a *meaningless* **metaphor**? But, *why* would the Creator *incorporate* such *language* unless there *actually* was **an** *eagle involved* in some way, *shape*, or form.

Well, to understand the *context*, we must understand the *animals* in **Genesis** 1 were, as we're told there, *made "after their kind"*. You can't make *something "after it's kind"* if *its* **kind** does not **first** *exist*. So, *what* existed *before* the **physical** animals? Well, **Job** tells us "*the stars* (angels) *sang for joy at the creation of the Earth*" and of course, the *creation* of the *physical* **animals** and *humans*! Obviously, the **physical** animals were created *after* their **angelic** *proteges*. (Stars, and/or sons of God)

In fact, we see the *one* that *deceived* Eve in the Garden was also an angelic "*beast*". We're told in **Genesis** 3, it was the "*craftiest of all the beasts*"! Obviously we are not talking about your average *cow*, **dog** or *goat*! In fact, according to **Revelation** 12, that *angelic* **beast** was a *dragon* that *launched* a *war* **against** the Creator!

Revelation 12 also tells us the *dragon* (one that was in the Garden) *conscripted* one *third* of the *angels* (other angelic *beasts?*) to **war** *against* the arch-*angel* **Michael** and *His* angels. Well, the *dragon* **lost** the *battle* and was *thrown* to Earth where it's been very *influential* in **manipulating** *things* from *behind* the **dimensional** *veil* ever since. We must keep in mind *here,* that II **Peter** 3:8 tells us **one** *day* in the *spirit* **realm**, is like 1000 years in *ours!* That said, we just don't *know* how *many* **thousands** of *years* ago that *war* occurred.

When the *dragon* fought against *Michael,* why would we **not** *assume* he was anything *other* than a beast (*animal)* of *sorts* as well? In the book of **Daniel** (chapter 10) we find *references* **angelic** *princes* (spirit kings) that had been *assigned* to *influence* and/or *control* those *nations* from *behind* the *scenes.* In fact, in **Daniel** 10 we find the angel *Gabriel* telling *Daniel* he had been *delayed* due to *fighting* (warring against) those **angelic** *princes* with *Michael,* and had to get *back* to the *fight.*

With the *thought* of **angelic** *princes* (beasts) in mind, **Daniel** 7 tells us of *four* **beast** kingdoms that *rise* and *fall* beginning with a *lion* with **eagles** *wings.* Then the *eagles* **wings** are *plucked* off the *lion* (to become a **separate** *nation*). Of course, we know the **lion** is the **angelic** *prince* of Great *Britain* and the *US* is the **eagles** *wings* that were *plucked* off. After all that's *exactly* **what** *happened* when the US *succeeded* from Britain!

Obviously, there's some **metaphor** *involved,* but the **real** *picture* is still quite *clear.* In fact we see *evidence* of that **eagle** *everywhere* in the US. Again, where did the **eagle** icon *originate; w*as it not from *Britain,* whose primary **animal** *icon* is the *lion* (eagle secondarily)? Just *who* or **what** is the Eagle *Icon* of the US? Does **that** *Eagle* have a **name**? If so, do the scriptures *tell* us? Well, we do have to *assemble* **many** *bits* and *pieces,* but we can *arrive* at a *fairly* **solid** *conclusion.*

First, we have many scriptures *making* the *connection* between the *stars* and *Angels* being *one* and the **same,** considering we are *told* the Creator calls *every* **star** (angel) by *name*! Adding more, we see Jacob *assigning* guardian **angels** (animal) to each of his sons in **Genesis** 49.

To *whom* the Eagle is *assigned* is shown *elsewhere*, but we do see how the *lion* was *assigned* to *Judah.* Then, with a little more digging (into non- Biblical records) we discover the prophet *Jeremiah* took the daughters of King *Zedekiah* to the **British** *Isles*, which they became the *first* **Jewish** *rulers* there. That's why we *see* **lions** on virtually **every** *family* crest in Britain.

Actually, we have **many** *clues* to whom *Michael* (the arch-angel) was *assigned*, like his *connection* to the *Israelites* **coming** *out* of *Egypt.* Plus, we saw the *eagle* **connected** to the *lion* in the *British* Isles. British, by the way, means "*Covenant man*". With whom did the Creator make **His** "*covenant*"? Was it not *Abraham,* **Issac**, and *Jacob*?

Interestingly, many very credible *genealogists* have *concluded* descendants of **all** the *tribes* of *Israel* are currently **here** in the US. In this *physical* world, there are *many* **degrees** of *rank*, which is also a *reality* in the *spirit* world.

Just as **every** *person* has apparently been *assigned* a **guardian** *angel* (lesser ranking angels) so has every *family,* **community** and *nation*! With that in mind, it seems *Michael* is the **angelic** prince *assigned* to the *people* of **Israel** as a *whole.*

We find more *evidence* of this in **Revelation** 12. There we find a *dragon* going after *a "Woman"* which we can only *conclude* is a *remnant* of the *Creator's* **chosen** people. What's *interesting* is how "*she is given two wings of a great eagle to fly her to a place*" (of safety). What a coincidence it was an **eagle** that *led* the *Israelites* out of Egypt as well. That said, how can we not *conclude* it's the **same** *Eagle*?

As for the *identity* of that *Eagle*, we find Him actually *named* in **Daniel** 12. There we find it's **Michael**, the Arch-Angel that "*stands **up** to **save** His **people***"! How interesting also, we find "*the **wings** that were **plucked off** the lion are stood **up** on two feet like a **man***" in **Daniel** 7! We can only *honestly* conclude it's a reference to *Michael* the great *Eagle* standing ***up*** (as a man) to **save** his *people*.

To recap; we see an *eagle* involved with *leading* the *Israelites* ***out*** of bondage (Egypt). Then in **Revelation** 12, we once again see an ***eagle*** *saving* a **remnant** of modern Israel. Again **Daniel** 7 tells us how the *eagle* (eagles wings) is "*stood **up** on two **feet** like a **man** and a **man's heart** is given to it*". Again, **Daniel** 12 tells us exactly who that one who "***saves his people***" is; *Michael* the **Arch**-*Angel*! He is the *great **angelic** eagle* and *savior* of *modern* **Israel**!

Chapter 58

New World (Solar) Order

Most everyone has heard of something called the *New **World** Order*; a new *One **World** government*. That one world order first *existed* in ancient times (Book of Enoch) and according to **Daniel** and **Revelation**, was prophesied to be *resurrected* in a *future* time from them. In fact, according to **Ezekiel** 28, there was *originally* a *One **Solar** Order* in ancient times.

According to **Ezekiel**, the ***perfectly*** *created* **Nachash** (dragon) was the *head* of that *solar **system** wide **trading*** empire! After going to *war* with *Michael*, and His Angels, it *lost* the *battle* and was *sentenced* to *live* on *Earth*, where it consequently *turns **up*** in YHWH's *Garden*. (Of Eden)

The *wise* man (Solomon) *proclaimed* there is "***nothing new*** *under the sun*" which seems *impossible* to comprehend in this modern *age* where we see so many *marvels* of *technology*. But, *archeology* has discovered *technology* we have ***not*** yet *duplicated,* ***existed*** *thousands* (even millions) of years ago. But then, the watchers (angels) have been around *millions* of years, *learning* and *developing* all sorts of *amazing* tec. and ***marvelous*** *machines*.

Also existing *thousands* of years ago, was a *solar **system** wide **trading** empire* which was *destroyed* in the ***war*** in *heaven* (Rev.12). Naturally, that ***dragon***, after being *marooned* on Earth, has been working to *reestablish* its ***trading*** empire. Unfortunately, that *trading **empire*** has been *confined* to the Earth and has *attempted* a *few **resurrection** efforts*.

The ***first** resurrection* of that ***trading*** empire was obviously *before* the great flood. We have very ***little*** *evidence* of it, but no doubt it *happened*. After all, *creatures* (animals and birds) always *rebuild* the ***same*** *kind* of *nest* or *den*. And the ***dragon***, being a *creature* of *habit* as well, has never stopped *attempting* to ***resurrect*** *its* ancient ***trading*** empire. We see many more *attempts* in the scriptures after the flood.

The *first* after the flood, was Babylon (tower of Babel). The second was Tyre (Phoenicia) which was the *trade **capital*** of the ancient world before being *destroyed* by Alexander. The *next* attempt was with the **Roman** empire. Rome opened up ***trade*** *connections* all-but worldwide. But then it was *destroyed* in the fifth century CE only to be *replaced* by the *British* Empire. The Brits *bragged* how the sun ***never*** *set* on the British *empire* because it really was a ***world**-wide* empire of which *trade* was very much a part of!

When we look *around* these days, *what* do we see virtually *everywhere* we look? Well, *advertising*! We are continually **bombarded** by *ads*, and we can't open a *magazine, newspaper*, turn on the *TV,* **computer** or *phone*, without being inundated with ***lures*** to *buy* virtually any *product* or *service* imagined. Again, the dragon's *one **world** trading **empire*** is being *resurrected* right *before* our eyes!

In fact, the NWO globalists have *divided* the world into **10** *"trade"* regions! But, most amazing is how we can see what is *happening* in our modern world simply by looking into **ancient** *history*. We must bear in *mind* with all this; *"**one** day"* in the time *continuum* in the **sprit** *world* is comparable to something like a **thousand** of *our* years! There really is **nothing** *new* under the sun, at least *outside* of Chokma and YHWH. Only they *create "**New** Things"*!

Unfortunately, every *recreation* of the **dragon's** *trading* **empire** is *doomed* to **fail** in that *those* **trade** *empires* are all based upon *greed* and *pride* (need to *impress* one's self and others) which are all *recipes* for *failure*.

On the other hand, a wonderful *concept* to *entertain* is how Bible *prophecies* tell us there will also be a *truly "**new**" world* **order** with **none** of the *evils* (lust, greed, hate, etc.) that are now being *fed* humanity. But, along with the new *peaceful,* **loving,** and *prosperous* **new** *Earth*, there will be a *new "**solar**"* order as well! We are told the **old** *world* will be *burned* (along with the evil watchers and their demonic nephilim *offspring*). Also *burned,* will be all those (humans) that *reject* YHWH and His *Torah* of **respect** and *love*.

Again, not only *was* the *Earth* **destroyed** in the **dragon** *war*, but the **solar** *system* as well. NASA has *found* **remains** of *civilization* **all** *through* our solar *system,* on *planets* (like Mars and Venus) and *moons*. The *evil* **watchers** and their *offspring* have *desperately* been *keeping* the **truth** of their *past* **actions** secret. In *maintaining* that *monstrous* **secret,** they have been able to **manipulate** *humanity* in every way, to ultimately *facilitate* our *eternal* **demise**.

But again, just as in *ancient* times, *they* **will** *fail*. In its *pride*, the *dragon* and its cohorts (offspring also) simply are *unwilling* to accept the *truth* that they **cannot** *defeat* the Creator(s) and their **righteous** *angels*. Pride, unfortunately makes *people* (and angels) **stupid**. Pride *flushes* **all** *reason* and *logic*. Because of their *pride*, they will go *down* in **flames** *fighting* an *un-winable* battle. Unfortunately, they are a **necessary** *evil*; *adversaries* for us to *fight*.

Getting back to the *subject* of the "*New* **Solar** *Order*" we are told that with the **new** *Earth* (after the great burning) will be a **new** *heavens*. Heavens have been thought by most to be **etherial** *realm* where the Creators and their *angels* **dwell**, but in this *context* of a *renewing* of a **physical** *Earth*, the *new* **heavens** can only mean **one** *thing*, **physical** heavens. (Solar system)

Obviously, to say this is *referring* to all **new** *stars* and *galaxies*, is silly. Considering Isaiah 45:18 tells us the Earth was **not** *created* in a *destroyed* **state** *implies* the *solar* **system** was also created *perfect* until *destroyed* by the dragon war with one *third* of the *angels*. New *heavens* can only mean one thing, a *perfectly* **restored** *solar* **system**!

Chapter 59

Oh My Stars!

Growing up, one of the popular *oaths* was to **swear** *by* the *stars*, as in; "*Oh my stars*". At the time, it didn't *mean* much to me, but as always, *knowledge* has a **cascading** *effect*. Each *time* we **gain** *understanding* in one *area*, it *triggers* understanding *in* **others**; like another *piece* of a *puzzle*. That said, just "**what**" *are* the *stars* that people would **swear** *by* **them**? After all, it's always been *customary* to *swear* by a **deity** or *God* (OMG) but what sense does it make to **swear** *by* a *burning* **ball** of *hydrogen*?

Well, it makes *no* sense until we *assemble* a few Biblical *clues* that seem to have been *buried* in the ever-shifting *sands* of **time**. The first is *found* in **Psalms** 138:8 (an *echo* of **Genesis** 1:16) where YHWH *ordained* "*the lesser lights*" (*moon* and *stars*) to "*rule* the *night*"! That said, doesn't a *person* have to be a **king** or *deity* to "*rule*"? As usual, it's one of those scriptures *shrugged* **off** as mere *metaphor*. But *what* if **it isn't**!?

If we put that scripture *together* with a *couple* more, it gets even more interesting! For instance; we find in **Psalms** 147, YHWH has **named** *each* of the *stars*! How interesting, but *why* in the world would YHWH **name** *each* of those *trillions* and *trillions* of *burning* **balls** of *hydrogen*? Wouldn't that be about as *redundant* as *naming* **each** grain of *sand* on the *sea*-shore? Hmm? What would be the point?

What's so *special* about these **supposed** lifeless **stars** (suns) for *them* to be personally *named*? Numbering, I can understand, but *naming*? What exactly are we are *missing*? Well, there's another scripture in **Job** (38:7) telling us how "*The stars sang for joy*" at the *creation* of the *Earth*" (and mankind)! Can *stars* really *sing* unless they are *alive* in *some* way? Again, just another scripture *dismissed as* **metaphor.**

We just read how the *stars* that **sang** for *joy* at the *creation* of Earth, were all *given* **names** by the Creator, and let's *not* forget; were also **ordained** to **rule**! To add more depth to *stars*, it's interesting to *note* the most oft used *word* for "*Angel*" in the Bible is "*Malak*". Malak also means "*king*" or (angelic) "*prince*"! What a coincidence the *Hebrew* word for "**stars**" is "*Kowkab*" which also *means* "**prince**" (princes) as well?

That information is enough to make a person's head *explode*, but there's still more! You see, scientists have *discovered* something very interesting about *light* in *experiments* such as "*The* **two slit** *experiment*". That *experiment* revealed *light* **cannot** be *consistently* measured. In fact, it **behaves** *differently* when *being* **observed** and when *not*! It's as if the *light* is **alive** and *conscious* and not just *lifeless* photons. (Charles-Chuck Missler) Remember, suns are **giant** *balls* of **light**, not just *heat*.

Adding even more *intrigue* to the *issue*, the book of **Revelation** speaks of the "*Great Dragon*" *gathering up a* "**third**" of the *stars*" (angels) with it! (Rev.12:3-4) Plus, the Book of **Enoch** (chap. 85) also speaks of **stars** *falling* from heaven in reference to the *watchers* as the context bears out.

Again, two more linking's of *stars* and *angels*! Maybe it doesn't make sense those *burning* balls of gas are **literally** *angels*, but is it not *possible* each *star* could be a *representation* of an *angel* in some way?

With those *thoughts* in mind, let's *examine* a shocking *truth* hidden right **in** *front* of our *faces* in reference to those "***watcher***" *stars* that **rule** the *night*! Remember, *night* is the *absence* of *sun* "**light**" with YHWH, Yahshua, both being *called* "*light*" and/or "*Light of the world*". That said, is it any *surprise*, that after Yahshua and YHWH's *Spirit left* in the *first* century it was called "*The* **dark** *ages*"? The truth is, it's been *spiritual* "**night**" ever since, and again, **Genesis** 1:16 informed us who "***rules*** *that* **night**"! (Moon and stars)

Taking a bizarre little *turn* in this study; an *author* named, Tom Stone, in *researching* his book "*Zeus*" was amazed to run into an old-timer in Greece, who boldly *declared*, in *response* to being *asked* about ***Zeus***; "*He was one of those* **Watchers** (angels)"! And no doubt he *was*, considering the *lore* shows him to be a *shape* **shifter**, *changing* between a *bird*, a **bull**, and *human*, among others. But, most interesting was his *penchant* for human *women; producing* beastly **half** *human* **offspring** such as the *Minotaur*!

That said, what a *coincidence* all the *attributes* of *Zeus* perfectly fit the 200 *watchers* of Enoch! And to top it off, these **rogue** *watchers* (angels) **taught** mankind all *manner* of **illicit** *knowledge* (Tree of the **knowledge** of *good* and **evil**) literally *destroying* humanity.

Interestingly also, is that watcher *Zeus* had 9 *offspring* called "*muses*" who were *instructed* to "**teach**" *humanity*. To make a *long* story short, YHWH finally put His foot down and sent His other *top* **watchers** such as **Michael**, **Gabriel**, **Uriel** and others to *arrest* the 200 and *lock* them in a *prison* called "*the pit*" and then *drown* all their *monstrous* **offspring** in a *flood*.

Enoch tells us in chapter 15 (v. 8-10) the *immortal* **spirits** of the **nephilim** (*offspring* of the *watchers*) would **not** be able to *return* to their **watcher** *fathers* and would be *bound* on Earth (like waterless clouds); *imprisoned* where they could still "contend, corrupt, oppress and bruise" humanity (if allowed)! Understanding that, can there be any doubt the **demon** *spirits* **possessing** humans (as well as *inanimate* objects) are literally the *spirits* of *these* nephilim?

Since the whole world was *filled* with them *before* the flood, there are probably *millions*, or even *billions*! With that thought, can there be any doubt what they're **doing** *now*? Would it not be *possessing* (reincarnating) and "*musing*" their **illicit** *knowledge* and *attitudes* to whomever *will* **allow** *them*? Let's not forget "*Muse*" is where the word "**music**" *originates* (of the muses)!

That brings us to the *conclusion* of this matter; *what* do we *call* those who *become* **great** in being *mused* (music, acting, and writing)? Well, aren't they are called "**stars**"? What a coincidence! And, *what* do they *call* the *great* **mused** pieces these **evil** *beings muse* (use) to **destroy** our *morality* and *families*? We all *know* that *one*; "*great* **hits**"! Uhhh, since when is being "*hit*" (**repeatedly**) a *good* thing?

Isn't that *called* "**abuse**"? Well, it seems those "*stars*" are quite *literally* **beating** (hitting) us *to* **death** and we shockingly just keep **taking** it and *taking* it (and loving it)! Well, it doesn't seem they can make **us** (our society) much more like *Sodom* and *Gomorrah*, which means their *reign* (rule) is about to *end*; at least for modern Israel! Fire and brimstone is about to once again rain *down*, but that's another study!

Chapter 60

Ode to Joy

The title of this *paper* has a ***familiar*** *ring*; it's a *beautiful* piece of *music*. But, the real *question* is; just ***what*** is *that joy*? Is it just a *fleeting **good** feeling* that *randomly **comes*** and *goes*? That in mind, is *Joy* the same *thing* as *happiness*? And, if not, what's the *difference*? How can we *know* we have "*that **joy***" a certain Bible scripture *references,* or is it something *else*?

Joy is an especially *prominent* subject in *Christian* and/or *Biblical* circles considering it's *listed* in scripture as *one* of the "*fruits*" of the "*Spirit*". That said, do those *fruits* also include *love* and *peace*? Of course, that begs the *question*; are they *connected* to, or a part of *joy* as well?

In fact, *how* is the *joy* of which the scripture *speaks*, any *different* from the *feeling* people *get* after *buying* a ***new*** car or *house*? In fact, Strong's Exhaustive Concordance of the Bible, tells us *one* of the *meanings* of *joy* is "*contentment*". Does *contentment* truly *encapsulate* the *average* persons *concept* of ***joy***?

Is the *Biblical* concept of *joy* just the *fleeting* joy of which we are all familiar, or "***continual***" *joy* and/or *contentment*?

Looking around, its quite obvious, no one *feels* **continual** *joy*, at least *not* in this world. But, again, there are those, especially in *Christian* circles, who *believe* we **should** *feel* **continuous** *joy* if we are *filled* with "**the Spirit**"; one of whose *fruits* being that *Joy*. But then, that *prompts* another question, *who* **has** that *Spirit* which brings that *joy,* and **how** do they *know*? In fact, if a person only *feels* **occasional** *feels* **joy**, is it *proof* they do **not** possess that **joy** *producing* Spirit?

That said, this whole *concept* of *joy* seems to be quite the *catch* **22** *conundrum.* Again **continuous** *joy* seems to be an **unknown** element in this *physical* world. But, even when filled with that *special* **spirit**, is **continuous** *joy* **possible**?

Can this *enigma* even be *resolved* in this *physical* **age** and *existence* at all? After all, how does a person feel *joy* when going through *horrific* **trials** such as **losing** a *loved* **one**?

Actually, isn't feeling *joy* in the *midst* of that *kind* of *terrible* **trouble**, a rather **morbid** and **masochistic** *oxymoron*? After all, how can this *idea* of **joy** *negate* the *concept* of **mourning**? Are we to no longer *mourn* tragic *loss* after discovering that (continual) *Spirit* of *Joy*?

With that in mind, maybe the *only* way to *find* or *have* **continuous** *joy,* is the complete *cessation* of **hurts** and *trials*? But again, is that *possible* in this *physical* existence? Maybe those occasional *fleeting* moments of *joy* we currently *experience* are just a *sampling* or **precursor** of the **real** *thing* to *come*, that is in the **next** *realm*?

With that in mind, is that joy *referenced,* only *possible* when we are *literal* **spirit** *beings*? After all, if all the *evils* of this **physical** *existence* are *removed*, as the *prophecies* of the "*new* **Eden**" tell us, wouldn't **continual** *joy* and/or *contentment* then be *possible*? Remember, **Isaiah** tells us there will be **no** *sorrow* or *death* there! What a *promise*! It is certainly something to look *forward* too!

But, the only way to **be** *there* is to *embrace* the Creator, by showing *honor* to His **exclusive** Name *YHWH,* and *practicing* His *Torah* of **Love**. In that **new** *coming* **realm** I have dubbed "the **New Eden**" everyone will be *walking* with YHWH and His *Torah,* and evil will *no* longer be *allowed* to **exist** and *metastasize* like a *cancerous* **disease** as in *this* world!

Chapter 61

Oh the Grace!

One of the prime *tenets* of Christianity is "***Saving Grace***". In fact, one of the most well-known Christian *songs* is one called "***Amazing Grace***". But, do the scriptures really *teach* we are **saved** "*by grace*"? And, just *what* does it mean to be "*saved*" in the *first* place? *Saved **from** what?* Are we *saved **from** calamity,* from **disease,** or maybe *saved **from** sin,* the *penalty* of which is **death**? Well, *looking* around, I *fail* to see *Christians* (or anyone else) being *saved* from any of **those** things.

So, what exactly **is** *grace* and just ***what** is **it** saving* us ***from***? If I were to *ask* the *average* Christian just what *grace* **saves** *them* **from**, I believe the primary *answer* would be "*hell*". But, then, **what** is *hell*? Well, the *Catholic* (universal) version is an *ever* **burning** *place,* apparently *deep* in the Earth, where *the* **devil** and his *demons* are *kept*.

That belief most likely *originated* with the **Book of Enoch's** *teaching* of the *200* **Watchers** (guardian angels) that **rebelled** and consequently were *imprisoned* in *a* **pit,** which **Revelation** 9 calls "*the bottomless pit*". It is from *there* those *watchers* (rebel angels) will be one *day* be **released**. (The *fifth* trumpet plague-Revelation 9)

The primary word *translated "Hell"* in scripture, is *Hades*. Hades is one of the Olympian *brothers* **Zeus** *saved* from their **evil** *tyrannical,* **father** *Cronos* (King of the Titans who *swallowed* them at birth). Using *poison,* Zeus caused him to *regurgitate* his *siblings* and then consequently *dethrone* him in a *coup*. Hades, Zeus's brother was the "**anointed one**" (Christ) to *rule* that *pit,* or *underworld* of the **living** *dead* (watchers).

Actually, the Greek word *Hades* basically means *underground*. In fact, the old English word for "*hole*" was "*hell*" the place people kept their *potatoes* and *apples* for the winter! It was also the *place* people were *placed* when they *died*! (Buried underground)

Other prominent *words* translated **hell**, are *Sheol*, and *Gehenna* (lake of fire). *Gehenna* is simply a *corruption* of the *Hebrew* "*Valley of Hinnon*". Hinnon was the *garbage* **dump** for Jerusalem, which was **always** *burning*. It was also the *place* where the *homeless* and *poor* were *thrown* after they *died;* in other words "**hell** *fire*". Considering everyone *dies* (in this age) and is **buried** or *burned* (cremation) so much for *grace* being *salvation* from *hell*! *Sheol* then, is a *Hebrew* word also *meaning* **underground** and/or *death*. Again, *what* does "*Grace*" *save* us *from,* if **not** *death*?

The other big *argument* is *grace* **saves** our "*souls*" from *another* hell; *eternal* **separation** from our *Creator*. Unfortunately, the **immortal** *soul* is **not** a *Biblical* teaching at all. **Ezekiel** 18 tells us "*the* **soul** *that* **sins,** *it shall die*"; **not** *live* **forever** in a *torturous* hell. (Or Heaven)

As for **eternal** *separation,* **actual** *death* **does** *exactly* **that**! In fact, **Ecclesiastes** 9 tells us; "*The* **dead** *know* **nothing** *at all*". Again, there's your **eternal** *separation*! In all honesty, how could a god, let alone the *God* of **Mercy** (YHWH) *condemn* people to an **eternity** of **torture**? Well, it certainly isn't a *god* I wish **any** *association*!

Getting back to *grace*, it's said it **saves** *us* from our *sin* (sins). But, considering the *penalty* for *sin* is **death** (Rom. 8:26) and last I checked, everyone is **still dying**! That means the *penalty* for humanities *sins* has **not been removed**! In spite of what people **want** to *believe*, the **proof** is in the *pudding* (as they say).

We can *deny* **what's** *happening* all around if we wish, but **fact** is *fact*! The *price* for our *sins* is still being *paid* **by** *our* **deaths**. But then, there's **no-one** *we* **lie** to *more* than *ourselves*! With that in mind, what about *grace* **saving** us from *calamity* and/or *disease,* at least?

Well, again, last I checked, the *rate* of **disease**, such as *cancer* and **heart** *disease,* covid. etc. is just as *high* among Christians as the *rest* of the *world*! And, thats *not* to mention **failed** *marriages.* Christians echo Pauls' teaching of "*grace*" as "*unmerited* **pardon**". But, *where's* **that** *pardon?* Well, it seems to be *imaginary,* at best!

It all goes *back* to why *Paul* and *Christianity* as a whole *teach,* that the *Law* (Torah instructions) was **replaced** by *grace* because *keeping* the *Torah* is just *too* **hard**; in fact, *impossible*! Replacing the *living* (loving) **instructions** of the *Torah* with *grace,* seems a *logical* **solution**, but unfortunately, is an *argument full* of **holes,** or "*holy*" (pun intended).

After all, why would the Creator give us *living* (behavioral) *instructions,* we **can't possibly keep**? Was He *not* **smart** *enough* to see the *problem* **upfront**, which supposedly *forced* Him to *resort* to a *plan B*? But, according to **Revelation** 9 the so-called "*Plan B*" was the **original** *Plan,* not an *alternative*!

With that in mind, *why* was it Paul *complained* of *doing the* **things** he *did* **not** *want* (sin) and **not** *do* the *things* he **wanted**? Does that not perfectly *explain* the **Christian** *condition?* No wonder *Christianity* **loves** *Paul* so much. Interestingly, **not** *one* of the **twelve** *apostles* **complained** of **Paul's** *problem?* (No, not one)

The Hebrew *Messiah* told His *Disciples* that *after* He *left*, He would **send** *them* a (Spirit) "*Helper*". In fact, the *day* after He *departed* into the *sky*, "*Pentecost*" that "*helper*" *YHWH's* **Spirit,** fell on *120*! But, Paul was **not** one of those *120*.

The bottom line; because of the *spirit* of the *dragon* (pride) was *instilled* into humanity ever since the *Garden*, it's *impossible* to stand *against* that *spirit* **without** the *help* of the Creator's *Spirit*. Since Christianity has **not** *received* that *great* **outpouring** either, they are in the *same* **sinking** *boat* as Paul!

Yes, *grace* is **unmerited** *pardon; shown* in the **blood** of the OT *animals*. When a *sin* is *committed*, that can't be *undone*, **someone** or *something* has to *shed* its blood (die) to *pay* the **price** for that *sin*. That's *unmerited,* or undeserved *pardon*. That *price* (blood) is *grace*.

Unfortunately, Christianity has been *duped* into *believing* the 1st century Messiah *shed* His *blood* for them and **removed** *their* **sins**, but they are *forgetting* one *major* **fact**. The Hebrew Messiah fulfilled the *Passover* **rehearsal** of *shedding* His blood for the "**First-born**"! He died **only** for the <u>*first-born*</u>, which was His *Priesthood*. They (the first-born) had the **death** penalty **removed** when they *received* the *great* **outpouring** of the *Spirit* of **Life** in **Acts** 2! Bottom line, *grace* is **forgiveness** and/or **atonement**.

Considering everyone's *still dying,* means *they still* need someone to atone (shed blood) for their *sins*. That someone is pictured by the *Atonement* **goat** that's *slain* for the sins of the *balance* of **house** of **Israel**. Considering the *Feast* of *Trumpets* has come in **real** *time* (Donald Trump-Trumpet King) that *sacrifice* is *still* **coming**; *shortly*.

How interesting it will be to see *exactly* who that *Atonement* "*goat*" is! Well, putting **Daniel** 7:3, **Daniel** 12 and **Revelation** 12 together, a strong case can be made, that "*One*" is **Michael** the *Arch-Angel*! He was also the One that led the people out of Egypt and is the one that takes the "*Woman*" to her *place* of *protection* for *three* and one **half** *years*! (Rev.12)

Chapter 62

Who is The Prodigal Son, Really?

If you're like me, you have probably heard *hundreds* of preachers *teaching* and *quoting* the *story* of the "*Prodigal son*" in **Luke** 15. I'm pretty sure I've never heard a single *one* use it as any more than a *personal* **story** of the **Father's** *forgiveness* of our *wayward* (gentile) ways. Is that *true* or is there much **more** to *that* parable than meets the average *eye*? I say that because of *what* Yahshua the *Hebrew* Messiah told **His** disciples in **Matthew** 13 when they asked Him "*why He spoke in parables*".

His *explanation* is virtually the *opposite* of *what* the *churches* and their **pagan** *god* **worshipping** *teachers*, **teach** their congregations. He told them He *spoke* in *parables* so "**no one**" except **them** (with His help) would be *able* to *understand*! With that in mind, *some* parables He *explained*, but others such as the **Prodigal** *son*, he did not; or should I say it wasn't written down for us. That said, does *pagan Christianity* really *understand* **what** that **parable** is all about? Do we?

The truth of the *story* of the *Prodigal son* is actually very simple if one keeps the ***big*** *picture* in mind. It was a story very *relevant* to Yahshua's ***first*** century ***disciples*** (not us). It's a truth that has been *hidden* from us right in *front* of our *faces*, which very few understand! You see, Yahshua *sent* His *disciples* (in pairs) to go "*only to the Lost tribes of Israel*" (the diaspora) who had been *scattered* throughout Europe *not* the *Jews*! (Matt. 15:24)

Just *who* then were the *lost* ***ten*** *tribes* or *diaspora* of Israel? Well, the story is clearly told in **I Kings** 12, when *Solomon* turned the kingdom over to his son *Rehoboam*. But, Rehoboam, unlike his *wise* father, *listened* to his ***foolish*** *young* ***advisers*** who told him to basically *turn* the people into ***slaves*** of the *king* with ***high*** *taxes* and *heavy* ***burdens***.

Obviously, that was extremely ***unwise*** *advice* for Rehoboam to *accept of* his foolish young *advisers*, which caused a ***split*** in the *kingdom*. A servant of Solomon, Jeroboam *rebelled* and managed to *convince* ten of the tribes to *adopt* ***his*** *rule* (kingship) versus Rehoboam.

Jeroboam then set up a *new* place of worship in *Samaria* with the *statues* of *two* ***bulls*** (like the one at Sinai) as *depictions* of their *Watcher* ***god***. Apparently, the *bull* was (is) the ***spirit*** *watcher* ***assigned*** to the *tribe* of Ephraim. We still see ***that*** *bull* in New York at the *stock* exchange *building* in downtown *Manhattan*.

The *bull* is *believed* to be a ***blesser*** *of* the *people*, which is *why* when stock market *rises* in value, it is called a "*bull market*". Personally, I think ***expecting*** *blessings* from that *bull* is a *whole* ***lot*** of *bull!* But that's another subject!

Getting back to the *prodigal* son then, it's quite obvious just "*who*" *he* is. We need only understand that when the *ten* tribes (as a whole) *rejected* YHWH (their Spiritual Father) to *worship* the *bull* (a gentile practice of worshipping the angel (demon) watchers) they were *allowed* ***their*** *choice*.

The land they were given in Canaan was *their* **inheritance** from YHWH. And, of course, most know the story of how they *squandered* that *inheritance* with **unclean** (unrighteous) living and *worshipping* the **gentile** gods until being *conquered* by *Assyria*.

Because of that, the *northern* 10 tribes ended up being *conquered* and *enslaved* of the *gentile* **Assyrians** and eventually were *scattered* all throughout the **gentile** *lands* and nations of Europe. Fortunately, YHWH their *father* did **not** *forget* them and *welcomed* His **repentant** *son* (sons) back in the **first** century.

But, as the parable shows, the **other** *son* who *stayed* (Judah-Jews) was **not** *happy* with the Father's *acceptance* and *celebration* of His **wayward** *son* (Judah's brother) But the Jews in the *first* century *viewed* the **scattered** *tribes* (diaspora) the same as any *other* **gentiles**! In fact, *thats* **what** was *going* **on** in **Acts** when Paul (a Pharisee) *confronted* **Peter** for *eating* with these **lost** *Israelites* the *Jews* **called** *gentiles*!

YHWH, with the *vision* of the **unclean** *animals* being *lowered* in the sheet, was *showing* Peter His *wayward* son (lost tribes) had *become* **unclean**. But then YHWH told Peter that those *unclean* animals; the *Jews* **unclean** *brother* (the *diaspora* of the ten tribes) were now *forgiven* and **cleansed**.

Ironically, those *Jews* **still** to **this** *day* do **not** *accept* the fact the so-called **lost** *tribes* of Israel are **not** *lost* at all and are still very *valuable* and *precious* to their **Father** *YHWH*! We must keep in mind YHWH's *prophecy* to His *prophet* **Amos** that He would *sift* His people *Israel* among all the nations (gentiles) yet not the *smallest* grain (seed) *would* **fall** to the *ground* (be lost)! No, YHWH is not some **inept** *god* that "*loses*" His *chosen* people and even worse, *throws* **them** *away*!!

Unfortunately, that's the *kind* of *god* Christianity *worships*. If *that's* the *kind* of *god we **also** worship*, my *advice* is to *find **another***; one who *loves* His people *enough* to **not** *discard* them and who is *smart* and *powerful* enough to **not** *lose* them like the Christian father god did! I know I certainly *want* a *God* that **loves** *me* enough to **not** *throw* me **away** and/or **lose** *me*!

Actually, YHWH (the Father) has **great** *plans* for both *His **sons** working **together***. (Ez.37) You see, it's *Ephraim* (Joshua) and *Judah* (Caleb) who are **destined** to **lead** *modern* **Israel** into the *new* (true) **promised** *land*!

That's why all the *Muslim* nations (and most of the world) **hate** *us* so much (primarily the Jews-Israel and Ephraim-the United States). Their *demon **puppet** masters* know full well *what* YHWH has *planned* for *us*. Many scriptures show it is also **modern** *Israel* who is to be *the* **priesthood** to the *gentiles*; that is, the ones to **lead** *them* to YHWH!

Chapter 63

Prayer, What is it?

We often hear people *telling* others they would **pray** for them, but, *what* does that mean, even if they are actually *telling* the *truth*? Unfortunately, many people *promise* others *such **things*** just to make *them* ***feel*** *good*, but if they really **do** *pray* for someone, to *whom* do they *pray*? Does *praying* to *just **any** spirit* or ethereal *god* do?

Then, *what* do we **pray** *when* we do? Do we *ask* our *god* a **generic** *prayer*, like **bless** that *person*? If so, what does "*bless*" actually *mean*? And, if we do, what *kind* of *answer* do we *expect **if*** we *expect* to get an *answer* at all? In fact, *what **if*** the *god* you pray to *doesn't **want*** to *bless* the person you're *asking* to *bless*? Or again, *what* if that *god* is not a **real** *god* at all, but simply a *figment* of *imagination*?

think that **brings** us to the *point;* how do we *truly **know*** if we can really trust **our** *god*, or if our *god* is even *real?* And even if *real*, **why** do we *believe* we can *trust* that god to do *anything* for us? That said, if there is any *gage*, or way to *measure*, it would probably be **real** *time* **history** or *experience*, would it not? After all, isn't the *proof* in the *pudding*, as they say? For instance, *what* if we *pray* for *something* or *someone* and the prayer seems to be *answered*, how can we be sure it isn't simple *coincidence*?

On the other hand, say the *answer* comes in some **supernatural way**, how can *know* it came from a **good** source? After all, *witches* and *satanists* do many **supernatural** things. What is *their* **power** source? If we're to *incorporate* the *Bible*, we can be sure the *source* of **their** power is **not** *originating* from a *good* or **benevolent** entity. After all, the Bible speaks of many **lying** *spirits* which do *lying* **signs** and *wonders*. A *powerful example* is king Saul using the witch of Endor to necromance Samuel for *advise* on the *battle* against the *philistines*. That shows the *power* of the *dark* side! (I Sam. 28)

With that in mind, Hitler reportedly said; "*If you want **people** to **believe** you, **tell** them a **lie**"*! Is that *true*? Well, if history can be *trusted*, Hitler certainly *proved **that** conjecture* with *flying* colors! Why is that? Why and/or *how* was he able to **convince** people to believe such *outrageous lies* such as the *Jews* (and a few others) being *inhuman*?

With those thoughts in mind, how can we be sure it isn't the *liars* on the **other** *side* of the *curtain* using **magic** (think Wizard of Oz) to **trick** us into *following* and *believing* in **them** versus the *righteous* ones, like Samuel being *summoned* from the *dead* for Saul?

Besides, isn't it *important* for us to *fully* **know** and trust that *help* and/or *provision* will be *given* when *really* needed and not simply *hit* and *miss*? Looking around, *hit* and *miss* seems to be the *norm*!

Sometimes *prayers* are answered **when** *needed* and for *what* was *asked*, but most times, not so much. Again, why is that? Just *how* can we be *sure* who the *true* **God** *is* and if we can **trust** Him to take *full* **care** of us, not to mention to *answer* our *prayers* **when** and *how* we ask?

Well, a scripture *tells* us, the **steps** of the *righteous* are *ordered* (orchestrated) by *YHWH*. That leaves the over-arching *question*; what constitutes a **righteous** person? Well, *short* and to the *point*, **righteous** simply means; "*to **do** the **right** thing*" but *what **is*** the "**right** *thing*"?

Assembling all the scriptures, the **right** (righteous) *thing* is to adhere to the Creator's *Torah* (instructions) of **love** as roughly *outlined* in the Ten *Commandments* (literally, words of love instruction).

The **first** *four* show **love**, *respect*, and *honor* to and *for the Creator Father*; to *worship only* Him; to show *respect* to His **exclusive** Name, and to *honor* His **Sabbath** *celebrations*. The last *six* are about showing *love* and *respect* to each *other*. The last six were more fully *elaborated* upon by the *Hebrew* Messiah in the *first* century.

Another scripture tells us the **proud** *heart* is an *abomination* to YHWH. Personally *walking* with Him in humility is *how* we come to *know* how *real* and *trustworthy* He is. If we then mesh that with a couple other scriptures, such as "*pray without ceasing*" we begin to understand, **real** *prayer* is a literal *on-going* **conversation** with our Creator *Father!* With that *kind* of *relationship*, we begin to literally understand *how* He *thinks* and *what* He *expects*.

Suddenly, *prayer* becomes a **real** *thing* and not just *wishful* and/or **etherial** *thinking*. Also, we *begin* to see the *little* **miracles** He *consistently* **orchestrates** *for* **us** (as He *promises*). But again, to have that *relationship*, we must *recognize* and put *away* our *pride*. Considering *pride* is a **lying** *spirit*, seeing it **in ourselves** is **impossible;** without **supernatural** *help!*

Our *pride* can only become *visible* to us if we *fervently* **pray** to have it **shown** **us**. It's a **painful** *process*, but absolutely necessary. The reason YHWH **cannot** *walk* with the *proud*, is because *pride* is the **spirit** of His chief *adversary*, the **dragon**. That spirit, is the *spirit* of **death**, while the *Spirit* of *YHWH* is the **Spirit** *of* **Life**.

The two are entirely *incompatible* with each other. Again, we have to *educate* ourselves to **our** *pride* before we can **do** *anything* about it. In fact, we're told "*My people are destroyed for lack of knowledge*". (Hosea 4:6) The *greatest* of that **knowledge** is of **our** own *pride* and how to *replace* it with the *Spirit* of **Humility** and *life*.

Only with *true* (not false) *humility* can we *walk* with our Creator and truly *know* **how** to *pray* and **what** to *pray*. YHWH is the **only** *God* that can be ***fully*** *trusted* to *keep* His Word and be *there **for** us* **when** and *where* we *need* Him. All the *other* gods, of which there are *many*, are *fickle* and cannot be *fully* **trusted**.

They will *throw* us a *bone* (so to speak) occasionally, just to get our *trust*, but never constantly follow *through* with any **real** love for us. After all, they *hate* us because of their *hatred* for our Creator.

In spite of their *hatred* for **YHWH** and *mankind*, the ancient *writings* show us they also *loved* the *adoration* and **worship** of *humanity*. Their *spirit* of *pride* drives their *need* for our *idolization* of them. Plus, if they can get us *away* from *YHWH*, they *believe* they can *ultimately* take us into the "*lake of fire*" **with** *them*!

Again, a *close* **prayerful** *walk* with our Creator YHWH is **what** will *keep* us from the *death* they *desire* for us. But, it has to be **real** *prayer* and to YHWH, not *one* of the thousands of *other* gods! Also, what it's *not*, is how we *fold* our *hands*, are on our knees, or have our heads *bowed* or *covered*, eyes *closed* and/or hands *raised*. Those are all *traditions* meant to make **whatever** *prayer* we *pray* **feel** *real*. (But not necessarily bad)

Bottom line, for **our** *prayer* to be truly **real**, we must have a *literal* relationship with our Creator which can **only** *happen* if put **away** all the *pagan* and/or *false* gods, their *ways* and *embrace* YHWH and **His** *Torah* of Love!

Chapter 64

Rapture?

Interestingly, the word "*rapture*" is *not found* in the Bible's *original* manuscripts, but has come to be *viewed* as if it were. Although, a very good *case* for such a *concept* can be *made* by **privately** *interpreting* a few Bible passages, but upon **close** contextual *examination*, that *idea* is **no** *different* from their *belief* the **Hebrew** Messiah had a **Greek** *Name*; one *dedicated* to Zeus, no less!

With that in mind, the whole **rapture** *doctrine* is based upon a few *passages* in **Matthew** and **I Thessalonians**. Upon close *examination* of *one* of the passages in **Matthew,** we find it very *problematic* in regard to supporting the **rapture** *theory*. There, we find Yahshua telling His Disciples how "*-two men would be in the field; **one** would be **taken** and the other **left**; two woman will be grinding at the mill; **one** would be **taken** and the other **left**.*" (Matt.24:40-41) The common *conclusion* is those **taken** are *taken* to *heaven*; i.e. in a *rapture*.

To glean the *whole* truth, we need to back up to verses 37-39 and *notice* the *context*. Yahshua was *instructing* them how *His **return*** would be; "*as the days of Noah—*" where the *flood* came *upon* them and "*took them all away*". (Matt.24:37-39) But notice; the <u>ones **taken**</u> in *the **time*** of ***Noah*** were the *ones **drowned*** in the *flood* while those ***not*** taken (Noah and his family) were *saved*! One *thing's* for sure; in the context of those *couple* scriptures, *being* "***taken***" was to be *taken* in ***death***, and *not a good **thing***! So much for "***that***" *rapture*!

The other major scripture used to *support* the *rapture **theory*** is I ***Thessalonians*** 4:14-17. The *writer* of ***Thessalonians*** (not Paul, according to a world leading *expert* in NT writings; Bart Ehrman) speaks of *rising* into the *air* to meet "*the Lord*" at some point in time. Of course, to understand that set of scriptures we have to *understand **who*** was being *addressed* and *what* the ***time*** period was. One thing's for sure; it's ***not** us*!

Yahshua clearly told His disciples (privately) "*this* (their) *generation*" would "*not pass*" until all the ***things*** He had just *told* them, such as the ***destruction*** of *Jerusalem* and ***His*** return (for them- Matt.24:34). Unfortunately, everyone *argues* He was actually *preaching **over*** their ***heads***, but if that were so, how would he *not* be "*a **deceiver***"? After all, *three **major*** *apostles*; ***James***, ***John***, and ***Peter*** as well as the *writer* of ***Thessalonians*** "*all*" *believed* and ***taught*** Yahshua was *coming* in <u>*their generation*</u>!

The Apostles teachings *proved* they *believed* Yahshua was *speaking **to*** *them* and if He ***didn't*** come in ***their*** generation, those *chief **first*** century *apostles* were *definitely **deceived***! Were they?

Besides, if we pay *attention* to the ***fact*** the *Passover* (shedding of the blood) the ***wave-sheaf*** (death and *resurrection* of the *saints* of *old*) and ***Unleavened Bread*** (the filling with YHWH's Spirit) all *happened* in ***real*** *time* just as *rehearsed*; how is it the *process* of the ***spring*** harvest ***stopped*** right after the Spring Harvest *countdown* to its ***completion***, was ***initiated*** (by the Wave Sheaf ceremony)?

Let's not forget, the wave-sheaf not only symbolized a *resurrection* (the first mass resurrection) but *signaled* the "**beginning**" of the **spring** *harvest* (the balance-bulk of the *first* resurrection)!

That said, did the wave-sheaf (resurrection of the saints of old) which *signaled* the **beginning** of the *spring* harvest (of people) "count *fifty*" later, really **not** come to *fruition*? We must also not forget the *spring* harvest was called "*The **Feast** of **First-Fruits**". Who are the *First-Fruits*? Well, according to the Torah books (Leviticus and Exodus) they were the "*First- born*" which YHWH said were "***His***" and were to be *brought* to **serve** *Him* in *His* Temple; a good *example* being **Samuel**!

To bring this *together*, there can be no doubt the *completion* of the **spring** *harvest* was **completed** in the **first** *century* following the **starting** *flag* of the **real**-*time* **wave-sheaf** (resurrection of the **saints of old** in Matt. 27:52). Otherwise, not only would that have made the *Messiah* a **deceiver**, but the **outline** *rehearsed* from **Leviticus** 23 would also be *nonsense*! YHWH does **not** (did not) *make* **mistakes** concerning the *implementing* of His *Plan* (Feasts) which He *instructed* His people to **rehearse** all those centuries'!

No, after the "***fifty*** *count*" from the *wave-sheaf* (fifty years) the *beginning* of the **spring** *harvest*, there can be absolutely **no doubt** Yahshua **returned** to *complete* that **Firstfruit** (priestly) *harvest,* which by the way, was also the **Jubilee** (releasing of all debts-including *death*-the ultimate debt)! So, the *so-called* **rapture** *predicted* in **I Thessalonians** 4 *happened* in the **first** *century* and has *nothing* to do with us in this *fall* **harvest** *age* except to *confirm* <u>**our** *priesthood*</u> is with Yahshua in Heaven!

The bottom line; there's *nothing* in the Bible *predicting* a **rapture** of *any* kind during the **fall** *harvest,* which was *initiated* by Donald Trump (meaning Trumpet king) and the **Revelation** 12 *"sign of the woman"* *occurring* exactly during the *Feast* of *Trumpets* in September of 2017. By the way, all the *astronomers* I've heard said such a *planetary* **alignment** was **impossible**, at least *naturally!*

Also, **Revelation** 21 and 22 *predicts* "*heaven*" **comes** here at the time of the *end,* not the *other* way around! Yes, the *priesthood* along with the (24) *elders* (saints of old-Rev.4:4) went to *Heaven* in the **first** century when Yahshua *came* **back** for *them,* but that's only until the **fall** *harvest* begins and they apparently come *back* (trans-dimensionally) with Yahshua to *usher* in the **new** *Eden!* (New Promised Land)

After that, the first century *priesthood* will *reside* with YHWH in His new House (city) which, if we can *believe* **Revelation** 21:16, will be some *1500* **MILES** *square* as well as **high**! Just for perspective, that's many times higher than our satellites! Some believe it's a giant *pyramid* but there's no proof. At any rate, and again, it's in this city where YHWH, Yahshua and His *priesthood* will *live*! It will be YHWH's "**real**" eternal *temple* and **dwelling** *place*!

The only *honest* conclusion upon which to *arrive* **from** the *scriptures,* is YHWH's people (fall harvest) are *not* going to be *raptured* **anywhere**, and will be right *here* to *welcome* YHWH and His *new* city, along with our *High* **Priest** *Yahshua* and **His** *Priesthood!* (Ours too) How more *exciting* can it get?

Chapter 65

The Revival and Raising of Israel

It seems every *Bible* based *denomination* in *existence* has *fabricated* virtually every *private* **interpretation** of Biblical *prophecies* imaginable. Unfortunately the primary *reason* for all that **private interpretation** is **lack** of *understanding* "*who* is **who**" in this modern age.

Considering *understanding* begins with *honoring* (following-*exercising*) YHWH's "**Torah**" *instructions* (Ps.111:10) Christianity has unfortunately *cut* themselves *off* from even a *clue* as to *who* is **who** or **what,** is *occurring*. Sadly, they give a *somewhat* honest effort to *keeping* the *six* **Torah** *instructions* involving *loving* our *fellow* humans, but completely *flush* the **first** *four* in lieu of their *worship* of *pagan* and **false** *gods*.

Let's be clear, it's *not* their *fault* **directly**, considering the demons are extremely *powerful* and YHWH *allowed* them (by design) to *influence* the *translators* to **change** all the "*Quodesh*" (set apart-*exclusive*) *Names* in the Bible to **generic** and/or downright **pagan** *names*, like "**the Lord**" (Baal)! **Baal** is "*the Lord*" and/or "*master*" in the *Canaanite* tongue; the **favorite** *pagan* **god** of the *ancient* Israelites.

Of course, the *demons* have also *convinced* the *majority* of *Christianity* that modern Israel (basically the Western nations) *are* **gentiles**; that YHWH (our Creator Father) *somehow* "*lost*" His "*chosen*" *people*! How silly, considering **Amos** 9 *prophecies* that Israel would be *scattered* over the *world* but **not** one **seed** (Israelite) would be *lost*! Besides, what *kind* of God *loses* His **chosen** people anyway?!

Understanding "*who*" is **modern** *Israel* is, is extremely *imperative* to *understanding prophecy*. In *ancient* times (as now) *Ephraim,* the **younger** *brother* of *Manasseh*, was the **largest** *tribe* of *Israel*. In fact, many places in scripture (like Hosea) the entire *northern* **ten** tribes were referred to as *Ephraim*.

In light of the *prophecies* given to the sons of *Joseph* in **Genesis** 48 (v.17-22) it's easy to make the case that *England* (who still *possesses* the *scepter* of David) *qualifies* as **Manasseh** (first born). We must keep in mind these *two* Israelite *tribes* were to be *blessed* **above** all the *other* tribes.

But, it was the *younger* brother, *Ephraim* (*meaning "double fruit"*) who would become the **greater** of the *two*. We have seen that *play out* very clearly in our time! Obviously, the *US* became much *greater* in **population**, *wealth* and **power** than his *older* **brother** *Great Britain*!

Understanding *modern* **Ephraim** is the *US*; suddenly the Bible book of **Hosea** literally *comes* **alive**! You see, the *prophecies* given to *Ephraim* in that book are primarily for "**modern**" *Israel*; of whom *Ephraim* is the *largest* tribe. Although **Hosea** is full of amazing *insights* into the *conditions* of modern *Israel* and *Ephraim*, I'm only going to *focus* on **one** prophecy, which is *one* of the most *astounding* **prophecies** in the Bible; **Hosea** 6:4. This is one of *greatest* **proofs** the Bible has *great* **truth**!

This *prophecy* began with *what* was *about* to *happen* to **ancient** *Israel* (and Ephraim) in **their** *time;* their *impending* **captivity** to *Assyria* and subsequent *scattering* among the *gentiles*. The prophecy then *switches* to *what* will *happen* to them, literally *thousands* of *years* in the *future*! Let's take a look!

YHWH is *prophesying* through **Hosea** in chapter 6 saying; *"Come and let us return to YHWH* (after the scattering and captivity) *for He has torn, but He will bind us up. After two days He will revive us and on the third day, He will raise us up."*

It is easy to read right *over* that astonishing *prophecy* **without** even *seeing* it! You see, this *prophecy* was *given* just *before* Israel's (not Judah) *captivity* to *Assyria* around 720 BCE. So, His "*tearing*" and "*binding up*" were *still* **future** events as was the *rest* of the *prophecy*! That said, *what* He says *next,* is where it really gets *exciting!*

He goes on to say; "*after two days He will revive us*"! Obviously this was *also* a **future** *prophecy,* but *what* did He *mean* by "*after two days*"? Again, it certainly could not be a *reference* to **two** *literal days*, or even *two* years considering Israel was *never "healed"* (bound up) in *ancient* times. Well, we have the answer in **II Peter** 3:8; "*But beloved, do not forget this one thing; that with YHWH one day is as a thousand years and a thousand years as one day*"!

So, when *Hosea* said YHWH would "*bind up*" Israel after "*two days*" it's certain He was *referring* to *two* **thousand** years after being "*torn*"! Jumping *forward* 2000 years from 720 BCE, we *arrive* in the *middle* of the *13th* century. Considering the Assyrian king Sennacherib's *conquest* of Israel was between 690 and 710 (torn) it makes the 13th century *two* **spiritual** *days*. That said, *what* was *happening* in the 13th century?

Well, by 1300, the *scattered* **tribes** of *Israel* had *thrown* off the yoke of *Rome* and were *establishing* their own *lands* and **empires** (nations); that's *not* to *mention* the *great* **awakening** of *understanding*; especially *Biblical!*

John Wycliffe *translated* the Bible into the *common*-man's *language* for the *first* time in 1380! Then, the *printing* **press** was *invented* shortly after by Johannes *Gutenberg* in 1440. Those events fulfilled the **first** part of that *prophecy* to "*return to YHWH*"! Plus **technological** advances came like a **tidal** wave after *13th century!*

The *prophecy* of YHWH **binding** up and **reviving** Israel (in modern times) was *shockingly* **accurate** considering modern *Israel* (most all the Western nations)! But; what about the *last* part of the *prophecy* "*on the third day, He will raise us up*"? Well, this *one* should be *obvious*; "*raising up*" is a **resurrection**!

What *resurrection* would that be? All we have to do is go to **Ezekiel** 37 and *there* it *is*; the *resurrection* of the "*whole house of Israel*". After all, **Hosea** was *prophesying* to *Israel*. After *seeing* Hosea's *prophecy* of the "*reviving*" of *Israel* after *two* days, coming to *fruition* with such shocking *precision*, what *kind* of *fools* would we *be* to not *believe* or *accept* the **last** *half* of that *prophecy*?

I for one, have *zero* doubt it will *come* to *pass* **exactly** *on schedule*! Our *problem* has been, as is with all of Christianity, they *worship* **pagan** and *false* **gods** and consequently are *clueless* about **true** *prophecy*. In fact, they are still *predicting* Yahshuas' **return**, even though He made it very *clear* He was *returning* (and did) in the ***first*** century!

To be able to *accept* the truth, we have to *flush* all the *nonsense* we've been *taught* and **allow YHWH's true** scriptures to **teach** us! Oh, if you haven't already gotten out your *calculator*, the "*third day*" where Israel is "*raised up*" would be around the year 2280! Sorry, but that sounds *about* **right** considering **Daniel** 7 *predicts* the *rise* and *fall* of 3 *world* **ruling** *empires* **yet** *to come,* before it's **all** *over!*

Chapter 66

The Rock or Rock and Roll?

During the 1950's a new kind of *music* was born called "*Rock and Roll*". The credit went primarily to the *one* who was labeled "*The **king** of rock and roll*"; the late ***Elvis Presley***. That in mind, how interesting the word for "*King*" in *Hebrew* is the same *Hebrew* word for ***angel***! That's a very important bit of understanding we would do *well* to bear in mind! Even though Elvis was a "*king*" of sorts, he died *young*.

Interestingly, *three* elements became the *dominate **elements*** of ***that*** *music*; "***drugs, sex*** and ***rock*** and ***roll***"! I can't say I didn't (don't) enjoy much of it, but can we honestly say such a music *theme* was a ***good*** *thing*? Of course, when *good* people *stood **up*** and ***protested*** the *adulterous **sexual*** and *drug **promoting*** *lyrics,* they were shot *down* and *silenced* by the Hollywood *liberals* screaming *musicians **right*** to *freedom* of *speech*!

Well, the worst *fears* the *righteous* people were *realized* with *a **vengeance,*** and worse! As *drug* use became *epidemic,* the *entire* institution of *marriage* and *family* has ***crumbled.*** In fact, we've been *reduced* to a *society* of ***sodomites*** the average person a few decades ago could *never* have *believed* possible in a million years, let alone a *few* decades!

One thing's for *sure*, the *authors* of the "*Mus-ic*" *accomplished* their **illicit** *goal* with astounding *success*! You see, "*Music*" literally *means*; "*Of the* **muses**". We always hear people talking about their *muse* **inspiring** *them* in their *writing* and *composing*. But, just *who* are the *muses* who **inspire** the *music* (and movies)? Well, we have a wealth of *answers* to **that** *question* in the *story* (supposed myth) of *Zeus*.

A man named Tom Stone wrote a book called "*Zeus*" and *uncovered* some extremely amazing *things* I'm sure even he *didn't* realize! (I don't believe he did) While researching the book in Greece, he *encountered* an old-timer, that when *questioned* about Zeus, said something very interesting! His response to Toms' query of Zeus was that *Zeus* was one of *those* **watchers**!

You see, one of the well-known *attributes* of Zeus was his *weakness* for **human** *women,* which **Genesis** 6 and **Enoch** show of the *watchers*! Legend also says Zeus used his **shape-shifting** *abilities* to *seduce* the *human* women! Those two *attributes* alone speak *volumes* considering one of the words used in the Bible describing *angels* is "*shinnon*".

Shinnon means "*changeable*" or in our modern language "*shape-shifting*". In fact, we know by the **half** *human, half* **animal** *nephilim* offspring, these watchers were largely **animals** in their **true** *form*! In fact, the legend of Zeus relates a story of Queen *Pasiphae* of *Minos* (Knossos Crete) lusting for *sex* with a *bull*.

That idea is absurd unless we understand Zeus was an angelic *bull disguised* as a man. There can be no doubt these **animal** *watchers* **disguised** *themselves* as *handsome* dashing young *men* to *seduce* foolish **human** *women,* but, the *truth* of their **true** *form* was *exposed* in the resulting *animal-***human** high-bred *offspring*! Such was the *result* of the **illicit** *union* of Minos's *queen* and Zeus (the watcher bull). Their child was the *Minotaur*; a **human** *body* with a **bulls** *head*!

King Minos, in his shame, *retained* the *accomplished* architect "**Dadalous**" to *build* a *labyrinth* in Knossos to keep his *nephilum* son. Interestingly, the Book of Enoch (as well as archeology) tells us these *nephilim* were **cannibals**, just as with the *monstrous* **Minotaur**; even though it had a *bovine* head, it thrived on *human* flesh! To *provide* that meat, King Minos had *seven* young *women* and *men* brought in from all over his kingdom to be *fed* to the Minotaur; that is until a *prince* named *Theseus,* and his girlfriend, slated to be ***its* food**, were able to *kill* the vicious *man*-eating *beast*.

As a little *icing* to this fantastic *tale;* according to intellectual **history** *professor*, Rufus Fears, the **Minotaur** *labyrinth* was actually discovered after the turn of the 19th century by an archeologist named Sir Arthur *Evans*. Even numerous *emblems* of the *Minotaur* were *found* ***in*** the *labyrinth* and surrounding area!

Getting back to Zeus then, *legend* tells us he *spawned 9 nymphs* (apparently by his angelic wife). These nymphs were called "*Muses*". Interestingly, the **muses** *were commissioned* to "*teach*" humanity, which they have apparently been *doing **ever** since*! At this point, we need to *think* "**Tree** *of the* **knowledge** *of* **good** *and* **evil**". That *tree* was *symbolic* of the *watchers* whom Enoch *informs* us, not only *procreated* with human women, but **taught** *humanity* all variety of *esoteric* as well as *destructive* knowledge!

This should come as *no* surprise, considering Zeus *hung out* at the *palace* of King *Minos'* of **Knossos**, which is the Greek word for *knowledge;* the very *thing* the *watchers* (with their muses) *taught* mankind. In fact, it seems King Minos was also a *watcher* with his *human* wife *Pasiphae!* One thing's for sure, the *story* of Zeus certainly brings the Book of Enoch's *record* of the watchers *alive* and *upfront*!

Getting back to the *subject* of this study, **music**; namely, *rock* and *roll*, we can be certain of its *origins* considering the *information* we've just *seen*. Rock and *roll* **music** (of the muses) is certainly **not** a *blessing* to humanity, considering it's all about **destroying** *morality*, **family**, and modern *Israel* as a whole. You see, *rock* and *roll* is the *diametric* **opposite** of our *Creator*. He is called "*The Rock*" in a few *places* in **Isaiah**.

What makes YHWH so *valuable* is He *does* **not** *change* as He *declares* in **Malachi** 3:6. That means He can be *trusted* and isn't all *over* the *place* like "*rock and* **roll**"! In fact, if we *listen* "**honestly**" to the *music* (as they *command* us in many of their "**hits**") we quickly discover how **destructive** it *is* as well as *who* is *singing* it to us. In fact, they openly *admit* who **they** *are* in much of it, and their *plans* for us, as in the song; "*Behind blue eyes*" by the "*Who*"! How amazing they even **taunt** *us* with *riddles* as to **their** *names*!

Another "*star*" group with many *big* "**hits**" even has the name "*Guess Who*"! How's that for blatant *taunting*! In fact, they **openly** *admit* **who** *they* **are** when they **call** *themselves* "**stars**"! Stars are a *reference* to the *watchers* (as well as angels in general). Plus, they *freely* **admit** the *effects* of their *musings* by calling them "*big* **hits**"! That is exactly what they are; *destructive* **blows** to our people and *families*!

The bottom line is; if we *choose* **rock** and **roll** (the watchers-Tree of the knowledge of good and evil) over "*The* **Rock**" we will be *destroyed* **by** *it* (them). They will continue **hitting** *us* until we are *dead* and gone! After all, the *last* thing they *want* is for **us** to *make* it to YHWH's **eternal** *family* as His *children*!

Chapter 67

The Feast of Trumpets; in Real Time!

One *major* **failure** in *Christianity* (and Judaism to a degree) is the **dismissal** of the **outline** and *keys* to the **Plan YHWH** has **prepared** *for us*. That *outline* and *key* to understanding is *YHWH's* **Feasts** and *Sabbaths*. Without those *guidelines*, humanity is but **blind** *people* **stumbling** through a **dark** *forest* at *night*! In fact, the axiom "*The blind leading the blind*" comes to mind.

What's so *fascinating* is Christianity's *shocking* **unwillingness** to *embrace* YHWH's *Feasts* even though (from a *physical* perspective) His *Feasts* are literally a **thousand** *times* better than any of the **pagan** *celebrations* Christianity and the *world* **wastes** *their* **time** *celebrating*!

Imagine, a *family* **Feast** *celebration* **every** *week*; not only a *day* of **family** *gathering* and *Feasting,* but a day *supernaturally* **blessed** by the Creator *Himself*. In addition, are two *annual* **Feast** *celebrations lasting* an **entire** *week*! Plus, adding *icing* on these wonderful **week** *long* Feasts, they *include* **gift** *giving,* only **without** the **lingering** *debt* to later have to *pay* off!

These Feasts aren't *mindless* celebrations involving **pagan** *gods* and *traditions,* but are *teaching* **rehearsals** of the Creator's *Plan* involving the *creation* of His **eternal** *Family*!

To understand, it's *imperative* we have the *big "**family**" picture* in mind, which is *what* was *shown* in the *Garden* of *Eden*. Adam and Eve were the *first-born* of YHWH's to begin YHWH's eternal Family, which will no doubt *consist* of **billions**! That *number* is undoubtedly the *reason* for the *lengthy* **time** *period* from Adam and Eve till *now*. We can be sure the *number* YHWH has in mind, *requires* just such a *period* of **time.**

The next *step* was to *gather* His People *out* of a *corrupt* **enslaving** *world ruled* by the *demons*, and *bring* them to His *House* (Mt. Sinai). Remember, that *first* step also *required* a **Messiah** (anointed one) to *redeem* a **priesthood** from the **devil's** *world*. That Messiah would *save* (purchase) those *first-born* from the **death** *angel* Mastema (Book of **Jubilees**) whom *YHWH*, at that *point,* had *chosen*. This step, of course, was **Passover** *outlined* in **Exodus** 12.

The next **ceremony** (inset) was the *resurrection* the *saints* of old (elders) *depicted* by the **wave-sheaf** *ceremony* **three** *days after* the *Passover*. That ceremony wasn't able to be *celebrated* until the people had been *brought* into their **Promised** *Land* (the new Garden of Eden (YHWH's place).

The wave-sheaf (waving of a *sheaf* of *barley*; down and up) signaled the *beginning* of the *spring* (first-fruit—Priestly) *harvest* to be *celebrated* 50 days (representing years) later. That *spring* **harvest**, of course, was a *rehearsal* of the **real** *harvest* of the *human* **priesthood**!

The step *leading* up to *that* harvest was to *clean* up (wash) the people of their *pride*, which is *pictured* by **leaven** in the Feast of *Unleavened* Bread. That *washing* was *accomplished* by the *putting* **away** (and/or controlling) our **pride** *pictured* by the mass *baptism* (symbolic washing) of Israel in the Red Sea as they were *led* out of *bondage* to YHWH's Mountain.

This *cleansing* was **required** then as well as *now*, for the people to *enter* into the **presence** of the *supreme* **Sovereign** of the universe! This washing was also *practiced* (rehearsed) *regularly* by the priests every time they *entered* the Temple, by washing in the *Brazen* **Laver** (brass pool in front of the temple).

We saw those *spring* Feasts *played* **out** in **real** *time* in the *first* century. The Lamb (the Messiah, Yahshua) *sheding* His *blood* for **His** *priesthood* (He was to be the eternal high-priest). The *wave-sheaf* then *occurred* in *real* time as the **graves** in Jerusalem *opened* (exactly three days as rehearsed) and the *saints* of *old* came into the city. Of course, since the wave-sheaf *happened* in **real** *time*, it also *signaled* the **beginning** of the *spring* harvest in **real** *time* (exactly as rehearsed) 50 years later! (Count was exact)

Considering we have *historical* **proof** all the **spring** *Feasts* (Sabbaths) came to *fruition* in **real** *time,* are we not to *expect* the **fall** *Feasts* to *come* to *fruition* in *real* time as well; exactly as *rehearsed* (including the timing)? After all, a *play* is not *rehearsed* over and over only to do *something* **different** on **opening** *night*, which Christianity believes. Such foolishness has been their *undoing*.

With that in mind, when the *spring* harvest was **completed** (80 CE-50 years after the wave-sheaf countdown) the spiritual *fields* were then **plowed** *under* for the *planting* of the *fall* crop (harvest). After all, was it only a *coincidence* the **time** period *after* the *first* century was dubbed "*The* **dark** ages"? Yahshua *returned* to *receive* His *priestly* (first-fruit) *harvest* just as He *promised,* which once again *left* the *world* in **darkness** (under the *rule* of the *dark* **ones**-*nephilim* spirits). But, at some *point,* the *fall* **crop** *sprouted* and is growing *into* the *light,* bringing us into the *fall* **harvest** season!

But, how are we supposed to *know* exactly **when** that *time* is *here*? Obviously, the *fall harvest* season *begins* with the **Feast of Trumpets.** With that in mind, would the *Feast of Trumpets* not also include the "*Trumpet*" *plagues* listed in **Revelation** 8-11? A close *examination* of those **Trumpet** *plagues* reveals a *hellish* rain of *asteroids*, and *meteors*, as well as **red** *dust* and *debris* (like blood) which *blocks* out the sun and *moon*.

A well kept *secret* our **ruling** *elite* have been *hiding* from **most** of the *population* is a *binary* **solar** *system* (Nemesis) has been spotted *approaching* our system over *forty* years ago. It is now **close** enough (in the right locations) for even **phone** *cameras* to get *videos* and *pictures*! The truth *cannot* be *hidden* from the general public much longer.

Interestingly, the *outermost* (large) planet *orbiting* that *brown* **dwarf** *sun* is a *red* planet (Nibiru) which will be the planet to most *closely* **interact** with Earth, bringing with it a *hail* **storm** of *debris* and **red** *dust*!

Thankfully, YHWH tells us that He does *nothing* without *first* **warning** His **people,** which many *times* **comes** in the *form* of **prophetic** *names* like "*Methuselah*". *Methuselah* meant, "**When I die, it** (the flood) **will come**" which is *exactly* what *happened*. The *world* before the *flood* was literally *warned* of the *impending* **doom** of the flood for 950 years! How many listened? Well, we know the answer to that one!

With all that in mind, is it only a *coincidence* we were *given* a *president* named "***Trumpet King***" (Donald Trump)? I have absolutely, no doubt **he** was the **announcement** (prophecy) of the *Feast* of *Trumpets* with the *Nemesis* **solar** *system* approach as *proof*. After all, we are way overdue for a *moral* **reset** of the *Western* (modern Israelite) *nations*.

We have become *blushingly* **immoral** like *Sodom* and *Gomorrah*! It's time for the *commencement* of the *Fall* Harvest (of humanity) with *inconceivable* **horrors** for those **not** protected by *YHWH*, which *begins* the *process* of YHWH *leading* **His** people out of *modern* **Egypt** to His *true* "**Promised** *Land*"!

Chapter 68

The Resurrection and Final Demise of Babylon

In at least *three* places in scripture we find many *detailed* **prophecies** of *Babylon*. It's interesting that they are all so *similar*. The *predominate* ones are *found* in **Jeremiah**, **Ezekiel**, and **Revelation**. More *prophecies* adding to those *three* are found in **Zekariah** 5. But, before looking at those extremely fascinating and *little known* **prophecies**, let's step back and *analyze* the *big* picture.

Almost *from* the *beginning*, there has been a *competition* (battle) *between* **two** entities. One is the *Creator* and *His,* and the other, His *Adversary* or **satan**. Satan is simply the *Hebrew* word for "*adversary*".

We see this *adversary* referenced in many places, first in **Genesis**, **Isaiah** 14, and also in **Ezekiel** 28. **Ezekiel** 28 shows us it (she) was the *most* **beautiful** and *perfect* of all the **created** *beings* (angels) and was to be *one* of the Cherub's which *covered* the Creators (YHWH) *throne* with *its* **wings**.

Ezekiel 28 goes on to tell us its *beauty* (vanity) and *greed* (trading) **corrupted** *it* and a **battle** *ensued*. **Isaiah** 14 gives us, not only more *details* of that *battle*, but also its *name*, **Heylel**. (The name was *replaced* with *Lucifer* by Jerome in the 4th century) Its *vanity* and **ego** became so *elevated*, it felt *it* **deserved** a *throne* of its *own*, next *to* or *above* the Creator YHWH, whose *throne* it was *designated* to *cover* with its *wings*.

Well, as can be *assumed*, the *battle* went *badly* for Heylel and she ended up on *Earth*. In fact, not *only* is she *found* on *Earth*, but in the *Garden* of **Eden**, which **Ezekiel** 28-31 alludes. She was the Nahash (class of Angel) that *tempted* and **deceived** *Eve* (wrongly translated *"serpent"*). Putting all the pieces *together*, *what* she *actually* was (is) is a *dragon*, which **Revelation** 12 makes *abundantly* clear.

Though, she *lost* **everything** in the *battle* with Michael (YHWH's Archangel) the *main* **thing** on her *mind* at this point was *revenge!* **"Vengeance is a dish** *best served* **cold"** goes a **Klingon** *proverb* from Star Trek. That said, and along with *attempting* to *destroy* everything YHWH was *doing*, her *secondary* **ambition** was to *reestablish* her **trading** (merchandising) *empire* which was *destroyed* in the **great** *battle* referenced in **Revelation** 12.

Again, **Ezekiel** 28 tells us her *merchandising* (trading) was one of the *things* that *corrupted* her. That's why *everywhere* we *look* in our world, we are constantly **barraged** with *advertising* to *buy*, **buy**, *buy!* You see, she's the god *ruling* this world from *behind* the *curtain* which we call the *"devil"*. And, just as the Creator *YHWH* set up His temple in **His city Jerusalem**, she also *built* a temple (tower) in **her** *city*, Babylon. Unfortunately (for her) YHWH **never** allowed **that** temple to be *completed*.

Though her *tower* (temple) was *destroyed* and city (Babylon) eventually came to *ruin*, the *prophecies* tell us, her city and *temple* finally **do** *get* **rebuilt**. Apparently the **new** *tower* of **Babel** is going to be the most *amazing* **structure** this world has ever *seen!* Unfortunately (again for her) her **new** *tower* will once again be *destroyed*. (Rev.16-18)

We find that *prophecy* for the *rebuilding* of *Babylon* in **Zechariah** 5 (verses 5-11) where we see *wickedness* being put into a *basket* and set *back on her base* in Shinar, (Babylon). Shinar was what *Babylon* was *originally* called and where the *tower* of Babel was being *constructed*.

After being *rebuilt*, we're told *Babylon* will be *destroyed* in **one hour** (Revelation 18:10&17) *never* to be *rebuilt* again. Let's look at those *prophecies* beginning in **Jeremiah** 50, verses 39-40. There we are told Babylon will be *destroyed* like *Sodom* and *Gomorrah* "*never to be inhabited again*".

Jeremiah 51, verses 7&8 echo what **Revelation** 18 tells us, that the Earth was made *rich* by the **trading** of *Babylon*, which again is **suddenly** *destroyed*. Remember, ancient Babylon was *never* destroyed **suddenly**! What we need to keep in mind here, is *what* II **Peter** 3:8 tells us; that the **time** *continuum* in the *spirit* realm is radically *different* from our *physical* dimension. The *example* given there is *one* **day** in **that** realm is like a *thousand* years in *this* one, so, **ancient** *Babylon* was just a *few* **days** ago.

Again, people will *argue* that Babylon **was** destroyed *anciently*, but it was a **gradual** *decline* over a *thousand* years, and to this day still has *shepherds* pitching their *tents* there, which the *prophecy* we just read says will *cease*. Obviously *this* **Babylon** of which **Revelation** and **Jeremiah** speak, is a *new* **rebuilt** one.

Revelation 22 tells us about a **new** *Jerusalem* coming down from *heaven,* which is a shocking **1500** *miles* square and **tall!** We can't even wrap our minds around a structure so *massive*. But, one *theme* we see all through the *Bible* is how the *devil* always *does* its **counterfeit** version of what YHWH is *doing* **before** *YHWH* (the Creator) does the **real** thing.

When we read the *fifth **trumpet*** plague in **Revelation** 10, we find the *pit* (angelic prison) is *opened* and the 200 watchers (angels) ***incarcerated** there* are *released*! Considering there's no mention of them being *re- incarcerated* during the *millennial* period (800 years) it's a very *logical* bet they will be *instrumental* in helping *build* that **new** *tower* of ***Babel*!** No doubt it will be the most *amazing* and *shocking* building ever *built*. Again, it's the *devils'* ***attempt*** to *out-do* YHWH *ahead* of Him.

According to **Revelation**, this *new **tower*** of *Babel* will be the *jewel* of the world! It's *possible* it could be ***miles** high*, again considering it's the watchers *attempt* to out-do YHWH's *new **Jerusalem*** that's apparently *1500 **miles** high*! We can only begin to *imagine* all the *new **technologies*** that will be *incorporated* in the construction of the **new** *tower* of *Babel*! Again, **Revelation** tells us how the *whole **world*** *mourns* its *demise*! It's no doubt going to quiet *spectacular*! But, YHWH will not be *up-staged* by the devil! *His **New** Jerusalem* will make the *new* tower of *Babel **pale*** in *comparison*!

Chapter 69

Red versus Blue

Considering the fact our *founders* **chose** the *colors* of **red** and **blue** (with the white background) makes one wonder (me for instance) *why?* What made them *choose* **those** *precise* **colors**; *blue* and *red?* Is there any *significance*, or was it just a *random* **coincidence** *those* particular *colors* were *chosen?* Is there a *message* being *conveyed* with *those colors,* or again, is it just *random* coincidence?

Well, we don't have a *record* of *what* went on in the **artists** *head*, but we can make some *observations* such as the color *red* is obviously the color of *blood* (sacrifice) while the *sky* and *ocean* appear *blue*. That's another thing; *what* are the *stars* **telling** *us* as they *whisper* from the *corner* of that great *American* **symbol** of *patriotism* and **pride?**

If we google the *meaning* of the *colors* on the US flag, we're told they *originally* meant *nothing* except being the *colors* on the **Union** *Jack* (British flag). Digging a little deeper, we find that **red** is the color of *hardiness* and *valor;* while **blue**, is the color of *vigilance, perseverance* and *justice*, while *white* symbolizes *innocence* and *purity*.

Again, the *British* flag used the **same** *colors* but apparently for **different** *reasons*, such as the *melding* of nations. The *royal* **blue** was not just the color of the *sky*, but the *chosen* **color** of *Scotland*. The **red** supposedly *represented* the *crosses* of *St. George* (dragon slayer) and *St. Patrick;* both *martyrs* on a background of *white* which, again, symbolizes *righteousness.*

But, are those the **real** *meanings*, or did the **spirit** *muses,* **controlling** the *world,* simply *muse* their *puppets* to *incorporate* those colors for **higher,** *not* **so** obvious, *reasons?*

People can say anything, which *may* or *may* **not** have anything to do with the *truth*, but considering this world is *run* by *watcher* (and demon) *spirits* from behind the great *dimensional* curtain, we can be certain there's much more *meaning* to the picture!

We may not *see* or *hear* them, but their **finger** and **footprints** are everywhere. For instance, Frank Sin-atra sang a song *proclaiming* how he **did** *it* "**my** (his) **way**"! Well, **his** *way* got him **dead**! Imagine that!? Strangely, he also had **blue** *eyes,* which *a*nother group called "*The Who*" sang about called "*Behind* **Blue** *Eyes*".

It was a song about someone with **blue** eyes in some kind of *prison* **plotting** his **revenge** (vengence) for those he *blames* for *putting* **him** *there* (mankind)! And let's not forget Hitler's **blue**-*eyed* arian *super* race!

We will get to more of that later, but first, lets take a *look* around at *how* and *where* those *colors* are *used* around the world. For instance, we see the *United Nations* extensively uses the *color* **blue**. Their *flag, helmets,* and *uniforms,* are *blue,* as well as many of their vehicles. Why did they choose **that** *color?*

Well, they don't give a reason except they supposedly used **blue** to distinguish them from other world *organizations*. Again, I believe the reason for the **blue** goes much *deeper*. (New world order) That said, how interesting to notice all the *leftist* states (Democratic-socialists) are also "*blue*" the **same** *color* as the UN *globalists*! Besides *sporting* the UN's color, they are also the ones *supporting* (promoting) the **murder** of our *unborn* babies!

Plus, they are the same people *promoting* and demanding *legalized* **sodomy** and the *destruction* of *traditional* **heterosexual** *marriage*! How interesting! Suddenly, the *color* **blue** is taking on a whole *new* **shade** of *meaning*!

Another interesting *fact* about *blue* is the Priests of YHWH wore *white* robes with a *blue* thread. The blue thread apparently symbolized a *hint* of *authority*, while the *predominate* color was *white*; the symbol for *righteousness*. In other words, they had *authority*, but were not **control** *figures* as we see in this world; *blue* is all about *complete* **power** and *control*, which has certainly become an **obvious** *fact* these days!

Under the *socialist* (Nazi) *one* **world** *government*, they plan to *control* every **tiny** *aspect* of our lives. That's *what* the so-called "*health care*" is all about. To be frank, there is *nothing* in our lives that cannot be *connected* to **health**; *what* we **eat, drink, drive,** *live* **in**, *work*, and even **what** we **believe**!

How interesting the one crooning "*I did it my way*" (old blue eyes) was actually indirectly *promoting* **outside** *control*. The demon world is *desperate* to keep us from *doing* **it** "**YHWH's** *way*".

Unfortunately, old "*Blue eyes*" doing it the "**my way**" (the **selfish** *way*) got him dead! People are unwittingly *giving* themselves over to the **control** of the **demonic** *realm*; the *spirits* of **selfishness** and **pride**. The *last* thing in the world the *demon* **puppet** masters **want** is for us to **control** our **own** *behavior* under the *Creator's* **guidelines** of *unselfishness* and *love*!

With that in mind, *what* we *see* on *our **flag*** is the *battle* between **blue** and **red**! We have addressed *blue*, but what is the *red*? Well, for one thing it symbolizes the ***blood** spilled* for our *freedoms*. It was also the *blood* spilled for the **sins** of *Israel,* not to mention the *color* of the Messiah's *redemption*! Is it any wonder why *blue **hates** red*?

The **red** *states* in the US are the *conservatives* who *believe* our *constitutional **freedoms*** are great *gifts*! They also *believe **murdering*** babies is **evil,** and that *marriage* was *created* by the Creator to be between a *man* and *woman*! They also, for the most part, *believe* in the *Bible* and the *Creator.*

What really gets interesting is to *understand* the **blue** *square* in the *corner* of that flag with the **white** *stars*! Using the Bible, we can *deduce* that each *star* is a *symbol* of the **spirit** *prince* (or puppet master) of each state. We have a few scriptures that make the connection between *stars* and *angels*.

We also have a few scriptures comparing the *gentiles* to the (blue) *seas*. Of course, the angels, both *good* and *bad*, live in the (blue) heavens, showing the *reason* the *stars* are shown on a *blue* background!

No doubt there are **other** *meanings* associated with **those** colors of *red* and *blue* in the **spirit** *world whose meanings* are much greater than we can possibly understand in this *physical* realm.

One last *thought* to *end* this *study* is to consider the *origin* of the term "**blue** *bloods*". Blue *bloods* are a reference to the **aristocracy** or *rulers*. How interesting to go back to the old Testament and discover the word for *king* (malic) is the **same** *word* as **angel**!

These **watcher** *angels* were the *original **kings,*** which *legend* claims (watchers) literally had "***blue** blood*"! Of course, they were working to *control* and literally *destroy* those with the *red* blood, humans; a *battle* obviously still *raging* to this day!

Chapter 70

Strong Delusion

It's easy to *view* our world and *conclude* it has gone *completely* **insane**! But, how is that remotely *possible*? If so, is there a *cause* and/or *reason*? But, before going there, let's look at just a few of *those* **insane** issues. To begin with, one of the biggest **issues embraced** by the *West* is "**civil rights**". Lately, it's the *civil* **rights** of the **trans**-gender and *homosexuals*. Even though they are only around 3% of the *general* **population**, why are **their** *supposed* **rights** so much more *important* than the *majority*?

Secondly, just where do these *supposed* **rights** *originate*? After all, aren't the Western *democratic* nations *founded* upon the *will* of the **majority**? What ever *happened* to that? Isn't *rule* by the *minority* (autocracy) where the **few** *impose* their *will* upon *everyone*, a **dictatorship**? This is all so *insane* considering the *majority* of the **Western** *peoples* **believe** in the *traditional* (Biblical) family. Why is the *majority* **no** *longer* in *charge*?

Let's look at *another* **insanity** connected to **civil** *rights*. Western **civil** *rights* are *based* upon the *idea* of all *men* (people) being *created* **equal**, with the *same* **god-given rights**. But, at the *same* time, the schools are *forced* to **teach** *evilution*, with *no* Creator and the *philosophy* of **survival of the fittes**t. Isn't that the **opposite** of the *concept* of **anti-racism** and *civil rights*? Isn't the *conquering* of the **weak** nations and *peoples* what **evilution** *teaches* and exactly what *Adolph* **Hitler** was *attempting* to do? Of course, it was!

Hitlers' NAZI (German acronym for "*National **Socialist** Party*") is roundly *condemned* as *horrific*, but why is it **forced** venue in *Western* schools? On top of that, the *ones* most openly **condemning** the *NAZI's*, proudly *admit* (boost even) to *being **socialists**!*

The *truth* is, they are the *new **nazi's**!* In fact, the neo-*socialists*, i.e nazi's, are *ruling* the **Western** *world,* led primarily by the US! After all, thousands of *nazi's* were brought here after WWII under *operation* **paperclip**! With that in mind, *Hitler* told his SS officers that if you want people to *believe* you, *tell* them a **lie**, and the *bigger* the **lie** the *better*!

Interestingly, the *truth* of what's *leading* our modern *insanity* is *found* right in *plain* **sight** in II **Thessalonians** 2, verses 10 and 11. There we are told "*those who reject truth are **given over** to **strong delusion** and the lie*" (lies). The *essence* of *truth* is, of course, our Creator YHWH and His *Torah* **instructions**. And, the *present* world, especially the *Western* world has *strayed* further *from* YHWH and *truth* than we have ever.

"*Strong delusion*" is, if you haven't *guessed*, a *supernatural* (spiritual) **blinding**. After all *truth* comes *from* YHWH, while the devil **mixes** *endless* **lies** into *what* **little** *truth* we have. After all, we are told by the first century *Messiah* (Yahshua) the *original* **liar** is the devil.

That's **where** the *lies* began, right *there* in the *Garden* of **Eden**, with the Dragon's **lie**; "*You **won't** surly **die**, you will be **like** the **gods***" i.e. *immortal* (If they partook of the **dragon** *fruit*). So, we have been *living* in a **lying** *world* ever since, except for YHWH occasionally *stepping* in to **restore** *truth* and *direction*!

That said, another *insane* **lie** being *propagated* is *man-caused global* **warming** and that *carbon* and *Co2* are also *man-**made*** *pollutants* causing that warming. But, even engaging a couple gray cells, we understand that it's *carbon* and *co2* that **feed** the *plants*, which in turn, *give* us *oxygen,* and without *oxygen,* we're all *dead*!

If we take *away* the *carbon* and *reduce* co2 levels *below* about *200 ppm* (we are currently at about 400) it will be an **extinction** *level* event! The only honest conclusion upon which to *arrive,* is **whoever** is *behind* man-**made** *global* **warming** is actually trying to **destroy** *humanity*!

Of course, that's *what* they **told** us on the *Georgia* **guide** *stones,* the *first* **commandment** to a *happy,* **healthy,** and *prosperous* world is to *kill* off 7 **billion** *humans.* No doubt, the ones *promoting* the **murdering** of *babies* in the *womb* (and even afterwards) are the **same** *ones,* which is *another* **accepted** *insanity*!

II Thessalonians 2 is generally *accepted* as a *warning* to *individuals,* but, it no doubt *applies* **nationally.** We are *told* that *when* we have **righteous** *leaders,* the people *prosper.* Otherwise, not-so-much! Our *prosperity,* **given** *us* by our **more** *righteous* leaders of the *past,* is currently *being* **stripped** *away.* One of the *greatest* of these *blessings* is, of course, **freedom**!

We are *currently* being *delivered* into the *hands* of our *enemies,* just as *happened* to our ancestors *over* and **over**! Let's not forget the *admonition* of the *wise* man; "*There is* **nothing new** *under the* **sun**"! He also *said*: "**Pride** *comes* **before** *destruction*"! So, *what* have our *leaders* **done**? They have *established* a *celebration* of the **proud** *sodomites*!

Not only **one** *day* as they give our *presidents* and *military* **heroes** that *gave* their *life* for our *freedoms,* but an *entire* **month**! The president even had a **pride** celebration at the *white* house during *that* month, with *bare*-breasted *trannies*! We can be sure, *celebrating* **pride** *month* (sodomy) is a *national* **death** *sentence*!!

Again, if *there* is **nothing** *new* **under** the *sun* and everything is *cyclical,* we need only remember *Sodom* and *Gomorrah.* Actually, Sodom is where we get our modern *term* **sodomy.** (Homosexuality) Remember, they became so *immoral,* the Creator decreed they be **exterminated** by *fire.* The *righteous* **patriarch** Abraham was *warned* of *impending* **doom** of *Sodom* and *Gomorrah* and *argued* with the Angel of YHWH that the cities be *spared* if only *10* **righteous** could be *found.*

If you remember the story, only *Lot* and his *family* were found to be *righteous* enough to be *spared.* But, Lot's *wife* **loved** her *life* in Sodom so much she couldn't *quite* **leave** it and was *destroyed* also! Well, we in the US, and most *Western* (modern Israelite) *nations,* have *come* to that **decadent** *level* and have been *decreed* for **destruction** (for the most part). But, YHWH sent two *solar* eclipses (heavenly signs) to tell us He has **not** *forgotten* His *covenant* with our ancestors for us *not* to be **completely** *destroyed.*

Revelation 7 tells us that *144,000* will be **sealed** from *death.* He also sent a *prophecy* by *John* in **Revelation** 12 that **another** *segment* of His people, called "*the Woman*" are given (apparently metaphorically) *two* **wings** of an *eagle* to be *flown* into a *place* of *protection* for 3 and 1/2 years during the *worst* of the **tribulation.** That second eclipse, arriving in the spring of 2024, is the *signal* for the *woman* to **flee**!

We don't know *exactly* **who** *she* is exactly, but **Daniel** 12 tells us *Michael* the **ArchAngel** has a *book* with the *names* of those to *be* **saved** and is *given* the *responsibility* to **save** her. How interesting He was the *one* to get the *Israelites* out of *Egypt* anciently at the **same** *time* of the *year,* **Passover**! **Malachi** 3:6 tells us *YHWH does* **not change**, so for Him to *follow* the **same** *pattern* as *anciently,* should come as **no** *surprise*!

Chapter 71

Space Ship Earth

This life is full of little *things* that reveal the **big** *picture* if we are only *awake* enough to **notice**. Some of them are incredibly shocking in their *obviousness* and *how* they've been *hidden* right in *front* of our *faces*! Of one *thing* we can be sure, our *awesome* Creators did **not** leave any part of their Creation to *happenstance*. We can also be sure, *nothing* in this *existence* is *accidental* or *coincidental*. Even *free* *will* and supposed *coincidence* are not here by *chance*!

With that in mind, a book written by the late Sci-fi author, Robert A Heinlein, was about a small *community* of people *placed* on a *spaceship* to *travel* and **colonize** *another* **planet** in another *star* system.

Unfortunately, the lack of *wormhole* technology made the trip a *several* generation *endeavor*. So, the ship was *designed* to be **self**-*contained* to *provide* all the *living* **needs** for the *many* generations *required*. Unfortunately, *early* in the *voyage*, there was a **falling** *out* between those with the *responsibility* of the more *mundane* **functions** and those monitoring the **higher** *functions*, such as the *helm* and the ships *progress*.

An ensuing *battle* resulted in a **nuclear** *explosion* that *rendered* the *bridge* and **upper** *levels* **uninhabitable**. Consequently, those parts of the ship were made *off-limits*, and *gained* the label *"**forbidden** zone"*. Fortunately, the *designer* of the ship *foresaw* the *possibility* of such an *event* and **programed** the *ship* with **auto** *pilot*.

After a *generation* or *two*, the *reason* for the **forbidden** *zone's off* limits (radiation) was lost and became a *thing* of *superstition*! Ironically, the *surviving* **scientists** became the **religious** *leaders* with **sudo**-*science* as **god***!*

A large part of that *superstition* was the societal *outcasts* and the *banished* would **escape** to the *forbidden* zone to *hide*, where the residual *radiation* **killed** them and/or caused *deformities*. That gave those parts of the ship the *concept* of **monster** *land*, making it even more *frightening* and *formidable*.

As the generations passed and considering there were **no** *windows* on the *lower* levels, the people literally **lost** the *knowledge* they were *on* a spaceship *flying* through *space*. Of course, they also *lost* the **knowledge** of *planets* and the **new** *world* they were *traveling* to **colonize**.

As time passed, a teenage boy, in his curiosity, *discovered* a *way* into the *forbidden* zone. By this time, the *radiation* had *dissipated* to a *tolerable* level and he ended up **befriending** *one* of the *mutants* living there. Of course, the few *surviving* mutants had *discovered* the *bridge* (control room) with *all* the **windows** and had come to understand they were actually on a ship *flying* through *space*.

The boy tried to *tell* his **family** and *friends* that shocking *truth*, but was called *terrible* **names** and *demonized,* but, he eventually *persuaded* his little *girlfriend* to go with him to see!

Ironically, the ship had just *arrived* at the new *planet*, but due to the peoples **fear** of the *forbidden* zone, not to mention to *accept* the **insane idea** of being on a *ship*, they were *completely* **unwilling** to *entertain* the possibility! Consequently, *only* the *two* **teenagers** and a *couple* mutants were willing to *board* the **shuttle** *prepared* and **programed** to take them *down* to their *new* home *world*.

It's an amazing story, especially considering it completely *encapsulates* the **current** state of *humanity*! You see, *Earth* is a **space** *ship* and our *destination* **orchestrated** and *designed* by our Creators, has become **lost** in the *millennia's* of *time*.

The *keepers* of the **Plan** (Israel and the Jews) which are YHWH's *Feasts* and *living* **instructions**, utterly **failed** in their *obligation* to *preserve* and **teach** *it*. Instead, they **replaced** it with *fables* and **nonsense**, just like **what** happened in Heinlein's' novel of the *spaceship*.

We can be *assured*, the Creator's of our *Earthship* have not *negated* Their *Plans*, prompting the *big* **question**; will *we* be *courageous* enough to *accept* the *truth* of our **actual** condition and leave this *comfortable* **familiar** *existence* for the *new* **spiritual** *world* (Eden) like the young people in the story? Or will we *allow* our **fears** and social *programing* to *dissuade* us from a *destiny* we *can't* **begin** to *imagine*, like most of *those* on that *ship*?

Again, the **new** *world* is a *new* **spiritual** *existence*, but, to get there we have to *believe* and *accept* the *truth* the Creators have *provided* and *follow* Their *protocols*. Sadly, those *guidelines* are a mostly *forgotten* and **discarded** set called *the* **"Torah"** which literally means *"instructions"*!

Whether we *accept* those Torah *instructions* or not, the *Plan* will be completed, **with** or **without** us! We have the *choice* to **stay** on our *current* Earth *ship,* in the **perceived** *safety* of its *familiar* **belief** systems.

It's easy to look around and *conclude* this **physical** *world* and *society* is not any different from *what* it *looks* and **feels** *like*. Thats exactly the mindset of those people on the spaceship.

All they *knew* is *what* they could **see** and had been *taught.* But, just as on that *spaceship*, there are a *courageous* **few** who *want* **more** and are *willing* to **brave** the *limits* set by their *society.* And, I do mean "*rise* **above**" not "**sink** *below*" as is *encouraged* in this *evil* world! It seems there is *no depth* people are not *willing* to **sink** *these* **days**!

We live in a *world* that has *morally* **parked** in the *stream*, or is *content* to take the easy *feel* **good** *morality* of *floating* **downstream** *with* the *current*. Only the **few** truly *courageous* are willing to *leave* their **comfort** *zone* to swim *upstream* **against** the *current.* After all, who in their **right** mind would *chance* **leaving** their **comfort** *area* to *expend* great *energy* to **go** *somewhere* **unfamiliar**? But then, that's *what courageous* (and righteous) people do; they don't *follow* the *crowd*; or should I say "**lemmings**"?!

Again, there are *clues* all around that *something* is very *wrong.* It seems *nothing* we've been *taught*, when given *any* **real** *thought,* adds up to anything *meaningful* in the **long** run. It seems the only **two** *choices* we are *offered* are to *do* as we *please* and *die*, or *do* **good** and supposedly *go* to *heaven.*

Unfortunately, *religions'* **heaven** is an **ethereal** *place* whose *location* no- one *knows* or even *what* people do when *they* **get** *there.* Interestingly, and shockingly, the Bible does **not** *teach* we *go* to that *ethereal* **place** when we *die* at all! That's something *religion* **invented** and Christianity *adopted.* But, the *truth* is still *right* **there** in that **operations** *manual* called the *Bible,* for anyone who *dares* look at it *honestly*! It *teaches* of a "*New*" *existence* in a *coming* **new** *Heavens* and **Earth**!

Chapter 72

Signs

There was a pop *song* in the seventies called "*Signs*" with one of the main *lyrics declaring* "signs" **everywhere**. "*Who*" knows **what** signs, but the Bible also mentions "*signs*" many, many, times as well, *beginning* in **Genesis** 1:14. There we are told the *sun* and ***moon*** were *placed* in the sky for "*signs*" *and* "*Moeds*" (badly translated "*seasons*" by the KJ). Moed is the ***Hebrew*** *word* for "*Feasts*" and/or "*sabbaths*". That's *what* we find in **Leviticus** 23:3; "*These are my **Feasts***" (Moeds) with the *first* Moed (Feast) listed, being the **weekly** *Sabbath*.

Then, in **Matthew** 24, **Luke** 23, and **Mark** 13, we find the Messiah *prophesying* to His *disciples* of all sorts of *heavenly* **signs** that would *precede* the *end* of the **age** and *His* **return**. The *first* century ***historian***, *Josephus*, chronicled many of those *shocking* **signs** in "*The wars of the Jews*".

No doubt there's something to the idea of ***heavenly*** *signs* **proceeding** *major* **events,** for instance more recently; a *solar* **eclipse** across Europe preceded the *two* **world** *wars* as well as the *Spanish* ***flu*** which killed *millions* of people. Another *major* **heavenly** *sign* (for the Jews at least) has been the ***blood*** *moons*.

Virtually every *major* **event** in the *history* of the *Jewish* people, *good* and **bad**, has been *preceded* by *blood* moons. (John Hagee) That said, there were *two* **blood** *moons* in 2014; one on *Passover* and one on the *Feast of Tabernacles*. Even more interesting, shocking actually, there were **two** *more blood* **moons** the *following* year; again on *Passover* and *Tabernacles*! Considering those *blood* moons, the Jews *believed* their long awaited **Messiah** would **appear** in their calendar year of 5777 (2017).

With that in mind, what a coincidence President *Trump* announced the *moving* of the US embassy to *Jerusalem*, in 2017, officially making *Jerusalem* the *capital* of Israel!

That *act* has led many of the *Israelis* to *proclaim* Donald *Trump* the **Messiah** for whom they've been waiting! That move also **opened** the *door* to the *reclaiming* of **all** *Jerusalem* and the **rebuilding** of the *temple*! So, having *four* **blood** *moons* in *two* years has indeed been a *major* **heavenly** *sign* for them; so far for *good*.

Considering those *signs* involving the *sun* and *moon*, was the **arrival** of the *fall* **harvest** *season* with "**Donald Trump**".

Donald Trump loosely means "*Trumpet King*" and the *fall* harvest season *begins* with the **Feast** of **Trumpets** (fall new moon) just as the *first* century *harvest* season (of humans-priesthood) was *initiated* (in *real* time) by the *shedding* of the **Lambs'** *blood* (Yahshua). And, as *rehearsed* anciently, *Passover* was to be *followed* by the **Wave-sheaf** *offering* (waving a bundle of green barley in the temple) *exactly* **three** *days* later.

The *wave-sheaf* was a *picture* of **death** (down wave) and **resurrection** (up wave). That said, was it only a *coincidence* the Messiah and the *saints* of *old*, **both** emerged from their *graves exactly* **three** days *after* Passover?

The Wave-sheaf not only *proclaimed* the **resurrection** of the *Messiah* and *saints* of old, it also *initiated* the **countdown** to the **completion** of the **spring** *harvest* **50** *days* later. Of course, the *50* **days** represented *50* **years** in *real* time, which means the *spring* Harvest (Yahshua's return) was *completed* around **80 CE**. Unfortunately, the Jewish *rabbis* who *founded* the "**Universal**" (Catholic) *Church* attempted to **bury** that *truth*.

Thankfully, our loving Creator *diligently* left enough of a bread-crumb *trail* for us to **find** and *see* the *truth*, such as the letters governor *Pontius* **Pilate** sent to Cesar *Tiberius* concerning the *opening* of the *graves* in Jerusalem and the saints *coming* into the city! (British Bible History Museum)

Getting back to *signs*, we have been given a *plethora* of *signs* announcing this **fall** *harvest* **season** as well! Right after the announcement of the Feast of *Trumpets* in *real* time by the *miraculous* election of *Donald* **Trump**, was the August 21 *full* **solar** *eclipse across* the **heart** of the US. That's an *event* which has **never** *occurred* since the *founding* of the United States. Even more amazing is the *coming* of *another* **solar** *eclipse* in 2024 that **crosses** the *first* exactly over the *heart* of the nation!

The *crossing* **point** is a *place* in southern *Illinois* called "*Little Egypt*" (by Cairo and Memphis) close to the "*Gateway Arch*" of Saint Louis. How interesting those two eclipses *form* a "**tav**" which is the last *letter* of the Hebrew alphabet. Astoundingly the *tav*, has **three** *meanings*; "**sign**" "**covenant**" and "**covering**"!

When we put those *three* **meanings** *together*, the solar eclipses are a **heavenly** *sign* where the Creator *remembers* His **covenant** with our *ancestors* to **save** and *protect* their *descendants*!

It's worth *noting* the *first* **solar** *eclipse* made a **direct** *path* over 7 *cities* and *towns* named "**Salem**"! *Salem*, in Hebrew, means "*peace*" which was a *heavenly* **sign** there would be "*peace*" (in the US) until that *second* solar **eclipse** *arrives*! Which is true!

But, without a doubt, the most *important* (astonishing) **heavenly** *sign* that *brings* the others together, is the *sign* of the "*woman*" in **Revelation** 12. That *sign* is the *constellation* **Virgo** (virgin) with the *moon* **under** *her* **feet**, the *sun* **shining** on her *face* and a *garland* of *12* **stars** (number of Israelite tribes) *over* her *head*. Normally there are only **nine** *stars* (constellation Leo) over her head, but because of the **impossible** *alignment* of *Venus, Mars,* and *Mercury,* the *stars* (lights) over her head *totaled* 12!

All *astronomers* I have heard *talk* about such an *alignment,* say it was **impossible** (*naturally*)! What was just as shocking was to see *Jupiter* (on stellarium) move **down** into Vigo's *abdomen* area in the *spring* of 2017 only to see it move **backwards** for a few months, to then *resume* and end up *between* her *legs* in September (Feast of Trumpets) when the *alinement* of **9** *stars* and **three** *planets* occurred! Though, no-one can *explain* the **unnatural** motions of *Jupiter, Mars, Venus,* and *Mercury,* it certainly **happened**!

This **Revelation** 12 *sign* announces the **dragon's** *coming* **attack** on the *woman,* (China) which is a *metaphor* for YHWH's **righteous** *remnant* of modern Israel. Then "*the* **woman** *was given two* **wings** *of a great* **eagle** *that she might* **fly** *into the* **wilderness** *to her* **place**" (Rev.12:14) that "*covering*" in the *tav meanings,* is *a place* of *safety.* Interestingly, the *plagues* in **Revelation** come in *sevens,* which is the *number* of years **between** Donald Trump becoming president and the second *eclipse.*

What that tells us is the *natural* **disasters** and *calamities* between the *eclipses* have increased exponentially. But, when that **second** *eclipse* arrives in April of 2024; *three* and **one** *half* years before *Atonement,* it's the *announcement* for the "*woman*" to *flee* just before *all* **hell** really *breaks* loose! That *hell* is going to *come* with the *arrival* of the **Nemesis** *solar* **system** bringing **meteors, asteroids, tsunamis, earthquakes**, and of course, **war**!

Chapter 73

The Trouble with Time

One of the great *enigmas* in the *science* world is *time*. There are *those* who will *argue* **time** doesn't even *exist* in the true *reality* of the space-*time*-continuum. And of course, there's the whole *time* **travel** *conundrum* that supposedly was *proven* true by Einstein. That *argument* is if one were to *travel* at the speed of *light*, time passes much more *slowly* than someone standing *still*.

Many books (most Sci-Fi) have been *written* about *someone* going on a **space** *mission*, only to *return* to Earth, and find everyone has **drastically** *aged* compared to them. Personally, *time* travel is extremely *confusing*, considering the *chaos* that would ensue if one **could go back** in *time* and **change** *events*, which would make *reality* more like a *dream* than real.

My *perspective* of *time* is that it's simply a **measurement** of *decay* and the **aging** *process*. But then, *what* do I know? I'm no Einstein or *scientist* who *understands* the *physics* involved. But, it's obvious to me, *time* is not a **physical** *entity* that can be *manipulated*, but simply a *record* and/or **measurement** of **changes** in the world.

Another case can be made about *time* if were we *immortal,* **what** would *time* be then? Since there would no longer be *physical* **decay** *occurring,* **what** would the *passing* of **time** *become? Irrelevant?* Could we go *back* and **recreate** the **past** *physical* situations; like actors on a stage *reenacting* a *play?* After all, one could make a *case* that's a *type* of **time-***travel,* could they not?

Scriptures tell *us* the Creator *knows* the **end** from the *beginning.* Can that not *also* be said to be *something* akin to **time** *travel?* Is that scenario *possible* because the Creator is in *control* of *everything* like the *director* of a movie? After all, the writer, *producer,* and *directors* of a movie *know from* the *beginning* how the *movie* or *play* is going to *end.* Is that how it is with the Creators in leu of **time** *travel?* Is *mankind* and the Earth then, simply part of a grand **scripted** *movie* **production**?

If so, do *we* as *actors* and *actresses* on the *human* **stage** have any *say* in this *production?* Are we *allowed* to **ad-lib** or are we *required* to strictly *adhere* to a script of which we are *not* even *aware?* Are we simply *programmed* to **act** and *perform* the lines *required* for our **small** *part?* And, just *where* is that line between *fiction* and *truth* in this production? Is it all *fiction,* or is it all *truth?* Is it really a *combination* of the two?

Getting back to the *issue* of time, we find a very *strange* scripture in the Bible that *addresses* this very bizarre *issue* concerning the *reality* of **time** (or not). That scripture is found in II **Peter** 3:8, where we are *told* the time **continuum** *between* the Creator's *realm* and ours is *radically* **different**. There, and also in a couple *other* **Bible** *related* books, we are informed **one** *day* in the **spirit** *realm* is *comparable* to about a **1000** *years* from **our** *perspective* and in our *physical* realm.

Obviously, I'm *incapable* of *answering* many of those previous *questions,* but there are some major *problems* upon which that scripture *sheds* **much** light. One of those big questions is; *why* does *humanity* seemingly **never** *learn* from the *mistakes* of *history* and continue to *repeat* them? That said, is *time* involved in this *conundrum* as well?

One thing's *obvious*; **behavior** is *definitely* **cyclical**. It seems every *third* generation (or so) *undoes* the moral *gains* of the *previous*. Why? Maybe we really are simply *actors* on a *stage* as the "*Bard*" proposed; *rehearsing* the **same** basic **play**? Regardless of the *answer*, we need to keep in mind **time** in the **other** dimensions is *certainly* drastically **different** from *ours*.

And, if the **spirit** *realm* is really in *control* of what's *happening* in our *physical* dimension, maybe we should be **wise** *enough* to *listen* to *what* a scripture found in at least *three* different books tells us; that *time* in the other dimensions *passes* incredibly *slow compared* to our *physical* **perspective**.

An *honest* look at the Bible *scriptures* show there's an orchestrated *plan* for *humankind **from*** the *beginning* with a *timeline **rehearsed*** in the Creator's Feasts. Unfortunately, those *feasts* were not *faithfully* **kept**, and the *purpose* and **timeline** *became* **lost**. If those scriptures such as II **Peter** 3 are giving us a *glimpse* into the *true **reality*** of *time*, then the Garden of Eden was just *earlier* in the **week** *viewed **from*** the *spirit* **time** *perspective*. Ancient *history* as *viewed **by*** *us* is just *days* ago there!

In the *spirit* dimension, *all* the *major* **events** of *history* are as *fresh* as a **few** *days* ago. Unfortunately, from our *physical* **human** perspective, those events are **so** *ancient* as to be *relegated* to **legend** and *myth*. That's an *unfortunate* **fact** which keeps humanity as a whole from accepting **ancient** *history* as *real*.

If we cannot *accept* or understand the *reality* of ancient *history*, such as the *gods worshiped*, and why, we become **lost** in the *present,* and of course, are *unable* to understand the *past* and **accept** the *future*.

An ancient book called "*The **book** of **Enoch***" tells us about *200* **beings** from another *realm* (dimension?) came to Earth and **procreated** with *humans*. Their *offspring* called Nephilim were **bizarre** *creatures* ranging from a *myriad* of **half** *animal, half* **human** creatures, to *massive* **giants** which Enoch tells us grew as large as **600** feet in *height*!

We don't have *conformation* of that *extreme* size, but **giant** *skeletons* have been *unearthed* in every country of the planet, as *large* as 35' and *rumored* by local lore to be 250' (according to Steve Quayle, author of a book called *"Book of Giants"*).

What's shocking is Enoch *chronicles* for us those *"creatures"* were then *imprisoned* in some type of *dimensional* **prison** for their *scandalous deeds* until they will be *released* in just a few *years,* according to the long *forgotten* Biblical *timeline.*

Because humanity has *forgotten* this **essential** *history*, they for the most part, are going to be *totally* **blind**-*sided.* But, according to the Creator's **plan,** *there* will be a *place* of *protection* from these *creatures* which will be the *true* **fulfillment** of the **original** *physical* **Garden** of *Eden.*

Those *blessed* enough to *discover* the new *Eden,* will not only be **supernaturally** *provided* **for** and *protected,* but will attain **immortality**! But, to truly *understand* and *accept* **that** *future,* we have to *understand* and *accept* the *time* **difference** between our physical *dimension* and the *spirit.* Only then does it all come *together* into one *amazingly* shocking *package.*

Another scripture (Hosea 6:4) tells us, YHWH's (the Creator's Hebrew Name) *"people are destroyed for "lack of knowledge"*. One of those *essential* understandings is that time *difference* between *dimensions.* The *lack* of that lack of *knowledge* **spawned** the *axiom*; *"Those who **fail** to **remember** history* (including ancient) *are **doomed** to **repeat** it"*! We don't need to be a *time-**traveler*** into the *future* to *understand* what's *coming*; we need only *look* at **history**! Human *nature* does **not** *change*! (On its own)

Chapter 74

Is Revelation 12 for Real?

When I was younger, I used to *wonder* if we could really *trust* the *Book* of **Revelation** to be *real* and/or *true*. After all, being a *dreamer* and one who *sees* **visions**, that's *exactly* how the book *appeared* to me. Like John's *visions* (whoever he was) and/or *dreams*, I didn't know *what* to *think* of most of *my* **own** *dreams* and *visions*, as to how much I could *trust* them, even if they made complete *sense* (which most didn't).

Considering the Bible is *full* of *dreams* and *visions*, most having **come** to *fruition*, leaves us in a *quandary*. Although *many* of my *dreams* and visions did come to *pass, most* did not! But, this *dilemma* brings a scripture to mind; the one *telling* us; "*without* **faith***, it's* **impossible to please** *Him*" (our Creator). I suppose that's the *object;* we are *required* to *exercise* **great** *faith* in our Creator and that He was *involved* in the *inspiring* of the *book* of **Revelation**.

If I'm honest, I must *admit* I'm no *paragon* of **great** *faith*, like the kind *needed* to **move** *mountains* or to fully wrap my mind *around* the *visions* of **Revelation**. But, I have *strong* **faith** our Creator has *wonderful* **plans** for His *people* (and humanity) in the end.

And, considering the *plethora* of **miraculous** *prayers* He personally *answered* for *me*, **helps** *drastically*! That's why I *chose* to *accept* **Revelation** as somehow *real* and that its *contents* would *eventually* **live** up to **its** name to be "**revealed**".

With that in mind, I'd come to *understand* the *spiritual* **fall** *Feast* (harvest) **season** would be *initiated* with the **arrival** of the *Feast* of **Trumpets** in **real** time. After fully *understanding* the *spring* **harvest** *season* (of people) came to **real** time *fruition* in the **first** *century,* kicked off by *Passover,* it left me *praying* for understanding the *real* **time** *arrival* of the *Feast* of **Trumpets**. Considering the current *decadence* of the world, I *knew* it had to **arrive** *soon*.

Finally, a *seeming* **answer** *came* with a man named Donald *Trump* (loosely meaning "**ruling** *trumpet*") *running* for *president*. I had come to understand how *most* **names** in the OT, not to mention the *new*, were *prophecies*. The Creator (YHWH) **always** *announces* His *intentions* in *advance*, many times through *names*. Well, being a bit of a "**doubting** *Thomas*" I wasn't quite willing to accept Donald *Trumps'* run for the presidency as enough to *convince* me the Feast of *Trumpets* was *here* in **real** time.

Well, when He *won* in spite of **all** *odds*, I was coming to *accept* his name really **was** the *announcement* of the **arrival** of the Feast of *Trumpets* in **real** time. But, there was still a *spec* of *doubt* floating around in my head, which was finally put to bed after the Feast of *Trumpets* **celebration** in 2017! This is *where* **Revelation** 12 *enters* the equation. You see, there's a *prophecy* in **Revelation** 12 of a *woman* "*clothed* **with** *the* **sun**, *the* **moon** *under her* **feet**, *and a garland of* **12** *stars over her* **head**".

Well, the **only** *woman* in the *heavens* we *can* **see** is the *Virgin* otherwise known as the *constellation* **Virgo**. That **exact** *alinement*, with all the *astronomers* I ever heard, was *impossible*, but it was *seen* **precisely** during the Feast of *Trumpets* in 2017! The reason it's normally *impossible* is because the stars over *Virgo's* **head** is the *constellation* **Leo**, which is only *nine*, **not** *twelve*.

In order to make a *garland* of **12**, *three* of the *planets* had to **join** the 9 *stars* of *Leo*, the **natural** *motions* of which make such an *alignment* **impossible**, but I *saw* it with my **own** *eyes* (on stelarium).

Besides *confirming* the *real-***time** arrival of the **Fall Harvest season**, it also *confirmed* the *authenticity* of **Revelation** 12! Of course, the *context* of the **Revelation** 12 **sign** of the *woman* is the **announcement** of *coming* of the *dragon* to *destroy* the (physical) *woman* (chosen remnant) who is then *given* **two** *wings* of a *great* **eagle** to *fly* to a *place* of *protection* for 3 and 1/2 years. That leaves us wondering *exactly* **what** that *dragon* is.

We are given a couple *clues* in those *same* **passages**; it's *something* that *causes* a *monster* **flood** (tsunami). Well, what can cause such a *flood*; an *asteroid*? Well, a man named Tom Horn had a *vision* of exactly *that*! He wrote in his *book* that he was in *space* **above** *Earth* in a *vision* and looking *into* **space** *saw* what appeared to be a **dragon** *approaching* him. But, as it passed, he *realized* it was a *monster* **asteroid**! As he *awoke*, he heard a voice say; "*It's* **name is Apophis**"!

He looked up the *name* and discovered *Apophis* is the *Egyptian* **god** of **chaos** and *destruction*! He was then able (through his DC connections) able to get a *meeting* with a *high* **ranking** *individual* in NASA who was *part* of NASA's asteroid **tracking** division. To make a *long* story *short*, they are currently *tracking* an **asteroid** (about 4 thousand feet long) which if not *deviated* from its **present** *course*, will *land* in the **Pacific** *ocean*.

The most **shocking** *part* of this, instead of giving this *asteroid* a *number* as with the other *thousands* being *tracked*, they *gave* **it** a *name*! Yes, Apophis!

That brings us back to **Revelation**. Now that the **Revelation** *12 sign* of the woman has come to *real-**time** fruition*, it gives *authenticity* to the *rest* of **Revelation**! That said, if we step back to **Revelation** 8, we find a *series* of **plagues** called "*the **Trumpet** Plagues*".

They are the *reason* the woman has to be *whisked* away to a *place* of *safety*. What is most shocking is to understand, NASA is not only tracking this *asteroid* but a *binary **twin** solar system* that's about to *smash* through **our** *solar* **system**! It's *one* of their *best* **concealed** *secrets*!

What is *incredible* is to see how **Revelation** 8-9 *describes* the **arrival** of that **Nemesis** *system* to a tee, with the first *Trumpet* plague *describing* **meteor** *showers* that *burns* up *much* of the Earth. The *second* is a "*flaming mountain that is **thrown** into the sea*"!

Is an *asteroid* not a **flaming** *mountain*? Of course it is, but according to the Biblical time line, along with the *heavenly* **eclipse** signs, that *asteroid* strikes right *after* the *woman* **flees**! It causes the **monster** *tsunami* that is *then* **swallowed** up by a monster *Earth split*! (Earthquake)

That earth-split is also *expected* by NASA where much of the **west** *coast* is going to **split** *away* from the *continent* and *sink* into the *ocean*! How *much* is widely *debated*, but no doubt there's a *modicum* of *truth* involved, especially since the *prophecies* **predict** *it*!

Chapter 75

What is Sin?

Considering the *title* of this piece, it may seem like a real *no-brainer*. After all, doesn't *everyone* **know** *what* **sin** *is*? Unfortunately, after *listening* to *thousands* of preachers *pontificate* over 50 years, I can most assuredly tell you, *most* are **clueless** as to the **real** *meaning* of sin! How bizarre is that?

Unfortunately, it seems everyone has *their* own **personal** *definition* of exactly *what* **sin** *is,* with much of *those* **beliefs** being *anything* **but** *Biblical.* Some of those non-Biblical *sins* are *dancing*, coffee, *alcoholic* beverages, and many others.

One of the big *problems* with much of modern Christianity's ideas of **what** *"sin"* is, has trickled down from such ancient **pagan** *sects* as the Eastern *"Janes"* and later such *cults* as the *"Essenes"* who concluded every **physical** *pleasure* was *sin.*

This *absurd thinking* trickled down into the *universal* (Catholic) Church; which gave *birth* to the medieval ages *concept* of **monasteries** and *convents*. Such *pagan* residue even crept down to some of the modern *Protestant* churches. Of course, that's not to *forget* the Amish who *believe* modern **conveniences**, like *electricity*, are also *sin*!

But, anyone with even a *modicum* of understanding of Bible scripture (and our Creator) understands we were created to **love** and *enjoy life*; just as long as it's **not** at the *expense* of others. After all, our five *senses* are all about *seeing*, **feeling**, *tasting*, and *hearing* all the **good** *things* YHWH *created* for us to **enjoy**!

I can't imagine concluding *things* such *dancing* (non-sexual) as King David, good *clean* food, good *wine* (or beer) in moderation etc. can in any way be *sin*. Fortunately, all those things are **not** *condemned* or called *sin* in the Bible. In fact, they're **promoted**!

Actually, if we are to *accept* the New Testament's *definition* of *sin*, it's in **Romans**.6:23; where we are told; *"sin is the transgression of the law"*. Unfortunately, that scripture is **invalidated** by those who *base* their *religion* on the NT and teach *"the **law** is **done** away"*! If we are *honest*; **no** *law* (which defined by the Hebrew Messiah is **love**) equals *no **sin*** and **excuses** <u>all</u> manner of **evil** *behavior*! I **John** 3 tells us *"lawlessness* is *sin"*! So much for doing away with the Law (Torah of love-literally).

To say *righteousness* (sinlessness) is something **"given"** under **grace** and **not** *practiced*, and that our *behavior* (works) is *irrelevant*, is the biggest *boatload* of pure manure (evil) **ever** *concocted*! Again, **every** *evil* on the planet **plaguing** mankind is **wrapped** *up* in *selfish*, greedy and **proud** *behavior*! Let's keep in mind, the Ten Commandments are all about **how** to **not** *hurt* and/or *abuse* each other, not to mention our Creator YHWH. Can our *treatment* of *Him* and *each* **other**, really be *irrelevant*?

Let's think for a moment; just how *different* the *world* be if only one **tiny** *instruction* (Torah) from our Creator, such as **not** *lying* was *obeyed*? We can be sure we would no longer *recognize* this planet! In fact, this world would be like a *Garden* of *Eden* if everyone would keep even a **few** of those *commands* to **not** hurt or *abuse* each other, such as *stealing*, **murdering** (hating) **adultery**, *lying*, etc.

Again, the Ten *Commandments* are *instructions* how **not** to *abuse* or *disrespect* the Creator and/or each *other*, which would *change* **everything**, but that's only *half* the picture. Those *Ten* Words (commands) are only the *negative* side of *love*!

A shocking *reality* is we can keep the Ten *Commandments* by literally *doing* **nothing**, considering they are all about **not doing hurtful** *things*! But, what about the *other* side; the *things* we should "**do**" for each other, aren't they just as, or even **more** *important*?

Again, just *honoring* the **negative** *side* of *love* would completely **change** the *world*, but *imagine* what incorporating the **positive** *side* of **love**, would do?! Isn't that exactly what the Messiah was *trying* to get *across* in His "*sermon on the mount*" and in His teaching of the *beatitudes*? In fact, we're told in I **John** 3:17 to **not** *help* someone we see is in *need*, is **evil**!

Interestingly, **not doing good** when we **know** to, *constituting* **sin**, is a *truth* few are willing to *acknowledge*! With that in mind and in consideration of the Ten *commandments*, the greatest *sins* of all are **not** *showing* **respect** and **honor** to our *Creator*.

Sadly, virtually all of humanity (mostly ignorantly) *refuses* to give the Creator the "*honor* **due** *Him*" and "*His Name*"! Even Christianity is very *guilty*! After all, what a *slap* in YHWH's face (sin) to worship **pagan** *deities* such as *God, Jesus* (the *three* **headed** *Trinity* **god**) and The *Lord* (ancient pagan god Baal).

Also *making* YHWH's **Exclusive** (*Set Apart*) *Name* **worthless** (vain) by calling Him *the* **Lord** (Baal) as if He's *no* greater than some *snooty* **British** *lord*, is *abhorrent*. Just as *dishonorable* is **reducing** *Him* to the **same** *level* as all the **pagan** *gods* (angels) in the *generic* **title** "God" (*Elohim* in Hebrew). Elohim, by the way was the **father** *god* of the Canaanites. (See Unger's Bible dictionary under false gods). Of course, He certainly is not the *Greek* god *Iesus* (Jesus) either.

And finally there's the blatant *disregard* for YHWH's special *celebrations* (Sabbaths) which ironically, are *all celebrations* of *what* He *has **done*** and is *doing **with*** and ***for*** His children! Just imagine being the greatest *man* the planet has ever *known* and *inviting* your *children* to come **celebrate** the *things* you have *done,* and are *doing* for them, only to have them ***ignore*** your *invitation?* And even worse, they *do* their ***own*** *things*, and even *attend celebrations* with your *enemies **instead***?! Can you imagine?

With that in mind, how bizarre to see the *monstrous **lengths*** the churches go to *find **excuses*** for ***dismissing*** and ***not*** *honoring* YHWH's ***special*** *celebrations*! But then, it couldn't be because this world is *ruled* by the ***demon*** *gods,* YHWH's *enemies,* could it?

Obviously, they will *do whatever* they must to ***keep*** *people **from*** *understanding* the ***blessings*** that ***come <u>with</u> honoring*** our Creator *YHWH's* ***special*** ***celebrations***! Of course, we must keep an important *fact* in mind; YHWH's celebrations (Sabbaths) are by *"invite" only*! Crashing His *parties* would also be very *unwise,* but *snubbing* His ***invite*** (as Israel did) is even worse!

In conclusion; YHWH *cannot* and *will **not*** *sentence* His children to an *eternity* of *bickering,* ***fighting*** and *abuse*! We were made *physical* so we can freely *choose* to *exercise **love***, *respect* and ***honor*** (not sin) and of course, to ***fight*** for ***that*** *choice*! Only *fighting **for*** a *choice* makes it truly ***real***!

When we've done that, we're ready to *enter* YHWH's eternal *family,* and if not, we simply go back to *dirt* from whence we *originated*! This is an *example* how a loving *merciful* Creator such as YHWH ***does*** *things,* not this *evil **monster*** *God* who *sentences* those who *choose **not*** to *accept* or *listen* to Him (and each *other*) to an *eternity* of heinous ***torture***!

Chapter 76

What is Salvation?

Listening to virtually any Christian preacher, the *basis* of their message is almost always "*Salvation*" and "*Jesus*" (their savior)! In fact, that seems to be the *theme* of all the Christian *denominations* (cults) to "*save*" people. But, just **what** are they **saving** people *from*? Well, the most *common* answer is "*their **sins**". The *second* most *common* answer is "*hell*". But, *what* do those *things* even *mean*? Does being *saved **from*** our *sins* mean we *go* to *heaven*?

Well, for starters, there's **not** a *single* scripture in the Bible telling us we go **to** *heaven* when we *die* (or not). Considering **Romans** 8:23 tells us; "*The **wages of sin is death**"* wouldn't being *saved **from** our **sins*** mean "***not** dying*"? After all, *death* is clearly what **Romans** tells us is the **price** of *sin*! That said, wouldn't being "*saved from our sins*" mean being *saved* from **death** ("*the wages of sin*")?

In the Book of **Luke**, we're told: "*He who **seeks** to **save** his life shall lose it*"! Wait a minute; doesn't that mean all these *Christians* **seeking** *salvation*; i.e. *saving* their lives (souls) are going to *lose* them? Well, if we can *believe* it, *that* "**is**" what **Luke** 9:24 *tells* us! So, **if** *saving* our own *skins* is *not* what the Bible is all *about*, **what** is? Well, it all goes *back* to the **Torah** (instructions). The *Torah* was *given* to us as *instructions* on how to be *happy*, **healthy**, *prosperous* and, of course, **alive**!

In **other** *words*, the Torah is **behavioral** *instructions* on *how* to *love*, *respect*, and *honor* our Creator *Father* **first**, and *each* **other** *second; that's* the Ten *Commandments* in a nutshell.

They are all about *how* to *love*, which is exactly what Yahshua (the Name of the Hebrew Messiah) told the *Pharisees* when *asked* what was the *greatest* **commandment**. His *response;* "***Love YHWH*** *with* **all** *your* **heart** *soul and* **mind**, *and your* **neighbor** *as* **yourself**". Actually, He was quoting **Deuteronomy** 6, where YHWH told His people that very *same* thing when He *gave* them the *Torah* (law) in the first place.

Well, there is *another* side to *salvation* referred to many times in the Old Testament. That *salvation* was *protection* from Israel's *enemies*. Still others were **salvation** *from* **disease**, *starvation*, and *natural* **disasters**. No doubt it's to those *kinds* of *salvations* Yahshua's disciples thought He was *referring*.

The disciples no doubt (judging by their reactions) *assumed*, just as today, that everyone **had** to *die*, so I'm sure it never *entered* their minds that Yahshua was referring to **literal** *salvation* **from** *death*! Unfortunately, as now, they had *lost* all knowledge of YHWH's *Plan* for His *children*!

YHWH's *creating* an **eternal** *family* and will **not** *tolerate* **selfish** *bickering*, **infighting**, *greed* and general *misery* in His family! His *desire* is for a *happy* **eternal** *family*, full of *peace*, **contentment**, *cooperation* and *Love*! We were created *physical* to *choose* either *selfishness* and *pride* (Tree of the Knowledge of Good and Evil) *or* **humility** (The tree of Life) to **love**, *respect* and *honor* YHWH and His Family.

If we *choose* the *former*, as did Eve and Adam, we simply *die* and go back to the *dirt* from whence we *came*. If we *choose* the *latter*, it will be an uphill *battle* for the rest of our lives to **prove** our *choice* to **love**, *honor* and *respect* YHWH *first* and *each* **other** *second*! And of course, that's the *reason* for the *adversaries* we were given to *fight* in the first place! Bottom line; *salvation* is YHWH's **salvation** not just from the *evils* of this world, but *death*!

Chapter 77

Saturday Sabbath versus Lunar

We find a bizarre *conundrum* in the Bible based *religions*, concerning the hotly debated, while largely *ignored* subject, the *seventh* **day** *Sabbath*. On one side we have those who *accept* the over **fifty** commands in the Old Testament to "*set it apart*" and *celebrate* it, many of which say "*forever*" or "*throughout your generations*" while most on the *other* side, *rationalize* it's been **done away.** That's so bizarre considering there's **not** a **single** scripture **changing** or *eliminating* that *command* to ancient Israel! Plus, **Malachi** 3:6 tells us *YHWH "does not change"*!

Christianity, for the most part, *refuses* to *accept* that very *plain* scripture in **Malachi** and *vehemently* **rejects** YHWH's *Sabbath* (as well as *annual* ones) while in the same breath, *professing* to "**love** God"! Can we really "*love* **God**" (YHWH) while at the same time **rejecting** His **special** *Days*, which He *ordained* to be *celebrated* with Him "*forever*"?

That's an **impossible** oxymoron considering we *cannot* **honestly** love someone *without* **loving** the *things* **special** to *them*! But, this *conundrum* exposes something *extremely* **important** about YHWH's (weekly) Sabbath; one so *important* as to be *integrated* with other *commands* (instructions) such as "*you* **shall** *not* **murder**"!

Obviously, the *weekly* Sabbath is *important* to *anyone* who *dares* to be **honest** with the *scriptures*, but how do we know exactly **which** *day* is the **seventh** *day*; the *day* "*set apart*" by YHWH in **Genesis** 2? That also prompts the *question*; did the Jews really keep *track* of **which** *day* is the **seventh,** since the *Garden* of *Eden* as they *claim*?

On the other hand, did the *pagan* world, *ruled* by the *demons* who **hate** YHWH, also *adopt* YHWH's **"same"** *seventh* day? Ironically, with *no* **written** *record* **proving** *it,* they (the Jews) still *expect* us to simply **accept** their **word**. But, considering their *absurd* **beliefs** and **rules** about *observing* it, why should we *accept* **their** *word*?

After all, would the Creator really *leave* such an *important thing* (to Him) as the "*sign between* **Him** *and* **His** *people*" in the *hands* of *people*? After all, can just any *pagan* **make** *themselves* **one** of YHWH's *chosen* people by keeping *Saturday*? (Or Sunday)

Another glaring *problem* with the **Saturday** *Sabbath*, is the fact that it's a *day* **dedicated** to the "*father god*" (Titan) of the Romans "*Saturn*" (Cronos in Greek). Considering *many* scriptures tell us **YHWH's** *Sabbath* is *Quodesh* ("Set Apart") would He really *share* that **exclusive** *weekly* **Sabbath** with the *Greek* and *Roman's* **father** *god*? In fact, **nowhere** in *scripture* do we find *Saturday* being *established* as the Sabbath. The **only** *day* we find is the "*seventh day*". (A counted day)

How on Earth could we possibly **prove** *Saturday*, a day *dedicated* to the **pagan god Saturn**, is really the **seventh** *day*? Besides, after Joshua's "**long day**" all the world's civilizations *changed* their calendars from a *360* day year to *365*. Finally, around 50 BCE Julius Caesar had a **new** *calendar* created with all the *days* of the *week* (and most months) named after **pagan** *gods*! It's the **same** *calendar* endorsed by pope *Gregory*, which we still use!

Obviously, YHWH did *not* give Adam and Eve the *Gregorian* calendar with most of the months *dedicated* to **pagan** *gods*, so what *calendar* did YHWH establish? Well, He tells us right *there* in **Genesis**, chapter 1 and verse 14; the *sun* and *moon*!

Unfortunately, the *human* translators **hid** *that* **truth** by *mistranslating* "*Moeds*" in **Genesis** 1:14 to "*seasons*". Yes, the *annual* Sabbaths involve *seasons*, but not the weekly. If we look up "*Feasts*" (Sabbaths) in **Leviticus** 23, we find it's the **same** *word* (Moeds) as in **Genesis**. And then, **Leviticus** 23 goes on to list the *weekly* **Sabbath** as the **first** of those *Moeds*. Considering the **weekly** *Sabbath's* **extreme** *importance* (the *sign* between Him and His people) would YHWH's Torah *instructions* really **"not"** *tell* us *from* "**where**" to *begin* the "**seven**" day *count* to that Sabbath?

Of course, considering He *instructs* us to *count* the *annual* Feasts **from** the New moon (which are all Sabbaths) why wouldn't the **weekly** *Sabbath* be *counted* from the New Moon as well? And, if the moon is YHWH's *calendar*, and no human can **change** the *course* and *speed* of the *moon*, there can be *no* honest *argument* **when** the Sabbaths are to be *kept*!

With that in mind, is it any *surprise* there are **seven** *days* between *moon* **phases**? Obviously, the **New Moon** marks the **first** *day* (Sabbath) of the *month* and each *successive* moon *phase* (every seventh day) are YHWH's **weekly** *Sabbaths*. How more *simple* can it get? But, this world is *run* **by** *demons* (authors of confusion) doing *everything* in their *power* to **hide** that simple major **truth**.

A simple *proof* about the *Saturday* Sabbath is shown by what Yahshua told the **Saturday** *keeping* Pharisees in **John.8:44**; "*you are **sons** of your father the devil*"! Obviously, they were <u>**NOT** keeping</u> YHWH's "*true*" (lunar) Sabbath (s)

Another very *profound* bit of *wisdom* found in scripture is; "*You know a tree by its fruit*". After all, people *say* all *kinds* of *things*, but it's *their* **actions** that *reveal* the **real** *truth*. So, for the *leaders* of a *religious* **sect** to **say** they've kept *track* of the *seventh* day since creation means absolutely *nothing*. After all, that **same** *religious* **order** *doesn't* even *accept* the *first* **century** *Messiah*, yet we should **believe** *them* on the Sabbath?

And speaking of *red* flags, when we check the *Saturday* keepers' *fruits*, it becomes overwhelmingly *obvious* they do not stand *up* to the **rotten** *fruit* **test**. After all, a large percentage of *Saturday* observing Jews *support* **murdering** *unborn* babies (abortion) and *sodomy* (homosexual marriage). In fact, many of the *mover* and *shakers* in the Hollywood (destroying our morality) are these **Saturday** *keepers*!

Just how wise are we to put **god-like** *faith* in *such* people versus *what* the Torah *plainly* **teaches**? Unfortunately, it's easy to get hung *up* on a **small** *issue* we **don't** *understand* and become **lost** in the (their) **black** *forest*. The scriptures are like a *puzzle* with all the *pieces* being of similar **shape**. Without a big (finished puzzle) picture to work *toward*, assembling the **correct** *picture* in the end is virtually *impossible*!

That said, another sure way to *prove* that YHWH's **lunar** *calendar* is the *calendar* He gave us *to* **use,** is to *attempt* to **prove** beyond a shadow of a doubt, **Saturday** is the *true* one. After all, there are *no* scriptures telling us its *Saturday*, but again, we do have the *words* of the *Messiah* **rejecting** *Saturday*-Sabbath keeping *Jewish* leaders. And, after *examining* their *illicit* fruits, how could we possibly think it's *wise* to take a stand on their *words* and *not* simple scripture?

No doubt; YHWH still has *plans* for His Israelite tribe of *Judah*, but that will be *after* He brings them *back* to Him!

Chapter 78

Sabbath Blessings

One of the most *misunderstood* aspects of the *Bible* and *Torah*, with both the *Christian* and *Jewish* communities, is the *Sabbath*. If we take all the scriptures *dealing* with, and *related* to the subject, and *combine* them with a little **common** sense and *logic*, we see *none* of the *common* **conclusions** *regarding* the *Sabbath* (on both sides) make any *real* sense.

I'm *not* going to launch into any kind of *in-depth* study except to point out a *few* of the *absurdities* involved on *both* sides. I will then point out some of the *ignored* and/or **unknown** aspects of the Creators true **7th** day Sabbath and the *blessings* that *come* with the *true* **respect** and *observance* of it.

Beginning with the Christian *community*, we find they virtually *ignore* all the scriptures instructing the *Sabbath* to be *observed* "*forever*" and "*throughout their generations*" (by Israel). Well, *forever* has **not** expired and **modern** generations of Israel are *still* **here**. Obviously, Christians and *Jews*, for the most part, teach Israel (the ten northern tribes) *no* longer *exist* even though the Creator said He would "*scatter*" them among the nations but "**not one** *seed would be* **lost**"! (Amos 9)

Secondly, they have to *conclude* YHWH, the Creator, *made a mistake* with His *commands* to Israel; or that He **changed** His *mind* even though **Malachi** 3 dogmatically tells us; "*YHWH does not change*" (or make mistakes).

Another *argument* is *Jesus* (the Greek Messiah) *became* and/or *canceled* the Sabbath, which the scriptures **nowhere** say. Besides, any *honest* and *rational* person can easily see what an *absurdity* that widely *popular* conclusion is. In fact, it thoroughly *destroys* the Bibles' *message* to humanity!

Even the Jews, who *claim* to *keep* the **7th day** Sabbath **as** *commanded*, have *turned* it into an *absurdity*. In fact, one of the chief *Christian* arguments is to *point* to the ridiculous *orthodox **Jewish** traditions* connected to their **Saturday** *sabbath*; things like not being able to *turn **on*** a *light* switch or *push* an *elevator **button*** because it's equivalent to *lighting* a fire, which *they* have *deduced* was *forbidden* by the Creator on the Sabbath.

With that thought in mind, they apparently *believe* He took *pleasure* in their being **cold** and/or hot (no air conditioning, or heat) and basically *miserable* on **His** *Sabbath*.

Considering YHWH commanded His Sabbath be *a **joy*** as well as a *feast*, how can that be possible with only **cold**, left-over *food*!?

The Jews also teach "*no work*" (at all) was to be *done* even though YHWH gave His priests a **double** *work* **load** (double the sacrifices) on His Sabbaths. (See Leviticus) I guess the Creator is just a *hippocrite* of the *grandest* order. Even though the work load of the priests was *doubled*, the Jews consider even *walking **work***!

In fact, they *rationalize* just how *many* steps can be *taken* (like *50*)! Honestly, if *what* the Jews keep is the *true* Sabbath, I can understand *how* and *why* the Christians say it's *absurd* and **did** *away* with it! Who can *blame* them?

One thing's for sure; the Jewish *Saturday* sabbath is **not** *YHWH's* (the true Creator) Sabbath, especially considering Yahshua called those Jews (Pharisees) who kept it in the first century "*sons of their father the devil*"! How interesting *Saturday* is **dedicated** to *Saturn*, a pagan god, the *chief* of the Greek *titan* gods!

Obviously, **neither** *side* is anywhere *close* to *correct* conclusions considering YHWH's Sabbath (s) are to be *celebrated* **forever.** In fact, *future* millennium *prophecies* show it's still being *celebrated* in **Ezekiel** and other places. Besides, the true *seventh* day Sabbath is the **heart** of the **Ten** *Commandments,* and how can you **rip** the **heart** out of the **Ten** *Commandments* without *destroying* them **all**! It's simply *not* possible.

Again, the Sabbath is *commanded* to be a **joyous** *feast,* not a *burden* of *dos'* and *don'ts.* It all boils down to *understanding* **what** the **Creator's** *Sabbath* is really *all* **about** and **what** it *means* to YHWH (and us). Again, if we conclude it's just a bunch of *meaningless* **hoops** the Creator wants us to *jump* through, only to *see* if we *will* **obey**, it becomes shallow and *redundant.* There are so many *other* ways to *test* our *obedience.*

With all that in mind, let's *notice* a few Sabbath *facts* that are *ignored* and **not** *taught.* First of all, the Sabbath is *a* **gift** from *YHWH* (**Exodus**.16:29 and Ez.20:20) It's not some meaningless "*do-or-**die**"* *command* just to *humor* the Creator. He's *not* that kind of **dictatorial** *god*! Plus, the Sabbath is a *perpetual* (eternal) "*covent*" and "*sign*" between YHWH and **His** *special* people, **not** *humanity* as a *whole.* (Ex.31:16-17 Ez.20:12)

We are told in **Ezekiel** 18:21&31-32; "*Cast away from you all your transgressions which **you** have **committed*** (such as disrespecting His Sabbath (s) is one) *and **get yourselves** a **new heart** and a **new spirit***. *For **why** should you **die** O house of Israel? For I have **no pleasure in the death** of one who **dies,** says YHWH our God. Therefore **turn and live**!"* Obviously, His Sabbath is a *gift,* of **life,** that is**,** when He *gives* it; just like the "*Tree of Life*" in the *Garden*!

Besides YHWH's Sabbath being a *gift* of **life**, He *blessed* it to be a *literal **all-around** blessing* as we find *outlined* in **Deuteronomy** 30. (Remember, His Sabbath is the heart of His Torah) He says in **Psalm** 37:23-24 (and Ps.40:2) "*The steps of a good* (righteous) *are **ordered*** (arranged) ***by YHWH** and He **delights** in his way. Though he **fall**, he shall **not** be utterly cast **down**, for YHWH **upholds** Him* (personally) *with **His hand**!*"

People will *argue* these scriptures are *etherial* and/or *metaphorical*, but I can personally vouch for the fact they're literal considering that's exactly how YHWH has *personally* been taking *care* of *me* ever since I began *honoring* Him with His true Sabbath (s) (*dictated* by the *moon*).

Unfortunately, it's a *huge* step of **faith** to first *honor* Him with His "***exclusive*** (set apart) *Name* (s)" (Mal.1&2) and then *honor* Him with the *celebrating* (with Him) His *exclusive **Sabbath***! (Again, counted from the new moons) YHWH and *His **true** instructions* (Torah-promises) *do **not** lie*. The bottom line is; YHWH will *not* (cannot) give **His Sabbath** (s) and the astounding *blessings* that *come **with** it* (like immortality) to *those* who. **worship** *pagan* and **false** *names* and *celebrate* **pagan** and/or *false* sabbaths. He will *only* bless us with His amazing Sabbaths if we first *honor* Him with His *first **three*** Torah instructions (commands). Again, that's why the Sabbath is *couched* in the **middle** (heart) of His **Torah** *instructions* (Ten Commandments).

Chapter 79

Repentance and Forgiveness

A big *question* **wrestled** *with* by many is the *essence* of **repentance**. Along with that, of course, is the *actuality* of **forgiveness**. For example, the Universal Church (Catholic) tells us *confession* (to a priest) is *repentance* and that the *priest* has the authority to **grant** *forgiveness*.

After all, the Pope *believes* he walks in the *shoes* of the *Messiah* (Vicar of Christ) and has the *power* to *hear* the *sins* and *to* **forgive**. My question is, how do we *know* if **any** of *that* is true? How *wise* is it to simply *accept* **their** *word* as *gospel*, especially considering they *replaced* the *Hebrew* **Messiah** with a Greek **substitute**?!

First of all, don't we need *something* very *authoritative* to *found* our beliefs *upon*, such as the Bible (minus translation changes and errors)? Of course, if we are *unable* to *accept* the **authenticity** of the *Bible* and/or the *God* who *inspired* it, **anything** *goes*! But, they have a *word* for that; **chaos**! In order to have *order*, **all** *societies* have to be *founded* upon *guidelines* (laws) from *somewhere*.

Most *societies* have *developed* (or inherited) various *religions* to form those *guidelines*, but unfortunately, *few* **use** the *Bible*. On the other hand *communist* governments *maintain* **order** by *way* of **force** instead. Unfortunately, an *inherent* **need** of humanity is *freedom* (to one degree or another) so **communist** *societies* are rather *short* lived.

To keep this as *short* as *possible*, let's *assume* the Bible is the **best** *course* of **true** *guidelines* by which to *live*. With that *established*, we *first* need to *know* **what** *sin* is, to *understand* what **repentance** is all *about*. Of course, *sin* is to *break* or **transgress** the law (Torah instructions) which in this case are the **instructions** *outlined* in Bible scripture, such as the **Ten Commandments**.

Considering the Hebrew Messiah in the first century was asked *which* of those *ten* was the greatest or most important, He quoted **Deuteronomy** 6, where we are told *"to Love YHWH* (the Creator's Hebrew Name) *your God with all your heart, soul and might"*! (First four decrees)

The Messiah then *added*; *"and love your neighbor as yourself"*. (Last six) In other words, those *ten* guidelines are all about *loving* our Creator God **"first"** and *each* **other** second. But, that list is basically the **hurtful** *things* **not** to *do*, except for two. (5 & 6) Other scriptures (NT) tell us **not** *providing* someone *in* **need** with *help*, is **also** sin. That's the **positive** *side* of *love*.

Getting to the point, doing **hurtful** *things* and **not** *doing* **helpful** *acts* where **needed**, are both *defined* as *sin*. When we *realize* we've done *something* **hurtful**, either to our Creator God or another *person*, what is the *proper* **course** of *action* (repentance)? Can we simply say *"my bad"* and go on? How about when someone *wrongs* **us**? How can that be *resolved*? Are we fine with that person simply saying *"sorry"*?

Sometimes there's *nothing* they can *do*, but usually there *is*. For instance, the **torah** *instructions* in the OT tell us we must *repay* a person from which we *stole*, 7 times over. But, most times, a *hurt* is **verbal**. Words, after all, are the *most* **hurtful** *weapons* around, in spite of the *saying* children are **taught**; *"Sticks and stones can break my bones, but words cannot hurt me"*! There's a grain of truth there, but words *do* **inflict** *deep* **emotional** and **phycological** *damage*!

Well, the scriptures *instruct* us in *what* to **do** in **these** *instances*. In **Matthew** 18, we're *instructed* to *confront* the *person* who's *wronged* us **face** to *face* and *resolve* it. If that *fails* to *settle* the issue, we are instructed to *return* with *two* **trusted** *friends* and try *again*.

What I've *discovered* in my **personal** *experiences* is *most* of *these* **hurts** *never* get *resolved* simply because they are **not** *discussed* **face** to *face* because the **guilty** *one* does **not** *desire* resolution. In fact, it's very common for *splits* in *families* to **never** *get* **resolved** simply because the *hurts* are not *addressed one* on *one*. (Lack of real communication) How sad to see so many *lives* **enduring** a *lifetime* of *pain* for *no* **good** *reason*!

In fact, we're told to "*confess our sins one to another*" in **James** 5:16. Unfortunately the word "*sins*" is a **bad** *translation*. The *essence* of that *admonition* is *confronting* those whom **we** *have* **wronged** to *make* it *right* and *vise-versa* as the Hebrew Messiah *instructs* in **Matthew**. It is **not** about *publicly* **airing** our *dirty laundry*! It's simply about *peaceful* **resolution**!

Personally *confronting* **each** *other* with our *wrongs* is the *essence* of *repentance* and/or *forgiveness*! When a person is truly *sorry* for a *wrong* **done** and attempts to *resolve* and *rectify* it, it's the *wronged* persons' *moral* **obligation** to **forgive**. They say; "*to not forgive is like taking poison and waiting for the other person to die*"!! Forgiveness is really *for* **us**!

What about the Creator? How do we *right* a *wrong* (like disrespect) with *Him*? Fortunately, He's the God of *mercy* and is **not** *vengeful*. But, if we *refuse* to *acknowledge* our *disrespectful* behavior *towards* Him, He will eventually **withdraw** His **protection** and *provision* (that is for His *chosen* people).

YHWH *allows* our **wrong** *behavior* to come *back* on *us* (Karma). Honestly, that's about getting us to *acknowledge* **our** *behavior* and *change* it and then to **return** to *Him*. One *thing* He *promises*; to 100% *forgive* us if we are truly *repentant* (sorry) and are willing to *change*. But, He will **not** *forgive* if we do **not** *repent*; that is, make a **commitment** to *change* **our** *behavior*!

One *stumbling* block in many peoples *minds* is how in *ancient* times when *someone sinned*, they had to *bring* an *animal* to the priests in the *temple* to *sacrifice*. Unfortunately, **that** *sacrifice* did **not** remove the *ultimate* **price** of that *sin;* **death**. (Rom. 8:26) When the *first*-born *Son* of the Creator *shed* his *blood*, He *replaced* the **animal** sacrifices, but the ultimate *penalty*, **death,** was **still** *there*. (Which is why everyone is still dying).

Although, His *blood* did *wash* **away** the *sins* of the *first* century *priesthood* (the first-born). After His sacrifice, the *priesthood* (the "**order**" not **world** as Jn.3:16 was miss-translated to say) was *cleansed* to be *filled* with the *YHWH's* **Spirit** of *life* for them to be *born* **again** (of *actual* spirit).

But, the *other* thing the *sacrifice* of the Messiah *did*, was *open* the *door* to the Father. We can now *address* Him *directly* without going *through* a **human** *priest*. Actually, the *priesthood* is still *acting* on *our* **behalf**, but are now **spirit** *beings* in *heaven*.

They were literally **born** *again* (of spirit) when the Hebrew Messiah (Yahshua) **returned** for *them* as He *promised* in **Matthew** 24. The rest of us, *will* **have** our *sins removed* and be *filled* with YHWH's *Spirit* of **life** in the **real** *time fulfillment* of the Day of *Atonement*, which is another amazing study!

Chapter 80

What and Who are the Two Witnesses?

In **Revelation** 11, we find a *strange* reference to "*two*" *witnesses* who are *killed* and then *resurrected*. There has been *massive **speculation*** as to just **who** they *are* and **when** they *witness*. I have personally *heard* people *claim* to be ***those** witnesses,* **who,** *without **fail,*** have proven *not* to be.

Obviously, the really ***big** question* is *who* these *two* witnesses are, and for *what* are they **witnesses**? Just *what* did they *see* to which they are to *testify*? As we *know*, there are ***always** witnesses* at *trials,* so does that mean *this* is a *trial*? If so, just *who* is **on** *trial* and *for* **what**? Since we find this *account* in the Bible, does it **not** *make* sense that it's also *there* we find the *answers* to **these** *questions*?

First of all, the *Torah* (OT instructions) *instructed* that someone could *not* be *accused* and *brought **before*** a *judge* without a *minimum* of **two** *witnesses*. If this is true, **who** is on *trial* and for what are they being *accused?* Well, **Revelation** 11 points out the *whole **world** rejoices* upon the **death** of these *two,* which would *indicate* the **one** on *trial,* is **the** *world!* And, just like a *mob **boss*** that's being *brought* to *trial,* they will do **everything** *possible* to **dispose** *of* their **incriminating** *witnesses!*

Of course, if it's the *world* being *judged*, does it not *indicate* this is the *final* **judgement** *before* the "*lake of fire*" that *consumes* this **evil** *world* and *everything* in it. (II Peter and Rev.19) And obviously, the list of *evils* for which this world is being *judged*, are *myriad*; *wars*, **murder** (and of the *unborn*) **sodomy**, and of course the *worship* of the **pagan** and *false* **gods**.

Exactly *when* that *judgement* is *levied*, is wildly *speculated* by a **million** *different* people, but we can be sure virtually all are only *guessing*. To understand, we need to *incorporate* the **Biblical** *outline* given us by the *Feasts* of **Leviticus** 23.

The *Creator* is very *precise* in His *timeline*, which **Revelation** 13 tells us was *established* "*before* the *foundation* of the *world*". To *know* **His** *Plan* (for *us*) and its *timeline*, was the very *reason* for *instructing* His *people* to *observe* the **Leviticus** 23 Feasts.

Those *Feasts* were *physical* **rehearsals** of the **real** *spiritual* **fulfillments** they *portrayed*. But, to fully understand, we *also* need to **see** the **big** *picture*. Our Creator's are *creating* an **eternal** *family* for *themselves*.

Since true **respect**, *honor*, and **love** *cannot* be *forced*, they created us **physical** *first*, for us to *learn* and **choose** *to* **love**, *respect*, and *honor* our *Creator* parents *first* and *each* **other** *second*. Until we do that, we simply *cannot* be a *part* of **that** *family*.

If we *choose* to be **selfish**, *greedy*, **proud**, and *disrespectful*, we simply **die** and *return* to the *dust* **from** *whence* we were *formed*. On the other hand, if we *choose* to **respect**, *honor*, and *love* our *Creator's* **first** and *each* **other** *second* (the ten commandments) and spend our *lives* **fighting** *for* **that** choice, we're *ready* to join *their* **eternal** *family*! (Be born again of spirit)

Of course, the **demonic** *world* was a **necessary** *evil* to *give* us *adversaries* to **fight** (for the *good* **choices**). After all, a *choice* **not** *fought for* is **not** quite *real!* For a *choice* to be *truly* **real**, it must be **fought** *for*, which causes **that** *behavior* to *become* an **eternal** *part* of us! After all, to be completely *real* our Creator's need our *love* to be *uncorerced*.

Then, after everyone's *made* **their** *choice* to *embrace* YHWH's *Torah* of *Love* (or not) it's **judgement** *time*. At that point *all* that will be *left* on this world (including the evil spirits) will be *those* who **rejected** *YHWH* and His *Torah* of *love, who* will then be **judged** and *burned!*

Again, because YHWH's Torah *requires* at least **two** *witnesses* for *judgement* to be *served*, these two *witnesses* will have had *witnessed* **all** the *evil* that *occurred* on this Planet, which necessitates them to be *thousands* of **years** *old*. If they didn't *live* through *all* the *evils*, they would **not** be *qualified* **witnesses**, which *narrows* down the *list* of those *eligible*.

That said, that list could obviously *consist* of those that **never** *died*. That list starts with *Enoch* who the scriptures tell us was *taken* to *heaven* and did **not** *die*. But, the problem with Enoch, he *witnessed* the **pre-flood** *era* which was *judged* with the *flood*.

So, for Enoch to be a *witness*, it seems it would have been for that **pre- flood** *era*. Next we have *Moses*, which a **solid** *case* can be *made* did **not** *die*; after all, we find *Moses* and *Elijah* conversing with Yahshua in the NT. After that, we are told *Elijah* was also taken up to *heaven* **without** *dying*.

Obviously those two would *qualify* to be *witness* before the *first* century, but what of the since then. Well, a *good* case can be *made* there are also *people* (priesthood) the **first** *century* that **never** *died* and are still *around*, such as the *story* of the **wandering** *Jew*.

The spring harvest (of people) *happened* in the **first** *century*, and as the Torah *directed*, the *corners* of the *fields* were to be *left* for the *poor*.

Since the *field* was the *priesthood* (first-born) upon *whom* the great *out- pouring* of YHWH's *Spirit* of **life** (immortality) was *poured,* that means *some* of those *immortals* must **still** be *around* and would *qualify* as *witnesses* of the *age* from the *first* century. Bottom line; it will be virtually impossible to **predict** *exactly* **who** those *two* witnesses are, and only a *fool* would try!

Chapter 81

Women Power

The history of *women* is a very *interesting* and *strange* **one** indeed. It's quite a history of **pendulum** *swings*. It seems women *acquired* a *stigma* causing **subjugation** and *reduction* to **second**-*class* citizen, or worse. In fact, in spite of the modern *gains* in **Western** *female* **freedoms**, that *second* **class** *stigma* still *remains* for a **large** *segment* of worlds *women*. Many Eastern societies still see women as *only* **good** for *sex, having* **babies**, *raising* them, and *taking* **care** of their *men*, who in many cases **treat** *them* **no** *better* than *slaves.*

The big *question* is "*how*" did women *acquire* such a *stigma,* and is it *something* they **deserve**? After all, *why* was it *not* until *modern* **Western** *nations,* that women were *allowed* to *assume* **authoritative** roles. What's the *source* of that *mistrust* of women in **authority** *positions*? Are the so-called *fables* such as **Pandora's** *box* the *source* that *authorizes* and *feeds* that *mistrust*? But, how much **historical** *truth* is there to these *fables;* any?

Another popular *argument* is women are much *smaller* and *weaker* than men and can be *more* **easily** *dominated* (as in the evolutionary model) by the *larger,* **stronger**, men. But, for that *argument* to stand, means men have to *want* or **desire** *dominance.*

But, in my experience, **most** men have **less** desire to *dominate* the women they *love*, than those *women* **desire** to *dominate* their men. My own *observation* has been, it's usually the *women* who are the **most** prone to **manipulate,** *dominate* and/or **control** a *relationship*. In fact, most every man whose *married* for any *amount* of *time* has come to *understand* that. In fact, the *running* **joke** in *marriages* is the *wife* is the "***true***" *boss*!

Regardless, **another** *argument* for **not** *allowing* women the *authority* **positions** they seem to *desire* (more than most men) is they are more *emotional* and **can't** be *trusted* to make *logical* **unbiased** *decisions*. Is that true? Well, we do have major *support* for that *conclusion* in the Bible (Genesis) as well as in world *history*. You see, it was the *woman* (alone) the dragon *approached* to **seduce**, *not* Adam.

What was it about Eve that *caused* the *dragon* to **approach** *her* **versus** *Adam*, or Adam and Eve *together*? Well, apparently the *dragon* **knew** *something* about Eve, which virtually every good **salesman** *understands*.

Women are more easily *persuaded* and/or *influenced* than men due to *their* **emotional** *make-up*. With the **right** *words* (invoking the right emotions) *most* women can be *influenced* to **do** or *believe* (or buy) most *anything*.

In reference to Adam and Eve, it seems Adam was **not** *deceived* and *chose* **death** rather than *lose* his *love*! Actually, that seems to be the **predominant** *feeling* most men had or *have* **towards** their *women* and/ or *wives*. Again, when *push* comes to *shove*, most men are willing to do *anything* for the *woman* they **love,** versus *losing* them.

That said, a good *case* can be *made*, the *reason* women in history have been *kept subdued* was because of **what** Eve *did;* possibly the *source* of the **Pandora** *fable*, which it seems the *world* is **still** paying for. I realize most women *hate* that *conclusion*, but from a man's *logical* **view** point, it does make *sense*.

Obviously, men were ***never*** *intended* to *dominate* or *subdue* women or their *wives*, especially when seeing how YHWH took a *rib* from *Adam* to create her. That means she was *intended* to *walk* ***by*** *his* ***side*** in life, ***not*** *behind* him (or before him). She has the ***same*** *value* in the Creator's eyes as men.

Now, considering *women* have *been* ***given*** the greatest *freedom* in history, how is it working out? Are they *proving* ***men*** *right*, or *wrong*? Well, let's just look at some modern *issues*. These days, a majority of women have *left* the home and the *nurturing* of their *children* for ***careers***, leaving their babies to be *raised* by *strangers*.

Unfortunately, this has resulted in a *spike* of ***broken*** *homes* and children being *raised* by ***single*** *parents*. In fact, most *psychologists* tell us ***single*** *parents* raising *children* is *very* ***damaging*** to those children's *future* ***adult*** *relationships* and ***mental*** *health*.

Not only has extreme *damage* been done to the ***traditional*** *families*, but the resulting *moral* ***decline*** has *spawned* a major *spike* in ***non***-*commitence* to *marriage*. That in turn, has *birthed* a massive *increase* of *single* mothers, and ***abortions***, which unfortunately *comes* with the ***baggage*** of *emotional* ***traumas*** that eventually *catches* ***up*** to them. The realization settles in one day that they *murdered* their *sons* and/or *daughters*.

Of course, that *realization* ***doubles*** *alcoholism*, ***drug*** *addiction*, and of course ***suicides***! The truth is, with *great* ***freedom*** comes ***great*** *responsibility*.

Unfortunately, the *pendulum* ***swing*** from *little* to ***no*** *freedom* has *swung* completely the ***opposite*** *direction*. Sadly, women *rights* leaders are telling women, they're *equal* in *ability* or even ***greater*** *than* men, which is pure *nonsense* considering the *different* ***talents*** and *abilities* between the two *sexes*. They ***never*** have *been* the ***same*** or *ever* ***will** be,* in spite of the women's *rights* people's *foolish* rhetoric!

But, it's the *differences* between the *sexes* that's **beautiful**! The *differences* are to *be* **celebrated**, and *enjoyed*, **not** *condemned*! That said, and *due* to the *average* woman's *emotional* make up, they are *often* like a **rowboat** on the open *ocean*; all over the place!

On the other hand, the average man has a *logical* mind and is *able* to be the *perfect* **anchor** for the woman in his life. Also, women have the **nest-** *feathering* and **nurturing** *qualities* the average man *lacks*. So, together the two make a *perfect* **whole**, each providing *what* the other *lacks*!

Again, that's exactly *what* the Creator's *intended* when YHWH *formed* Eve from a *rib* of Adam. It shows they are to *walk* through *life* **side** *by side*, of **equal** *importance*, but with **different** *abilities*. But, for any *relationship* to truly *work*, the **final** *say* has to be given to *one* of them, or there will much *unnecessary* **bickering** and *fighting*. And, again, considering women's *emotional* makeup, obviously the **logical** *mind* has to have the *final* say.

To end this article; it's **not** a *dissertation* **against** women, but to *point* out the **power** women *actually* have, especially with the men that *love* them. And again, with great *power* comes great **responsibility**. Properly *exercised*, women have incredible *power* to *influence* **good** into *society*, while at the same time, that *power* **can** *be* and has **been** used very *destructively*, as in the *fable* of Pandora's box.

Chapter 82

Why do Good People Suffer?

We so often hear asked; "*why does* **God** *let* "**good**" *people suffer*"? It seems to be a very *valid* and **logical** *question*, but, we must *first* ask; **who** *defines* "**good**"? Is **our** *definition* of **good** the *same* as *God's*? And, **how** can we *know*? In *contrast* to all the *bad*, we see *promises* all through the Bible of **protection**, *provision*, and **healing**. So, *what* gives?

The first scripture we should probably *keep* in mind, is *where* the Creator tells us; "*For as the* **heavens** *are* **higher** *than the* **Earth,** *so are* **my** *ways* **higher** *than* **yours** *and* **my thoughts higher** *than* **yours**". (Is. 55:9) In other words, *why* the *ones* **we** *determine* "*good*" **suffer**, is way *above* our **pay** grade, although we do have some **basic** *promises* upon which to *stand* to *avoid* the **worst** of *things*.

On the *other* hand, some *things* are **necessary** *evils* **required** for our *maturing* and **humbling**. **Isaiah** 57:15 clearly tells us YHWH **only** *walks* with the **humble** and *contrite*! Does *adversity* not net *humility*?

Again, the *core* **problem** is **our** *deciding* for *ourselves* **who** or *what* is **good**. That said, just **what** *process* do we *incorporate* to *arrive* at our conclusions of *good* and/or **bad**? Let's not forget, the **evil** tree of which Eve and Adam *partook*, was the tree of the *knowledge* of **good** *and* **evil**! If we're able to take a *look* at *ourselves* in *relation* to **good** and/or *evil*, **what** would we *conclude*? Obviously, some honestly *know* **they** are **evil** and do *evil* things, but most of us naturally **paint** ourselves with a *whitewash* brush.

But, our Creator's *know* the **real** *us*, in spite of the *picture* we've **painted** of ourselves. In fact, we're told in **Romans** 6:23; "*The* **wages** *of* **sin** *is* **death**". That said, is there a person alive who has *not* or *does* **not** sin and *earned* the *wages* of that *sin* (death)? If you *believe* we all *sin*, then we *all* **deserve** *death*, right? That **reality** *nullifies* the original *question* of this draft. Technically, if we are **all** sinners, we are all *deserving* of *nothing* **less** than *death* and the **suffering** *entailed*.

That said, *what* makes us "*good*" or should I say, *what* is it that *brings* the Creator's to **see** us as *good* (righteous)? We are told by most of *Christianity* it's *accepting* the *name* of *Jesus* that makes us *good* and/or *righteous*. But, does that act *nullify* **evil** *selfish* **behavior**? Does *greedy*, **manipulating,** and *selfish* **behavior**, which is *causing* all the worlds *problems* (evils) suddenly become *irrelevant* if we **accept** *Jesus*? But, isn't *righteous* (good) *behavior* what makes us **good** *people* and the *world* a **good** *place*?

When we *listen* to Christian teachings, we're told *good*, **righteous** *behavior* is *impossible*, which is *why* the "*law*" (Torah) was *done* **away** and *grace* was *given* instead. Is that *correct*? Unfortunately, that *teaching* **originates** with the **self**-appointed (false) *apostle* that *complained* how he **did** the *things* (evil-selfish) he *did* **not** *want* to *do* and **did** *not* **do** the (righteous) things he *wished* he could.

Interestingly, **none** of the *other* (12) Apostles of Yahshua talked **that** *way*. Why? What was the *difference*? Was it because they *received* the great *outpouring* of YHWH's Spirit of *life* in **Acts** 2? Remember, Paul was **not** *among* the 120 **receiving** that *outpouring*!

Bottom line; the *spirit* of *pride* **imbued** *us* by the dragon, is far too *powerful* for us to *overcome* (control) without **supernatural** *assistance;* which Paul obviously had **not** *received!*

Just *before* Yahshua *ascended,* He *promised* His 12; "*You will receive* *power when YHWH's* **Spirit** *comes* **upon** *you*-" (Acts 1:8) It's taught virtually across the board *the* **power** they *received* was the *ability* to **perform** *miracles.* No doubt that's also *true,* but there was a much more *important* **reason** for that *power!*

That's exactly what Paul was *alluding* to when he said he **did** the *things* he **didn't** *want* to *do* and *didn't* **do** the (good) *things* he **wanted**. Again, the reason the 12 apostles of Yahshua didn't *talk* like *Paul* is because they *had* **received** the **power** *needed* to **overcome** the *spirit* and **power** of the dragon! The dragon is a **supernatural** *creature* and only with *supernatural* **power** can we do *battle* and *overcome* the *dragon's* **spirit** of *pride,* **selfishness**, and *greed!*

Getting back to the *premise* of this study; what *determines* a person is *good* or *not,* is if we have the *Creator's* **Spirit** of **humility** and **love**. Without that Spirit, all people *fall* into the category of "*carnal*" that is, of the *spirit* of the *dragon* (tree of the knowledge of good and evil). Only after *embracing* the "*Tree of Life*" are we technically *good!* To *embrace* the **Tree** of **Life**, we must **first** *give* our Creator the **Honor** "*due*" His **exclusive** *Name* (Names) and put away the **pagan** *gods* and *names.*

Secondly we must **Honor** *Him* by *attending* His **Sacred** *celebrations* (His special anniversaries) with Him. That shows Him we *care* about **what** He's *done* and **is** *doing* for us.

YHWH also tells *us* those **celebrations** are a "*sign*" between *Him* and His *People!* (Ex. 31-Ez. 20) Considering those *special* celebrations (Sabbaths) are *rehearsals* of *His* **Plan** for mankind (His Children). There's **no** *way* we can *honestly* say *we* "*Love*" Him without *participating* (honoring Him) in His *special* **anniversaries** of *what* He has *done* and *what* He is *still* **going** to *do!*

To *end* this study, it's imperative to *understand* we **all** "*will*" **reap** the *fruits* of our *actions,* good or *bad.* But, unfortunately, we sometimes *fail* to **understand** the *depths* and **consequences** of *our* actions. A perfect Biblical *example* is the *story* of Job.

The account *opens* with the devil (adversary) *approaching* the Creator and being asked *where* he had *been* and *doing.* He was then *asked* if he had *seen* YHWH's *servant* Job, the *most* **righteous** *man* of the East? The devil *challenged* Job's *obedience* to YHWH's **special** protection. To *prove* that, the devil was *allowed* to *take* **all** his *possessions,* including his **ten** *children.* Talk about **bad** *things* happening to *good* people!!

Due to the *compliers* of the OT canon **failing** to *include* all the *original* books, like **Jasher** (meaning "*true account*") the *story* **behind** *Job* was *lost* leaving us *scratching* our heads as to "**why**" *Job* was *fated* to *suffer* all those **terrible** *things*!

In **Jasher**, we *discover* **Job** was one of Pharoah's *chief* **advisers** (along with Baalim) that Pharaoh brought in to *advise* him on *what* to do with the **mushrooming** *population* of *Israelites* in his country. We find it was *Jobs'* advise to have all the **baby** *Israelite* **boys** *thrown* in the river, which the Pharaoh *adopted.*

That *prompts* one to *ask*; **why** would a *righteous* man give such *terrible* (too us) *advise?* Well, *obviously,* Job did **not** *realize* the *Israelites* were *YHWH's* **chosen** people. All he *knew* is they were a *threat* to Egyptian *sovereignty,* to which he simply acted *logically.* But his *actions* make **obvious** the *reason* all his **10** *children* were all *killed!*

Chapter 83

The Renting of the Veil

Upon the *death* of the Messiah, we're told a major *Earthquake* occurred *resulting* in the "*renting*" of the *curtain* that *separated* the Creator's Father's *residence* (in the west end of the temple) from the "***court*** of the ***priests***". **Matthew** 27:51 says; *"And behold, the **veil** of the temple was **torn in two** from top to bottom; and the earth **quaked**, and the **rocks** were **split**"*—

With that in mind, this *renting* of the *veil* has been *interpreted* virtually *cart-blanc,* to mean *access* to God who sits on the "**mercy** *seat*" (the Ark of the covenant) had now been **opened** to the *world*. But, honestly how can the **renting** of that *veil* between YHWH and the *Court* of the *Priests* have given **direct** *access* to YHWH to **all** mankind? Actually, a simple *examination* of the *layout* of the *Temple* shows us such a *conclusion* is *nonsense*!

The *outlay* of the temple, according to *scriptures* we find in **Ezekiel** (and elsewhere) basically show it to be *concentric* squares with the inner Sanctum (YHWH's quarters) in the **rear** *middle*. The *Veil* **rent**, was a *huge* **curtain**, 4 to 8" thick (depending upon which expert you ask) *separating* the *adjoining* court (court of the Priests) from YHWH's sanctuary.

No one was *allowed* to enter there except the ***High*** *Priest*, and then *only* **once** a year on the ***High*** *Day* called "*Atonement*". In the court, just *outside* YHWH's sanctuary *behind* the curtain, was the "***court*** *of the* ***priests***" where <u>***only*** the ***priests*** were ***allowed.***</u> No *regular* Israelite (and certainly no gentile) could ever "*see*" the "*veil*" let alone go *behind* it!

Then, just outside the ***court*** *of the* ***priests*** was the "***court*** *of* ***Israel***" also called the ***court*** *of* ***women***, where again, **no** *Gentiles* were *allowed*. In fact, it was only ***outside*** the *court* of *Israel* (*court of the Gentiles*) where a Gentile (non-Israelite) could *approach* the Temple in any way.

The *layout* of the temple is *EXTREMELY* ***IMPORTANT*** to *understanding* the **process** YHWH is *using* to *bring* His *children* into *His Family*. It begins with *Him* in the *center* (obviously) with the *High* **Priest** (His Son Yahshua) ***second*** and Yahshua's' ***priesthood*** (symbolized by the Levitical priesthood) *third*.

Coming ***fourth*** is the *nation* of *Israel* (all twelve tribes) with the Gentile nations finally bringing up the *balance*. Each of these groups *serves* the one ***directly*** *outside* their particular *placing*.

You see, YHWH, the Father *begins* the process, by *directly* **serving** His *Son*, the ***High*** *Priest* who in turn directly *serves* His *Priesthood*, who in turn *serves* Israel, who finally *serve* as *priests* to the *Gentiles*! A good understanding of the *layout* of the temple is absolutely ***essential*** to understanding the *meaning* ***behind*** the *tearing* ***in*** *two* of the *curtain* between YHWH's sanctuary and the *court* of the *Priests*.

That *knowledge* shows us the *renting* of the *curtain* was certainly ***no*** random *coincidence,* but an *essential* ***step*** in the *Plan*. What happened was, <u>the *barrier* between YHWH and His ***Priesthood***</u> was *torn* down with *Yahshua's* ***death***! Again, that *renting* of the *curtain* had *nothing* ***directly*** to do with the *rest* of *Israel* and certainly *not* the Gentiles! The *gates* and *walls* **separating** the *courtyards* between ***Israel*** and the *court* of the *Priests* ***still*** *remained* in *place* after the *tearing* of that *veil*! Of course, it definitely did not give the *gentiles* ***access*** to the *temple* and/or YHWH.

The bottom line is, Yahshua **DID return** (as He promised) to *receive* His Priesthood and *take **them*** to His Father (behind the dimensional veil) But, that was merely a *precursor* to a *far **greater** event,* the ***fall** harvest,* which has *begun.*

In this ***fall** harvest* (of people) referred to as the *Millennium* in **Revelation** 20-21 (the new Eden actually) all Israel that *chooses* our **Heavenly** *Father* will have *access* to YHWH (at least His Spirit at first)! What that means is the *wall* between *Israel* and the *court* of the *Priesthood* will finally be ***torn** down*! The *renting* of that veil gave the *priesthood,* which were Yahshua's *disciples* and *followers* direct *access* to YHWH's Spirit of *Power* (and life) they were *Israel's **literal** priesthood.*

Yahshua *promised* them that *power* after He left, which *they **received**.* (See Acts 2) But, the *rest* of Israel will *not* have *access* to ***that** power* until after the **Atonement** *goat* sheds its' blood for *Israels **sins**.*

There, all Israel, like the *apostles* in the *first* century will have *access* to that ***same** power* and *Spirit* (of life)! That is *power* over *behavior* and the *power* to do *miracles.* It will also be the *power **over** death* (immortality). After all, YHWH is called *"life"* and His Spirit is literally the *Spirit* of **immortality**. In the *new **Eden**,* we are told there will be **no** *death,* not to mention *disease.*

Chapter 84

There be Dragons!

No doubt virtually everyone has heard **Dragon** *tales* growing up, but how many ever *believed* that there was even a shred of *truth* to such *fanciful* and *mythical* whims, after all, they're simply tall *tales* of the valiant *Prince Charming* and *fairy* type, right? But, considering, we as little children (most of us) were taught *Santa Clause* and the *Easter Bunny* (that lays eggs) were *real*; so why not *dragons*?

Well, this is quite an interesting *conundrum* considering a *majority* of our modern, *Western*, **Christian**, *nations*, claim to put *their* **faith** in the *Bible* as well as its *God* and *Messiah*. But, that Bible, so many *claim* to *trust*, tells us that *Dragons*, or at least *one* for *sure*, is **real**! In fact, *dragon* (and/or *dragons*) is mentioned over *thirty* times in the Bible.

Of course, anyone *familiar* with the Bible to any degree, surely knows the most **dogmatic** *reference* to a *dragon* in scripture; **Revelation** 12, where that *"Great Dragon of old" being cast to Earth*. How ironic that those who *teach* their children that *Santa Clause* and the *Easter bunny* are **real**, shrug off *something* the **Bible** proclaims as **real**, like **dragons**, as some kind of *metaphor*! Go figure?!

With that in mind, is it also just an interesting *coincidence* that virtually **every** *culture* and people on the planet have *dragon tales* as if they were *real*? Do those tales come from some *kind* of **fact** and actually *substantiate* the Bible's teaching's of *Dragons*? Should we really *trust* the Bible is *telling* the *truth* in such matters? I for one, *accept* the *Bible* as **truth** (minus miss-translations) over what *people* **say** any day (like dragons are myth). Does that make *me* a *fool* or is it those *dismissing* **plain** *Bible* scripture that are the fools?

Well, if we only had that *one* scripture in **Revelation** 12, I suppose the case for *dragons* being *only* a *figure* of *speech* would have some *credence*, but, other Old Testament scriptures describe in very **plain** *language*; a *"dragon"*! The only problem is these *creatures* apparently had a **different** *name* or at least *title* in *Hebrew*, which the translators *dubbed*, *"Leviathan"*!

Taking a **close** *look* at the *features* and *attributes* of that *fearsome* **reptilian** *creature*, there is only one **honest** *conclusion* we can come to; it's a *dragon*! So, reading about it in **Job**, we see that it had **impenetrable** *scales*, **glowing** *eyes*, breathed **fire** and **smoke**, *had* **wings**, and yes, it *could* **talk**! Hello; did someone say *dragon*? Let's take a look at *those* shocking verses in **Job** 41!

To begin with, we find its *invincibility* (immortality?) referenced in v.9; *"Indeed, any hope of overcoming him* (it) *is vain!"* Then in verse 14, we find it had *"terrible* (fearful) *teeth* and *scales"*; definitely a *vicious* **reptilian** *creature*. But, look at what scriptures 18-21 reveal; *"His* (its) *sneezings* **flash** *forth* **light** *and his* **eyes** *are like the eyelids of the* **morning** (glowing red). (v.20) *"Smoke goes out of his nostrils"* (v.21) *"His breath kindles coals and a flame goes out of his mouth"*!

Wow, if those *descriptions* don't have **dragon** *written* all over them, nothing does; but there's more! Let's go back and look at versus 3&4; "*Will he make many* **supplications** (ask for things) *to you? Will he* **speak** *softly to you? Will you take him as a* **servant** *forever?*" This *creature* not only has *glowing* **eyes**, *breaths* **smoke** and **fire**, but has the *ability* to **speak** and **reason**!

Well, it *cannot* get more *dragonesk* than that, except for *one* **thing**, which we find in verse 5; it has *wings*! "*Will you play with him as a bird-*"? Yes, this **fire** *breathing* **reptilian** creature also had *wings*! There you go! A perfect *description* of a **supposed** *mythical* "**dragon**"! But, it is *what* is stated at the end of chapter that clinches it; versus 33-34; "*On* **earth**, *there is* **nothing like** **him** (it) *which is made without fear. He* **beholds** *every* **high** (heavenly) *thing! He is* **king** *over all the* **children** *of* **pride**"! What an amazing statement that is!

It is interesting how the *King* (Malak-angel) of **Tyre** (Roman name "*Mars*") in **Ezekiel** 28 was also in the *Garden* (of Eden) and had a *covering* (skin) of *jewels*. Were those jewels *actually* **angelic** *scales*? I personally have no doubt! But, of one *thing* there is no doubt, the *spirit* of **death** *imparted* to Adam and Eve by that "*fiery* **red** *dragon*" (of old) was the spirit of "*PRIDE*"! Of course, we know that "*pride goes* **before destruction**" **death** (Prov.16:18)!

That great *fiery* **red** *dragon* that was in the Garden was very much *real* (described in **Job** 41) and gave humanity its *gift* of *death*! But, it was not the **only** one, there were (are) *more*! But that is a shocking and *unbelievable*, but related *story* for another time! Considering that *creature* in the Garden of Eden, a *better* translation of *Nachash* would have been "*Leviathan*"; *serpent* was *what* it was *cursed* to **become** after its dirty *deed*!

Giving more credence to this idea is that a *dragon* skull was *found* in *Hell Creek* SD in 2003. It's called "**Dracorex Hogwartzia**" (no joke)! Anyway, there was a very interesting movie called "*Dragon Wars*" about an underground *cavern* (pit) in London that's broken into in which an *immortal* **dragon** had been *hibernating* for **thousands** of *years*. The dragon was inadvertently *released* and began to *multiply* and *devastate* the Earth; *reducing* the human *population* to only *thousands*. They *accomplished* this not just by *killing* them, but by **eating** them!

Interestingly, the pit in **Revelation** 9 no doubt *contains* **dragons** (among other species) and is *opened* by an *angel* (watcher-demon) where they **devastate** the Earth! Interestingly, the *design* of the *dragons* in the movie **dragon** *wars* looked shockingly like the *skull* they found in SD. Anyway, *Hollywood*, which is a major **propaganda** *machine* for the *demons* that *run* this world, obviously took this **movie** *seriously*, considering their using *major* "**stars**" like Christian Slater and Gerard Butler!

Ending this study, there's one more shocking Bible *fact* found in **Ezekiel** 28. There we find a *lamentation* to the "*King* (or queen) *of Tyre*" (Mars) a "*Cherub that covers*" which was also in the Garden of YHWH (Eden)! Of course, the Cherubim that *cover,* are the *ones* on either side of the Ark (throne) of YHWH, spreading their *wings*, but, that's a subject for *another* time!